81 GREAT COLLEGES
IN
FLORIDA, GEORGIA & ALABAMA

81 GREAT COLLEGES IN FLORIDA, GEORGIA & ALABAMA

Lookout Mountain
Covenant Coll

Florence
Univ of North Alabama

Huntsville
Alabama A&M Univ
Univ of Alabama in Huntsville

Dahlonega
North GA Coll and St Univ

Demorest
Piedmont Coll

Waleska
Reinhardt Coll

Gainesville
Brenau Univ

Athens
Univ of Georgia

Mt Berry
Berry Coll

Jacksonville
Jacksonville State Univ

Decatur
Agnes Scott Coll ♀

Birmingham
Univ of Alabama at Birmingham
Birmingham-Southern Coll
Miles Coll
Samford Univ

Marietta
Southern Polytechnic St Univ

Atlanta
Georgia Institute of Technology
Georgia State Univ
Atlanta College of Art
Clark Atlanta Univ
Emory Univ
Morehouse Coll ♂
Oglethorpe Univ
Spelman Coll ♀

Carrollton
Univ of West Georgia

Talladega
Talladega Coll

Macon
Mercer Univ
Wesleyan Coll ♀

ALABAMA

LaGrange
LaGrange Coll

Tuscaloosa
Univ of Alabama

Montevallo
Univ of Montevallo

Auburn
Auburn Univ

Fort Valley
Fort Valley State Univ

Marion
Judson Coll ♀

Columbus
Columbus State Univ

Livingston
Univ of West Alabama

Tuskegee
Tuskegee Univ

Montgomery
Alabama State Univ
Huntingdon Coll

Americus
Georgia Southwestern State Univ

Troy
Troy Univ

Albany
Albany State Univ

Thomasville
Thomas Univ

Mobile
Univ of South Alabama
Spring Hill Coll

Tallahassee
Florida A&M Univ
Florida State Univ

Pensacola
Univ of West Florida

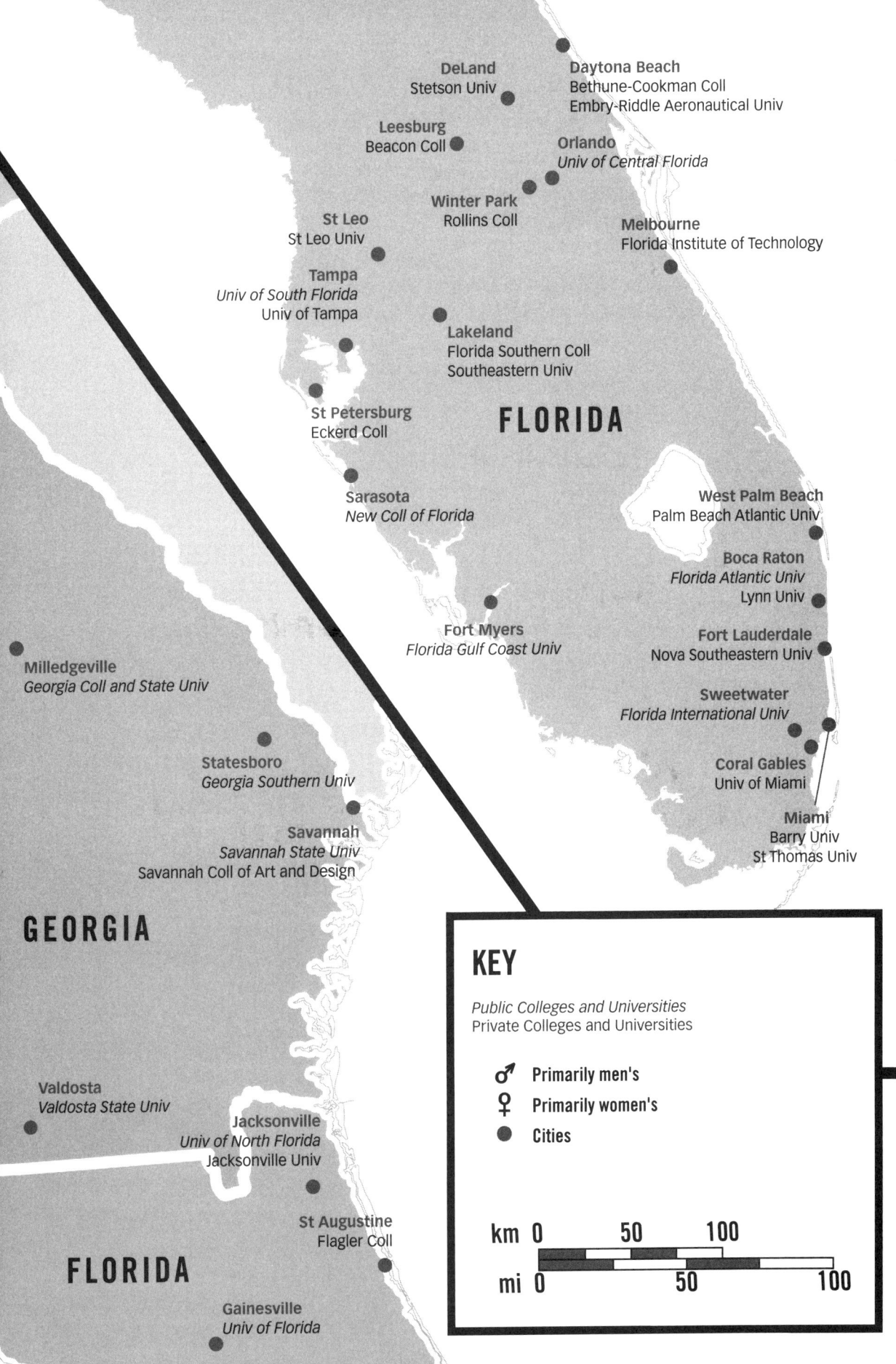

81 GREAT COLLEGES IN FLORIDA, GEORGIA & ALABAMA

SPARKCOLLEGE

AN IMPRINT OF SPARK PUBLISHING

WWW.SPARKCOLLEGE.COM

© 2006 by Spark Publishing

School data and in-depth descriptions: Thomson Peterson's, copyright (2005) Thomson Peterson's, a part of Thomson Learning Inc. All rights reserved.

All rights reserved. No part of this book may be used or reproduced, stored in a retrieval system, or transmitted, in any form or by any means electronic, mechanical, photocopying, recording, or otherwise, without prior written permission of the publisher.

SparkCollege is an imprint of SparkNotes LLC

Spark Publishing
A Division of Barnes & Noble
120 Fifth Avenue
New York, NY 10011
www.sparknotes.com

ISBN-13: 978-1-4114-9990-4
ISBN-10: 1-4114-9990-5

Library of Congress Cataloging-in-Publication Data

81 great colleges in Florida, Georgia, and Alabama.
    p. cm.
 1. College choice—Alabama. 2. College choice—Florida. 3. College choice—Georgia. 4. Universities and colleges—Alabama. 5. Universities and colleges—Florida. 6. Universities and colleges—Georgia. I. Title: Eighty one great colleges in Florida, Georgia, and Alabama.

LB2350.5.A15 2006
378.73—dc22

2006019079

Please submit changes or report errors to www.sparknotes.com/errors.

Printed in Canada

1 3 5 7 9 10 8 6 4 2

ACKNOWLEDGMENTS

SparkCollege would like to thank the following writers and contributors:

    Christina Couch
    Megan Elliot
    Grace Labatt
    Casey Levine
    Emily McCombs
    Karen Quarles
    Jordan Stokes

We would also like to thank the following students, parents, and educators at Freehold Township and Manalapan High Schools for generously donating their time to the SparkCollege guides:

    Cyndee Baumgartner, English supervisor
    Leanne Dinverno, high school graduate
    Elizabeth Higley, principal
    Lida Nagel, guidance counselor
    Kim Parks, high school student
    Jan Peterson, parent
    Maggie Rogers, parent
    Dani Rosen, high school student
    Jacqueline Thomas, head guidance counselor

Finally, we wish to thank Lynne Brett, educational psychologist and college admissions consultant, and Brandon Rogers, grant development coordinator, Clover Park Technical College, for their sage advice.

CONTENTS

INTRODUCTION xiii

FINDING YOUR BEST FIT xvii

GET OUT!
Amazing but True Off-Campus Options xxii

FLORIDA 1

Barry University	2
Beacon College	5
Bethune-Cookman College	7
Eckerd College	10
Embry-Riddle Aeronautical University	13
Flagler College	16
Florida A&M University	19
Florida Atlantic University	22
Florida Gulf Coast University	25
Florida Institute of Technology	28
Florida International University	31
Florida Southern College	34
Florida State University	37
Jacksonville University	41
Lynn University	44
New College of Florida	47
Nova Southeastern University	50

CONTENTS

Palm Beach Atlantic University 53
Rollins College 56
Saint Leo University 59
Southeastern University 62
Stetson University 65
St. Thomas University 68
University of Central Florida 71
University of Florida 74
University of Miami 77
University of North Florida 80
University of South Florida 83
University of Tampa 86
University of West Florida 89

COOLEST CLASSROOMS EVER 92

GEORGIA 93

Agnes Scott College 94
Albany State University 97
Atlanta College of Art 100
Berry College 103
Brenau University 106
Clark Atlanta University 109
Columbus State University 112
Covenant College 115
Emory University 118
Fort Valley State University 121
Georgia College and State University 124
Georgia Institute of Technology 127
Georgia Southwestern State University 130
Georgia Southern University 133
Georgia State University 136

LaGrange College 139

Mercer University 142

Morehouse College 145

North Georgia College and State University 148

Oglethorpe University 151

Piedmont College 154

Reinhardt College 157

Savannah College of Art and Design 160

Savannah State University 163

Southern Polytechnic State University 166

Spelman College 169

Thomas University 172

University of Georgia 175

University of West Georgia 178

Valdosta State University 181

Wesleyan College 184

AIR TIME 187

ALABAMA 189

Alabama A&M University 190

Alabama State University 193

Auburn University 196

Birmingham-Southern College 200

Huntingdon College 203

Jacksonville State University 206

Judson College 209

Miles College 212

Samford University 215

Spring Hill College 218

Talladega College 221

Troy University 224

CONTENTS

Tuskegee University 227
University of Alabama 230
University of Alabama at Birmingham 233
University of Alabama in Huntsville 236
University of Montevallo 239
University of North Alabama 242
University of South Alabama 245
University of West Alabama 248

SCHOOLS BY CATEGORY 251

INTRODUCTION

Another college guide. We know. But before you put this one back on the shelf with the others, hold on a second and let us tell you why this one is different.

Thanks.

So . . . you've probably noticed that choosing a college has become a pretty complicated process. Endless books, guides, websites . . . full of what? Rankings and statistics that are usually meaningless, obviously biased, or out of date? Search engines that suggest all the wrong schools? Thanks for nothing, we say.

Instead of fueling the hysteria, we decided to stop all the madness and deliver a college guide that actually provides you with some useful tools of measurement. In order to deliver the goods, we recruited a team that includes not only educational professionals and guidance counselors but also, and most important, students—high school students, college students, and college graduates. We found out about some pretty simple, but not so immediately apparent, concepts that can define the "best" college for you.

WHERE ARE YOU?

This was our first question.

We now know that more than 95 percent of students apply to a college within a 200-mile parameter of their home. And those of you who want to move farther away often know what region you'd like to live in. So (*duh*), we organized all of our college guides into regions that cut up the United States into clear, obvious segments.

WHICH COLLEGE IS THE BEST?

Wrong question. College is a different experience for everyone. That's not just one of those useless blanket statements . . . it happens to be true. The college experience is simply too varied now for the term *best* to have any real meaning. New colleges are popping up all the time. Older ones are changing and responding with new opportunities for class work, research, and exciting living-learning communities.

WHAT ABOUT COLLEGE RANKINGS?

Wrong message. Rankings provide great publicity for the few colleges that get selected as the "best," but what are those lists, really? Who makes them? Answer: a bunch of people at a magazine who look at a narrow range of statistics.

INTRODUCTION

The average SAT score of the incoming class isn't really going to tell you much about what the college is like. Rankings? Let's get over it.

THE NEW "BEST"

Gone are the days of a special elite, with their loafers and tattered books, attending a limited number of institutions to ensure their future in a higher income bracket and lifestyle. Forget the standard 20 or 30 majors your parents remember being offered at college. It's a different ballgame now.

We discovered there are a *lot* of really good schools out there, with programs and opportunities that we in our wildest imaginations (and our imaginations are pretty wild) would never have thought existed. Today, there are more than 4,000 colleges and universities in the United States, and the majority of them are in a near-constant state of development.

Our idea is this: The "best" college is now the "best fit"—the school with the right facilities, location, major, size, and attitude. Maybe you want to live on a farm and create art. Maybe you want to be in a different part of the world every single semester. Maybe you never want to step outside of a lab.

There is something for everyone out there.

A LITTLE OF THIS, A LITTLE OF THAT

We've categorized the schools using four identifying icons. But just like you, no college can fit neatly into one stereotype. So you'll often see a college listing with two of our icons, the larger one being its most predominant feature. Yale University is a perfect example. It's chiefly a Big Rep, but its comprehensive financial aid offerings make it a (surprising) Big Deal. Here they are:

BIG REP: Yeah, you want the sweatshirt. Going to one of these schools gives you automatic bragging rights. These schools are good, and everyone knows it. With heavy-hitters on the faculty, huge endowments, and loyal alumni who throw fistfuls of cash in their direction, these schools tend to attract academically aggressive students. Because students at these schools are almost always driven (if not alarmingly competitive), the atmosphere can sometimes be a bit much. If you're expecting a laid-back college experience, you may not get it here—pressure junkies, however, may feel right at home. Though no school can guarantee success, you'll be well set up for it at a Big Rep. This also means that you have a lot to live up to when you leave.

BIG DEAL: Students of all kinds can benefit from these schools. Big Deals are mostly, but not entirely, public; charge less than $16,000 per year for tuition for in-state applicants; or offer very generous financial aid packages. Some of these schools are nicknamed the "public Ivies." There's a good reason for this. These schools have surprisingly low student-to-teacher ratios (20:1 or less), and many offer seminar classes. Impressive research facilities, standout programs in the arts and humanities, and a faculty that rocks—you can find all this here.

BIG IDEA: Welcome to the world of the highly innovative, experimental learner. These colleges are unique, just like the students they serve, and come with innovative educational components, such as co-curricular studies, create-your-own programs, and a major emphasis on community service, hands-on experience, or study abroad. And don't make the mistake of thinking these are schools that have blossomed overnight—many Big Ideas are venerable institutions that have produced legions of forward-thinking graduates. These schools also vary tremendously in character—some have organic havens, others have monthlong programs where students learn on the "job," instead of being stuck in a classroom . . . you really never know what will turn up at a Big Idea.

BIG FISH: As in "little pond." Let's face it . . . some schools are so mammoth that it's nearly impossible not to get lost in the tide. Big Fish schools may not have crazy curriculums or fancy pedigrees, but they do offer a quality education and a chance to stand out. They frequently have a stand-out program or two and some high-profile faculty members or alumni. Big Fish schools are excellent choices for students who don't relish the thought of living on a massive campus with thousands upon thousands of other students. And you may not have to lie, cheat, steal, or kill to get ahead. You can be the star student, or just get a sterling education in a particular major.

WHAT HAPPENS WHEN YOU GET THERE?

UNIVERSITY 101: Used to be, you put your boxes in the car, drove off to your concrete cell-block of a dorm, picked up one of a standard selection of majors, signed up for the usual selection of core and major classes, and hoped for the best.

The twenty-first century has ushered in a new and growing interest in "first-year support." Both parents and students are very attuned to what specific programs and faculty are available to incoming first-years. Today students want to make sure they have "advocates" who can help them through the hurdles of what courses to take, which professors are good, which organizations they should join, and most important, how they can be successful at the school of their choice.

INTRODUCTION

Look for the University 101 icon throughout this book. We'll tell you what schools have to offer their incoming students.

THE $$$ QUESTION

We'd be doing you a disservice if we tried to pretend that money wasn't an issue when making a decision about college. College is expensive. But we also have this to say, and we mean it:

Look into every school that interests you—don't be put off by the price tag.

If you find a school you really love, no matter what the cost, you should absolutely investigate its financial aid offerings. You'd be surprised at what's out there. Many Big Rep schools, for example, have price tags that will send you into a dead faint. But don't think that just because your funds are low, you can't attend one of these prestigious schools—the truth is quite the opposite. Big Reps usually have large endowments and frequently provide very compelling financial aid packages. Some meet *100 percent* of demonstrated need.

THAT'S ALL, FOLKS!

Well, not quite. You'll still have a lot of work to do—college visits, application essays, and so on. Think of this guide as a starting point. We hope we get you a little closer to starting the process and moving onto what will probably be one of the most exciting experiences of your life.

If you've got something to say about this book, tell us! Your input makes us better. Go to **www.sparkcollege.com** and tell us what you think. We really read what you write!

Did you read this all the way to the end? How great are you? Now take a deep breath, grab a coffee, and have a look. *You're gonna do just fine.*

Laurie Barnett
Editor-in-Chief
Spark Publishing

FINDING YOUR BEST FIT

Okay, so you've got this book and you're ready to find your best fit college. Now what? Well, we've devised a short and painless quiz to help determine what college type might best suit you. It won't take long, and you won't need any extra sheets of paper.

The important thing here is that you *be honest with yourself*. Don't answer the questions in the way you think they should be answered—select the answer that comes to you first, your gut answer. If the answers don't fit you exactly, just go with the one that feels the most right out of the given choices.

1. **What do you envision when you think about life on a college campus?**

   a. I like the classic image: old buildings, tough classes, all-nighters. And I want it all—I want to pull a muscle when I lift the massive bulletin of classes and the list of extracurriculars. Gimme, gimme, gimme.

   b. A tight-knit community. I imagine walking into the dining hall or a classroom and knowing almost everyone I see.

   c. A kind of life laboratory. I'm sick of the standard "listen to a lecture, take notes, take a test, get a grade" formula. I'd enjoy developing my own major, working on long-term projects of my own invention, and getting evaluations instead of letter grades.

2. **Which of the following scenarios best describes how a weeknight at college might be spent?**

   a. I could be doing just about anything. Knowing me, I'll be working on some strange group project or show. I may make it to dinner, or I may get my hand stuck in a vending machine trying to get a bag of chips.

   b. After a well-scheduled, tightly packed day, I'd probably have a quick dinner with some friends at the nearest dining hall (or take out a sandwich and a coffee), go to a meeting, and then head home for some serious studying. I'll catch up on my phone calls as I walk from building to building.

   c. Everyone in my hall or building would gather together and head to dinner as a group. We might end up lingering there for a while. Then we'd all go back and study together, or watch TV, or a little of both.

3. **Which would you most like to have on your campus?**

   a. The mother of all research libraries. All other libraries must bow before it.
   b. A real, operational windmill.
   c. A student center where everyone on campus gathers each night.
   d. An old-fashioned social club, where a select group of members can gather for dinner and networking.
   e. One central green around which all the campus buildings are arranged.
   f. A dining hall run entirely by students—from the business end to the cooking and menu planning—which provides a healthy, eclectic selection of foods.

4. **Do brand names and labels matter? Tell the truth. No one else will see your answer.**

   a. Yes, absolutely. There's no point in denying it.
   b. Sometimes. Behind the hype, there is often some truth. In the end, though, I don't really care.
   c. No. I'm not really label or brand conscious.

5. **Do you already have a résumé?**

   a. Yes
   b. No

6. **Ice cream flavor challenge: vanilla or mint chocolate chip?**

   a. Vanilla, you fools!
   b. Mint chocolate chip, you philistines!
   c. I don't do dairy.

7. **What kind of professors would you like to have?**

   a. I'd like them to be approachable. I'd like to be able to grab a cup of coffee with them and talk about my work if I'm having trouble.
   b. People who work in the field and who treat me like a fellow practitioner.
   c. The biggest, best, and brightest. I don't mind if they are a little scary or crazy—bring it on!

8. **Would you ever consider working on a self-designed academic project by yourself, for an entire semester . . . *and* not get a grade for it . . . just for the sake of developing your own ideas?**

   a. Sign me up.
   b. You must be kidding.

9. **Would it freak you out if, instead of a letter grade, you got a long written summary of your progress? And you never had a GPA?**

   a. Yes. I would not be able to sleep at night.
   b. No. Sounds great!
   c. It's a little weird, but I could live with it.

FINDING YOUR BEST FIT

10. Complete the following statement: "I'd like my professors to be . . ."

a. Very involved with my academic progress and available if I need support.

b. Mentors I can work with on a personal basis.

c. Masters in their fields—my progress is my own problem.

11. Which would you rather be: the star in a small town, or one of the crowd of star-struck hopefuls in the big city?

a. Small-town star

b. Big-city hopeful

12. Fill in the blank: "I consider myself to be a(n) _____ student."

a. Excellent—I do well, bottom line. I may be a certifiable genius.

b. Very innovative—I tend to go out on my own a bit, and I work well independently.

c. Thoughtful—I like a nice, even pace in classes and a chance to talk concepts through in a small-group discussion.

d. Competitive—I embrace the system and its rules, and I play to win. Ask me my GPA. Go ahead. Ask me.

e. Not so good—The truth is, the thought of going to college is a little scary, and I'd like some support.

f. Frustrated—I'm way ahead of my school. They're constantly testing me when they should be letting me do my own thing. I have plans! Ideas!

THE RESULTS

On the next page, check your responses against the answers and place a check in the appropriate box for each of your Big Reps, Big Ideas, and Big Fishes.

You'll notice that there are no Big Deal questions in our quiz. This is because Big Deal schools are for all types of students. *Your financial need has no bearing on what you're like as a student.* Remember: Schools will often work with you to create financial aid packages, so don't limit your choices purely to schools with low tuition. If your dream school is a $40,000 per year Big Rep—and $40,000 is well beyond your means—check it out anyway.

FINDING YOUR BEST FIT

Question 1:
a. Big Rep
b. Big Fish
c. Big Idea

Question 2:
a. Big Idea
b. Big Rep
c. Big Fish

Question 3:
a. Big Rep
b. Big Idea
c. Big Fish
d. Big Rep
e. Big Fish
f. Big Idea

Question 4:
a. Big Rep
b. Big Idea
c. Big Fish

Question 5:
Give yourself an extra Big Rep point if you answered **a**.

Question 6:

This question has no bearing on your college choice—we here at Spark Headquarters were just curious. However, if you have a firm opinion on this matter, we might recommend going to a school in the state of Vermont. Vermont features a number of schools with on-campus creameries or connections to Ben and Jerry's, *as well as* schools that cater to vegan diets.

Question 7:
a. Big Fish
b. Big Idea
c. Big Rep

Question 8:
Give yourself an extra Big Idea point if you answered **a**.

Question 9:
a. Big Rep
b. Big Idea
c. Big Fish

Question 10:
a. Big Fish
b. Big Idea
c. Big Rep

Question 11:
Give yourself an extra Big Fish point if you answered **a**.

Question 12:
a. Big Rep
b. Big Idea
c. Big Fish
d. Big Rep
e. Big Fish
f. Big Idea

	Question #											
	1	2	3	4	5	6	7	8	9	10	11	12
BIG REP												
BIG IDEA												
BIG FISH												

WHAT AM I?

Which category has the most checked-off answers? Do you have a long row of Big Ideas? Are you Big Fish all over? Or are you a classic Big Rep? If so, pay special attention to those schools. In the back of this book, you'll find a list of which pages these schools can be found on.

It's possible that you might be evenly distributed over two (or even all three) rows. If that's the case, go back and take another look at question 12. That's the question about you, rather than the school. How do you see yourself as a student?

GET OUT!

AMAZING BUT TRUE OFF-CAMPUS OPTIONS

If campus life stifles you, consider the following:

Karlovy Vary Film Festival: Florida International University
Observe ground-breaking filmmakers in their natural habitat as you attend classes at the Prague Film School as well as the world-renowned Karlovy Vary Film Festival.

Global Communities and Health Care in Thailand: Florida Atlantic University
Learn about international health care reform in class, then see it in action as you tour local hospitals for both humans and elephants.

The Grand Tour of Europe: University of Miami
Why choose just one country when you can study in four? Bring comfortable shoes for this whirlwind architecture tour of Italy, France, Greece, and Spain.

Tropical Ecology and Ethno-biology in Costa Rica: Tuskegee University
The rainforest becomes your living classroom in this semester-long trip through one of the most ecologically diverse places on earth.

Antarctica, The Fragile Continent: University of Georgia
Perhaps the only institution in the country to offer a study abroad program to Antarctica, the University of Georgia gives students the once-in-a-lifetime chance to hop on board a 15-day cruise to the coolest place in the world.

Psychology in the South Pacific: Emory University
Begin your trip by stopping by the University of Hawaii to brush up on Micronesian culture, then spend the rest of the semester flitting between the Marshall Islands conducting child-development research.

Spelman Summer Art Colony: Spelman College
Get those creative juices flowing at an artists' cooperative in the Caribbean. Students of the visual and written arts gain inspiration and serenity from the beaches, rainforests, and people of the Republic of Panama.

Academic Adventure: Lynn University
Perhaps the most unbelievable one of all, the first-year Academic Adventure, an academic *requirement*, is a cruise to the western Caribbean. The cruise is intended as both an educational and social activity, and therefore the cost is included in your tuition.

FLORIDA

BARRY UNIVERSITY

11300 Northeast Second Avenue (305) 899-3000
Miami Shores, FL 33161 http://www.barry.edu/

 **BIG FISH**

 **UNIVERSITY 101**
Extended orientation program; optional first-year transitional seminar for business students; optional first-year residential learning communities; upperclassman mentors; optional first-year leadership program.

Uniting students from as many as 49 states and 80 countries, Barry University is one of the most diverse schools in the region.

But with a full-time undergrad enrollment of fewer than 5,000, Barry feels local as well as global. The school maintains a low student-teacher ratio and restricts class size to make sure that no student falls through the cracks. Faculty members are experienced in scholarly research and fieldwork and incorporate both academic and practical learning into their lessons. Independent studies courses and undergrad research projects allow students to truly get to know the faculty.

BARRY UNIVERSITY

WHAT IT IS

Barry University grads say that the best part of their education was the unique sense of closeness in the Barry University family. Students are encouraged to explore their individual interests and develop the critical-thinking skills needed to succeed. Small class sizes allow more personal interaction with classmates and professors, building one-on-one relationships that last a lifetime. Major divisions include the schools of Adult and Continuing Education, Arts and Sciences, Business, Education, Graduate Medical Sciences, Human Performance and Leisure Sciences, Law, Natural and Health Sciences, Nursing, and Social Work.

Students find the cultural diversity of South Florida and the Barry community a wonderful enhancement to their educational experience. Nine air-conditioned residence halls on campus and extended housing off campus accommodate residential undergraduate students. The university has a snack bar, cafeteria, post office, student union center, bookstore, performing arts center, television studio, radio station, game room, health and sports center, and an outdoor recreation center. There are 89 student organizations and numerous campuswide events. Since 1984, the Barry University Buccaneers have won six national championships, participated in 79 national tournaments, and won 30 Sunshine State Conference championships. Intramural sports include basketball, flag football, golf, sand volleyball, soccer, street hockey, tennis, three-on-three basketball, and volleyball.

WHERE IT'S AT

Barry's beautifully landscaped campus and Spanish-style architecture are located in Miami Shores, between Miami and Fort Lauderdale, giving students access to all the recreational facilities and cultural opportunities of South Florida. Golf, tennis, swimming, soccer, scuba and skin diving, waterskiing, and sailing are available all year long. Miami also offers pro football's Miami Dolphins, the Miami Heat, the Florida Marlins, and the Florida Panthers. The New World Symphony, Opera Guild of Greater Miami, Miami Film Festival, and Miami City Ballet provide a full season of highly acclaimed performances, as do the Coconut Grove Playhouse and Broward Center for the Performing Arts. Also easily accessible are the Florida Keys and the Everglades.

THE DETAILS

Campus setting:	suburban
Degrees:	bachelor's, master's, doctoral
Calendar:	semesters
Public/Private:	private religious
Number of full-time faculty:	346
Student-to-teacher ratio:	14:1

Admissions requirements:
- **Options:** common application, deferred entrance, early admission, electronic application
- **Application fee:** $30
- **Required:** high school transcript, SAT or ACT
- **Application deadlines:** continuous (freshmen), continuous (transfer)
- **Early decision:** —
- **Notification:** continuous (freshmen), continuous (transfer)

Average high school GPA:	2.97
Average freshman SAT verbal/math score:	488 / 484
Average freshman ACT score:	19
Number of applicants:	3,186
Number of applicants accepted:	2,236
Percentage of students from out of state:	15%
Total freshman enrollment:	548
Total enrollment:	9,207
Percentage of students who live in campus housing:	17%
Total tuition:	$22,430
Total cost with fees & expenses:	$30,050
Average financial aid package:	$14,855

BARRY UNIVERSITY

MAJORS

- Accounting
- Acting
- Advertising
- Biology/Biological Sciences, General
- Broadcast Journalism
- Business Administration and Management, General
- Chemistry, General
- Clinical/Medical Laboratory Technician
- Clinical Laboratory Science/Medical Technology/Technologist
- Communication Studies/Speech Communication and Rhetoric
- Computer Science
- Criminology
- Cytotechnology/Cytotechnologist
- Drama and Dramatics/Theatre Arts, General
- Ecology
- Economics, General
- Education, General
- Elementary Education and Teaching
- Engineering, General
- English/Language Arts Teacher Education
- English Language and Literature, General
- Finance, General
- French Language and Literature
- History, General
- Information Science/Studies
- International Business/Trade/Commerce
- International Relations and Affairs
- Journalism
- Kindergarten/Preschool Education and Teaching
- Kinesiology and Exercise Science
- Liberal Arts and Sciences/Liberal Studies
- Literature
- Management Information Systems, General
- Marine Biology and Biological Oceanography
- Marketing/Marketing Management, General
- Mass Communication/Media Studies
- Mathematics, General
- Nuclear Medical Technology/Technologist
- Nursing/Registered Nurse Training
- Philosophy
- Photography
- Physical Education Teaching and Coaching
- Piano and Organ
- Political Science and Government, General
- Pre-Dentistry Studies
- Pre-Law Studies
- Pre-Medicine/Pre-Medical Studies
- Pre-Pharmacy Studies
- Pre-Veterinary Studies
- Psychology, General
- Public Relations/Image Management
- Radio and Television
- Sociology
- Spanish Language and Literature
- Special Education and Teaching, General
- Sport and Fitness Administration/Management
- Theology/Theological Studies
- Voice and Opera

BEACON COLLEGE

105 East Main Street
Leesburg, FL 34748

(352) 787-7660
http://www.beaconcollege.edu/

 **BIG IDEA**

 **UNIVERSITY 101**
Extended orientation program; special academic advisors assigned to first- and second-year students; first-year residential learning communities; required first-year transitional seminar.

 BIG FISH

Learning disabilities don't stand in the way of academic achievement at Beacon College.

Beacon offers associate's and bachelor's degree programs exclusively to students with learning disabilities and maintains a supportive atmosphere that allows students to recognize their strengths and work with their learning differences. Classes are small, and professors are specially trained to make sure students get personal attention. In addition, students work with mentors to develop individualized learning techniques that will serve them academically, professionally, and in their daily lives. Beacon also offers study abroad trips to sites across Europe, and the Field Placement Program gives all students the chance to gain valuable experience in the workplace.

BEACON COLLEGE

WHAT IT IS

Some students with learning disabilities may worry that it will be difficult, if not impossible, to succeed in college because of the unique educational challenges they face. Beacon College, founded in 1989, counters that impression by affording an environment in which students with learning disabilities can excel. The idea for the school grew from the activism of a group of parents concerned about the lack of higher education opportunities for their children with learning disabilities. Beacon College has a staff of academic mentors and other professionals trained to address the unique needs of learning disabled students. Individuals with language-based learning disabilities, math disabilities, ADD/ADHD, auditory- and visual-processing differences, expressive/receptive language deficits, and reading and writing disabilities will thrive at Beacon. Classes are small, and students are guaranteed to receive the attention they need to complete their degrees. The college offers majors in three areas: human services, liberal studies, and computer information systems. Beacon also provides a welcoming social environment, and beyond the classroom, students can participate in several student groups, theme nights, and campus events.

WHERE IT'S AT

Beacon College is located in Leesburg, approximately 50 miles northwest of Orlando in central Florida. Fifteen percent of the land in Leesburg is dedicated to parks and recreation, and with more than 1,400 lakes in the county, outdoor activities like waterskiing, boating, and fishing abound. Students can also explore the town's art galleries, museums, restaurants, and nightclubs or take advantage of major area attractions, including Walt Disney World, Universal Studios, Kennedy Space Center, and Daytona Beach. The Beacon College campus is conveniently small, and students living in college housing can easily walk to class and other activities. The Stoer Building, which houses the dining hall, is central Florida's only existing example of pebble architecture.

THE DETAILS

Campus setting:	small town
Degrees:	bachelor's
Calendar:	semesters
Public/Private:	private nonprofit
Number of full-time faculty:	10
Student-to-teacher ratio:	7:1

Admissions requirements:
- **Options:** deferred entrance, early admission
- **Application fee:** $50
- **Required:** essay or personal statement, high school transcript, 3 letters of recommendation
- **Application deadlines:** —
- **Early decision:** —
- **Notification:** 8/16 (freshmen), 8/16 (transfer)

Average high school GPA:	—
Average freshman SAT verbal/math score:	—/—
Average freshman ACT score:	—
Number of applicants:	87
Number of applicants accepted:	47
Percentage of students from out of state:	75%
Total freshman enrollment:	33
Total enrollment:	97
Percentage of students who live in campus housing:	99%
Total tuition:	$21,700
Total cost with fees & expenses:	$28,860
Average financial aid package:	—

MAJORS

- Computer Information Systems
- Human Services, General
- Liberal Arts and Sciences/Liberal Studies

BETHUNE-COOKMAN COLLEGE

640 Dr Mary McLeod Bethune Boulevard
Daytona Beach, FL 32114

(386) 481-2000
http://www.bethune.cookman.edu/

 **BIG FISH**

 **UNIVERSITY 101**
Required first-year transitional seminar; upperclassman mentors; optional first-year learning communities.

Would you like to polish a spaceship?

Do you dream of feeding Shamu? Could Walt Disney World use a go-getter like you? Bethune-Cookman students have the opportunity to work at some of the world's most famous attractions, including Sea World, Universal Studios, and the Kennedy Space Center. Field experience is a chief component of several majors, and the college strongly encourages all students to take part in it. Paid and unpaid internships, co-ops, practicums, work abroad programs, research opportunities, and credited service-learning experiences can be incorporated into almost any program of study. In Florida alone, Bethune-Cookman students are eligible for internships at Anheuser-Busch, Walt Disney World, IBM, the American Cancer Society, Sony Pictures, Virgin Records, and the National Aeronautics and Space Administration, just to name a few.

BETHUNE-COOKMAN COLLEGE

WHAT IT IS

Bethune-Cookman College is an historically black career-oriented liberal arts institution that operates on a semester calendar and is affiliated with the United Methodist Church. The college is a result of a merger between the Daytona Educational and Industrial Training School for Negro Girls (founded by Mary McLeod Bethune in 1904) and the Darnell Cookman Institute for Men (founded in 1872). High academic standards, curriculum flexibility, concern for the individual student, and an emphasis on a Christian way of life are trademarks of the institution. The college enrolls promising secondary school graduates and adult learners from diverse social, economic, and educational backgrounds.

The students at Bethune-Cookman College come from 43 states and 35 countries. The campus cultural and social activities include choirs, band, drama, student publications, radio broadcasting, clubs, Greek letter organizations, and athletics. The Office of Student Activities provides programs, speakers and lecturers, and community service opportunities to enhance student growth and development.

WHERE IT'S AT

The 70-acre campus of Bethune-Cookman College is nestled in the heart of Daytona Beach, Florida. The Atlantic-coast city of Daytona Beach is a metropolitan area that has a population of more than 160,000. The college's location provides easy access to local business centers, churches, theaters, museums, beaches, recreational facilities, and bus and air terminals. The area offers good weather year-round, fine beaches, long-distance bus service, and an international airport. Within 100 miles of the campus are many major attractions to enhance students' personal and educational growth: the Kennedy Space Center, St. Augustine, Walt Disney World/EPCOT Center, Sea World, Silver Springs, MGM and Universal Studios, Marineland, and similar attractions.

THE DETAILS

Campus setting:	urban
Degrees:	bachelor's
Calendar:	semesters
Public/Private:	private religious
Number of full-time faculty:	150
Student-to-teacher ratio:	17:1
Admissions requirements:	

- **Options:** deferred entrance, early admission
- **Application fee:** $25
- **Required:** high school transcript, letter of recommendation, SAT or ACT
- **Application deadlines:** 6/30 (freshmen), 6/30 (transfer)
- **Early decision:** —
- **Notification:** continuous (freshmen), continuous (transfer)

Average high school GPA:	2.81
Average freshman SAT verbal/math score:	420 / 418
Average freshman ACT score:	16
Number of applicants:	4,134
Number of applicants accepted:	2,426
Percentage of students from out of state:	32%
Total freshman enrollment:	819
Total enrollment:	2,895
Percentage of students who live in campus housing:	57%
Total tuition:	$10,610
Total cost with fees & expenses:	$17,774
Average financial aid package:	$11,555

BETHUNE-COOKMAN COLLEGE

MAJORS

- Accounting
- Biology/Biological Sciences, General
- Biology Teacher Education
- Business Administration and Management, General
- Business Teacher Education
- Chemistry, General
- Chemistry Teacher Education
- Clinical Laboratory Science/Medical Technology/Technologist
- Computer Engineering, General
- Computer Science
- Corrections and Criminal Justice, Other
- Education/Teaching of Individuals with Specific Learning Disabilities
- Elementary Education and Teaching
- English/Language Arts Teacher Education
- English Language and Literature, General
- Gerontology
- History, General
- Hotel/Motel Administration/Management
- Information Science/Studies
- International Business/Trade/Commerce
- International Relations and Affairs
- Liberal Arts and Sciences/Liberal Studies
- Mass Communication/Media Studies
- Mathematics, General
- Mathematics Teacher Education
- Music Performance, General
- Music Teacher Education
- Nursing/Registered Nurse Training
- Philosophy and Religious Studies, Other
- Physical Education Teaching and Coaching
- Physics, General
- Physics Teacher Education
- Political Science and Government, General
- Psychology, General
- Social Studies Teacher Education
- Sociology
- Speech and Rhetorical Studies

ECKERD COLLEGE

4200 54th Avenue South
St. Petersburg, FL 33711

(727) 867-1166
http://www.eckerd.edu/

 **BIG IDEA**

 **UNIVERSITY 101**
Required first-year Western Heritage course; required first-year Autumn Term course; extended orientation program; required first-year learning communities; special academic advisors assigned to first-years; faculty mentors; required first-year service-learning project.

 BIG FISH

Palm trees, blue water, and academic excellence.

Mix that with a visit from Stephen King for the annual Paradise Conference, and you'll see why Eckerd is a magnet for creative and motivated students. An extra three weeks of classes for first-years may not sound appealing at first. But Eckerd's Autumn Term for incoming students gives new arrivals the freedom to make friends, explore the college's resources, and find their way around campus before upperclassmen arrive, while taking an Autumn Term course designed to introduce them to collegiate-level studies. Eckerd also has a one-month Winter Term, which many students use for international study. A spring-summer program is also available, during which students prepare for travel in the spring, then take off for a summer of adventure.

WHAT IT IS

A liberal arts institution of distinctive quality, Eckerd College was founded in 1958 as Florida Presbyterian College. Eckerd College is related by covenant to the Presbyterian Church (U.S.A.). Dedicated to excellence, Eckerd College has established a national reputation as a leading, innovative liberal arts college. Its student body, faculty members, and program attest to its founders' high expectations and a remarkable degree of fulfillment in the years that have followed. In addition, the college has been awarded a chapter of Phi Beta Kappa.

Sixty-nine percent of the student body comes from out of state. Dormitory life is one hub of the college's social environment. The dorms are small and informal, and friendships are easily developed in this setting. Upperclassmen may choose to live in the apartment-style town houses located right on campus. Through the Eckerd College student government, social and cultural programs are planned for the college community. Four buildings in the center of campus comprise the Hough Campus Center, which includes a pub, snack bars, lounges, student offices and meeting rooms, and a fitness center. The Campus Center is designed to accommodate meaningful interactions between all members of the college community. Students also have the opportunity to get involved with the campus television and radio stations, yearbook, and weekly newspaper.

WHERE IT'S AT

Bordered in part by a one-mile-plus waterfront, the 188-acre campus is located in a suburban setting on the southern tip of the peninsula that makes up Pinellas County. This peninsula is bound on the west by the Gulf of Mexico and on the east by Tampa Bay. St. Petersburg is a city of almost 250,000 people and part of the rapidly growing Tampa Bay metropolitan area of approximately 2.5 million, which has become the national and regional headquarters for many major corporations. Cultural and recreational opportunities are abundant, including art museums, symphony orchestras, professional theater and road-show engagements of Broadway plays, concerts, and year-round professional sports attractions.

THE DETAILS

Campus setting:	suburban
Degrees:	bachelor's
Calendar:	4-1-4
Public/Private:	private religious
Number of full-time faculty:	101
Student-to-teacher ratio:	13:1

Admissions requirements:
- **Options:** common application, deferred entrance, early admission, electronic application
- **Application fee:** $35
- **Required:** essay or personal statement, high school transcript, letter of recommendation, SAT or ACT, SAT Subject Tests (recommended)
- **Application deadlines:** continuous (freshmen), continuous (transfer)
- **Early decision:** —
- **Notification:** continuous (freshmen), continuous (transfer)

Average high school GPA:	3.30
Average freshman SAT verbal/math score:	583 / 569
Average freshman ACT score:	—
Number of applicants:	2,284
Number of applicants accepted:	1,696
Percentage of students from out of state:	69%
Total freshman enrollment:	468
Total enrollment:	1,688
Percentage of students who live in campus housing:	79%
Total tuition:	$24,116
Total cost with fees & expenses:	$31,688
Average financial aid package:	$18,961

ECKERD COLLEGE

MAJORS

- American/United States Studies/Civilization
- Anthropology
- Art/Art Studies, General
- Biology/Biological Sciences, General
- Business Administration and Management, General
- Chemistry, General
- Chinese Language and Literature
- Clinical Laboratory Science/Medical Technology/Technologist
- Communication Studies/Speech Communication and Rhetoric
- Comparative Literature
- Computer Science
- Creative Writing
- Drama and Dramatics/Theatre Arts, General
- East Asian Languages, Literatures, and Linguistics, General
- Economics, General
- English Language and Literature, General
- Environmental Studies
- Foreign Languages and Literatures, General
- French Language and Literature
- German Language and Literature
- History, General
- Human Development and Family Studies, General
- Humanities/Humanistic Studies
- Human Resources Management/Personnel Administration, General
- Interdisciplinary Studies
- International Business/Trade/Commerce
- International Relations and Affairs
- Literature
- Marine Biology and Biological Oceanography
- Mathematics, General
- Modern Languages
- Music, General
- Philosophy
- Physics, General
- Political Science and Government, General
- Psychology, General
- Religion/Religious Studies
- Russian Language and Literature
- Sociology
- Spanish Language and Literature
- Women's Studies

FLORIDA

EMBRY-RIDDLE AERONAUTICAL UNIVERSITY

600 South Clyde Morris Boulevard
Daytona Beach, FL 32114

(386) 226-6000
http://www.embryriddle.edu/

 **BIG REP**

 **UNIVERSITY 101**
Optional first-year transitional seminar (required for certain colleges); extended orientation program; special academic advisors assigned to first-year students; upperclassman mentors; optional first-year tutors; optional first-year extracurricular activities and social events; optional first-year residential learning communities; optional First Class special summer intensive academic program.

The term "higher education" takes on a literal meaning for students at Embry-Riddle.

The university is the biggest, oldest, and best-known aeronautics school in the world, with classrooms across the country and on military bases around the globe. More than 20 undergrad degree programs, all somehow related to the study of flight, allow students to major in a range of subjects. Students may even find themselves piloting one of the school's 93 instructional aircrafts during flight training. Ninety-six percent of all Embry-Riddle graduates find employment or decide to continue their education within one year of graduation.

EMBRY-RIDDLE AERONAUTICAL UNIVERSITY

WHAT IT IS

The purpose of Embry-Riddle Aeronautical University is to provide a comprehensive education of such excellence that graduates are responsible citizens and well prepared for productive careers in aviation and aerospace. In addition to its traditional residential campuses in Daytona Beach and Prescott, Arizona, Embry-Riddle serves the continuing education needs of the aviation industry through an extensive network of off-campus centers in the United States and Europe and through its division of continuing education training seminars and management development programs.

Students come from all 50 states and more than 100 countries, which makes Embry-Riddle truly an international university. Students take advantage of the many opportunities for personal growth and development through social and pre-professional Greek organizations, as well as cultural and recreational activities. Embry-Riddle's award-winning Precision Flight Demonstration teams offer students the opportunity to compete nationally in air and ground events. Embry-Riddle also has the largest all-volunteer Air Force ROTC detachment in the country and among the fastest-growing Navy ROTC units and Army ROTC battalions. Embry-Riddle athletes participate in intercollegiate and intramural competitions in many sports, including baseball, basketball, crew, cross-country, golf, soccer, tennis, and volleyball.

WHERE IT'S AT

The clear flying weather year-round and resort communities surrounding Embry-Riddle's residential campus in Daytona Beach offer students an excellent environment in which to study, fly, and enjoy recreational activities. Located adjacent to the Daytona Beach International Airport, the campus contains more than 20 main buildings set on 211 acres and is only three miles from the world's most famous beach. The high-technology industries located in Daytona Beach and nearby Orlando provide the university with an outstanding support base. In addition, the Kennedy Space Center is less than a two-hour drive away.

THE DETAILS

Campus setting:	urban
Degrees:	bachelor's, master's
Calendar:	semesters
Public/Private:	private nonprofit
Number of full-time faculty:	225
Student-to-teacher ratio:	17:1

Admissions requirements:
- **Options:** common application, deferred entrance, early admission, early decision, electronic application
- **Application fee:** $30
- **Required:** high school transcript, letter of recommendation, SAT or ACT
- **Application deadlines:** continuous (freshmen), 7/1 (transfer)
- **Early decision:** 12/1
- **Notification:** continuous (freshmen), continuous (transfer), 12/31 (early decision)

Average high school GPA:	3.25
Average freshman SAT verbal/math score:	544 / 575
Average freshman ACT score:	23
Number of applicants:	2,846
Number of applicants accepted:	2,396
Percentage of students from out of state:	71%
Total freshman enrollment:	935
Total enrollment:	4,788
Percentage of students who live in campus housing:	41%
Total tuition:	$22,820
Total cost with fees & expenses:	$31,356
Average financial aid package:	$7,570

EMBRY-RIDDLE AERONAUTICAL UNIVERSITY

MAJORS

- Aeronautical/Aerospace Engineering Technology/Technician
- Aeronautics/Aviation/Aerospace Science and Technology, General
- Aerospace, Aeronautical and Astronautical Engineering
- Airline/Commercial/Professional Pilot and Flight Crew
- Air Traffic Controller
- Atmospheric Sciences and Meteorology, General
- Aviation/Airway Management and Operations
- Business Administration, Management and Operations, Other
- Civil Engineering, Other
- Communication Studies/Speech Communication and Rhetoric
- Computer Engineering, General
- Computer Software Engineering
- Electrical and Electronic Engineering Technologies/Technicians, Other
- Engineering, General
- Engineering Physics
- Engineering Technologies/Technicians, Other
- Environmental Psychology
- Occupational Safety and Health Technology/Technician

FLAGLER COLLEGE

74 King Street, PO Box 1027
St. Augustine, FL 32085

(904) 829-6481
http://www.flagler.edu/

BIG IDEA

UNIVERSITY 101
Required first-year career explorations courses; extended orientation program; first-year seminars required for some majors.

BIG DEAL

Flagler's deaf education major is the largest and most developed program of its kind in the country.

Students who major in deaf education complete coursework in deaf and hard-of-hearing education and elementary education; they also participate in fieldwork in both hearing and deaf schools. Sports management, communications, business, administration, English, and graphic design are also popular majors at Flagler. One nonacademic reason to consider Flagler: the chance to live in Ponce de Leon Hall, a former resort hotel featuring Spanish Renaissance architecture and interior décor by Louis Comfort Tiffany.

WHAT IT IS

Founded in 1968, Flagler College is predominantly residential and small by intent. The college strives to develop qualities of civility, integrity, loyalty, dependability, and affection in its students. An atmosphere of friendliness and respect prevails throughout the college.

The focal point of the campus is Ponce de Leon Hall, formerly a famous resort hotel. Described as a masterpiece of American architecture, the Ponce de Leon is listed on the National Register of Historic Places. Ponce de Leon Hall contains a residence hall for 500 students, the dining hall, the student center, and the infirmary. The college offers a wide range of extracurricular activities that are designed to enrich students socially, culturally, and physically. There are 23 organizations and five honor societies for students to join. In addition, favorite pastimes of Flagler students include biking around town, walking through the restoration area, surfing at the beach, competing in a sports event or being a spectator, or just sunning by the pool. Athletic and recreational facilities include a gymnasium, eight tennis courts, and a swimming pool. A 19-acre athletic field for baseball, soccer, softball, and intramurals is located two miles from the campus.

WHERE IT'S AT

The 19-acre campus is situated in the heart of historic St. Augustine, four miles from the Atlantic beaches. St. Augustine is located on the northeast coast of Florida, about midway between Jacksonville and Daytona Beach. A famed tourist center, rich in history, and beautifully maintained in all of its storied charm, St. Augustine provides an attractive environment for a liberal arts college. Community resources complement the programs offered by the college. Flagler is an important part of the St. Augustine community and seeks to use the community's educational, cultural, and recreational resources to supplement and enhance the quality of life and education at the college.

THE DETAILS

Campus setting:	small town
Degrees:	bachelor's
Calendar:	semesters
Public/Private:	private nonprofit
Number of full-time faculty:	79
Student-to-teacher ratio:	21:1

Admissions requirements:
- **Options:** early admission, early decision, electronic application
- **Application fee:** $30
- **Required:** essay or personal statement, high school transcript, letter of recommendation, SAT or ACT
- **Application deadlines:** 3/1 (freshmen), 3/1 (transfer)
- **Early decision:** 12/1
- **Notification:** 3/30 (freshmen), 3/30 (transfer), 12/15 (early decision)

Average high school GPA:	3.32
Average freshman SAT verbal/math score:	575 / 575
Average freshman ACT score:	23
Number of applicants:	2,313
Number of applicants accepted:	704
Percentage of students from out of state:	32%
Total freshman enrollment:	493
Total enrollment:	2,106
Percentage of students who live in campus housing:	36%
Total tuition:	$8,600
Total cost with fees & expenses:	$14,590
Average financial aid package:	$7,683

FLAGLER COLLEGE

MAJORS

- Accounting
- Art Teacher Education
- Business Administration and Management, General
- Communication Studies/Speech Communication and Rhetoric
- Drama and Dramatics/Theatre Arts, General
- Education/Teaching of Individuals with Emotional Disturbances
- Education/Teaching of Individuals with Hearing Impairments, Including Deafness
- Education/Teaching of Individuals with Mental Retardation
- Education/Teaching of Individuals with Multiple Disabilities
- Education/Teaching of Individuals with Specific Learning Disabilities
- Elementary Education and Teaching
- English Language and Literature, General
- Fine/Studio Arts, General
- Graphic Design
- History, General
- Latin American Studies
- Liberal Arts and Sciences/Liberal Studies
- Philosophy
- Political Science and Government, General
- Psychology, General
- Public Administration
- Religion/Religious Studies
- Secondary Education and Teaching
- Social Studies Teacher Education
- Sociology
- Spanish Language and Literature
- Spanish Language Teacher Education
- Sport and Fitness Administration/Management

FLORIDA A&M UNIVERSITY

Foote Hillyer Administration Center
Tallahassee, FL 32307

(850) 599-3000
http://www.famu.edu/

BIG DEAL

BIG IDEA

UNIVERSITY 101
Optional first-year transitional course (required for undeclared majors); special academic advisors assigned to first-years; upperclassman mentors; first-year newsletter to help inform you of what's happening on campus; optional first-year extracurricular activities.

Florida A&M grads have work experience before they even think about entering the job market.

The school's cooperative education programs provide paid work for students in several domestic and international locations. Students can participate in business, government, and education co-ops on campus, in any U.S. state, or in such countries as Switzerland, England, and Australia. Other notable off-campus programs include the School of Architecture's semester (or year) in Washington, D.C., joint degree offerings in conjunction with Florida State University, the annual FAMU study abroad trip to the Dominican Republic, and a partnership with the College Consortium for International Studies that allows students to take courses in 80 countries.

FLORIDA A&M UNIVERSITY

WHAT IT IS

For more than a century, the primary goals of the Florida Agricultural and Mechanical University have been to promote academic excellence and improve the quality of life for those it serves. Founded in 1887 as the State Normal School for Colored Students, FAMU opened its doors with two instructors and 15 students. Today, it is a full and equal partner in the 10-member State University System. Although historically black, the university seeks qualified students from all racial, ethnic, religious, and national backgrounds.

There are more than 100 student organizations on campus, including nationally affiliated fraternities and sororities, honor societies, religious groups, fashion/modeling clubs, the Literary Guild, Orchesis Contemporary Dance Theatre, the Playmakers Guild, and the FAMU Gospel Choir, which released its first album in 1985. The School of Journalism and Graphic Communication publishes a weekly student newspaper and operates an FM radio station. The Marching 100, FAMU's 300-member marching band, has received national television and magazine coverage and, in 1985, became the first band outside of the Big Ten Conference to earn the Sousa Foundation's prestigious Sudler Trophy. Athletic facilities include Bragg Stadium (capacity 25,600), which features a track and field complex with an eight-lane, all-weather, 400-meter track; competition-grade tennis courts; two outdoor pools; baseball and softball fields; and a complex that serves as headquarters for the largest women's athletic program at any historically black institution in the country.

WHERE IT'S AT

The FAMU campus covers 419 acres of lush shrubbery, flowering plants, and massive oaks. The university is located on the highest of seven hills in Tallahassee (population 200,000) among the heavily wooded, rolling hills of northwest Florida, only 22 miles from the Gulf of Mexico. There are more than 1,000 acres of public parks and land, as well as numerous lakes nearby. The university is located eight blocks from the Capitol Complex, and bus service is available from campus to shopping malls; state, county, and city offices; and recreational areas. An intercampus shuttle (between FAMU and Florida State University) and on-campus shuttle run daily during class hours.

THE DETAILS

Campus setting:	urban
Degrees:	bachelor's, master's, doctoral
Calendar:	semesters
Public/Private:	public state
Number of full-time faculty:	621
Student-to-teacher ratio:	21:1
Admissions requirements:	

- **Options:** common application, deferred entrance, early admission, electronic application
- **Application fee:** $20
- **Required:** high school transcript, letter of recommendation, SAT or ACT
- **Application deadlines:** 5/9 (freshmen), 5/1 (transfer)
- **Early decision:** —
- **Notification:** 8/1 (freshmen), 8/1 (transfer)

Average high school GPA:	3.18
Average freshman SAT verbal/math score:	486 / 485
Average freshman ACT score:	20
Number of applicants:	5,709
Number of applicants accepted:	4,029
Percentage of students from out of state:	20%
Total freshman enrollment:	1,973
Total enrollment:	13,064
Percentage of students who live in campus housing:	—
Total in-state tuition, fees & expenses:	$9,084
Total out-of-state tuition, fees & expenses:	$22,428
Average financial aid package:	$7,926

FLORIDA A&M UNIVERSITY

MAJORS

- Accounting
- Accounting and Business/Management
- Actuarial Science
- Administrative Assistant and Secretarial Science, General
- African-American/Black Studies
- Agricultural Business and Management, General
- Agriculture, General
- Animal Sciences, General
- Architectural Engineering Technology/Technician
- Architecture
- Art/Art Studies, General
- Art Teacher Education
- Biology/Biological Sciences, General
- Business Administration and Management, General
- Business Teacher Education
- Chemical Engineering
- Chemistry, General
- Civil Engineering, General
- Civil Engineering Technology/Technician
- Commercial and Advertising Art
- Computer and Information Sciences, General
- Computer Engineering, General
- Construction Engineering Technology/Technician
- Criminal Justice/Law Enforcement Administration
- Drama and Dramatics/Theatre Arts, General
- Economics, General
- Education, General
- Electrical, Electronic and Communications Engineering Technology/Technician
- Electrical, Electronics and Communications Engineering
- Elementary Education and Teaching
- English Language and Literature, General
- Entomology
- Environmental Science
- Finance, General
- Finance and Financial Management Services, Other
- French Language and Literature
- Geography
- Graphic and Printing Equipment Operator, General Production
- Health/Health Care Administration/Management
- Health and Physical Education, General
- Health Information/Medical Records Administration/Administrator
- Health Teacher Education
- History, General
- Horticultural Science
- Industrial Engineering
- Information Science/Studies
- Jazz/Jazz Studies
- Journalism
- Kindergarten/Preschool Education and Teaching
- Landscape Architecture
- Management Information Systems, General
- Management Information Systems and Services, Other
- Mass Communication/Media Studies
- Mathematics, General
- Mechanical Engineering
- Medical Illustration and Informatics, Other
- Molecular Biology
- Music, General
- Music Performance, General
- Music Teacher Education
- Nursing/Registered Nurse Training
- Occupational Therapy/Therapist
- Ornamental Horticulture
- Parks, Recreation and Leisure Facilities Management
- Pharmacy (PharmD [USA] PharmD, BS/BPharm [Canada])
- Philosophy
- Physical Education Teaching and Coaching
- Physical Therapy/Therapist
- Physics, General
- Plant Protection and Integrated Pest Management
- Political Science and Government, General
- Pre-Dentistry Studies
- Psychology, General
- Public Administration
- Public Relations/Image Management
- Religion/Religious Studies
- Respiratory Care Therapy/Therapist
- Social Sciences, General
- Social Work
- Sociology
- Spanish Language and Literature
- Technology Education/Industrial Arts
- Trade and Industrial Teacher Education

FLORIDA ATLANTIC UNIVERSITY

777 Glades Road, PO Box 3091
Boca Raton, FL 33431

(561) 297-3000
http://www.fau.edu/

BIG DEAL

UNIVERSITY 101
Optional first-year transitional seminar (required for athletes and students who do not meet all admissions requirements); extended orientation program; optional first-year learning communities; optional first-year residential learning communities.

BIG FISH

Florida Atlantic holds its own when compared to other research-intensive universities in the state.

There are 42 university-operated centers and institutes, several of which run their own corporate and government-sponsored research projects. Interested in teaching? Try one of the several bachelor's degrees available in education. Additionally, the university operates its own dual-enrollment public high school. Students in grades nine through 12 can get a jump on their future by taking up to 75 percent of bachelor's degree coursework prior to high school graduation. Talk about a head start! Partnerships with the Florida Atlantic High School and other area school boards provide immediate jobs for education grads, which helps reduce local teacher shortages.

FLORIDA ATLANTIC UNIVERSITY

WHAT IT IS

Florida Atlantic University is a midsize university established in 1961, making it the fifth-oldest university in the state system. Since the original Boca Raton campus was founded in 1964, the university has expanded to six other campuses in South Florida: Dania Beach (SeaTech), Davie, Fort Lauderdale (two locations: Downtown Fort Lauderdale and Commercial Boulevard), Jupiter (John D. MacArthur Campus/Harriet L. Wilkes Honors College), and Port St. Lucie (Treasure Coast).

The residential campus in Boca Raton accommodates students in eight residence halls and a student apartment complex. Nearby is a 5,000-seat gymnasium, field house, swimming and diving complex, and athletic fields and courts (baseball, soccer, softball, and tennis). The Boca Raton campus hosts art exhibits and theatrical productions in its two galleries and theaters. The University Center's 2,400-seat auditorium enables students to enjoy performances ranging from rock groups to the Florida Philharmonic Orchestra. One of FAU's newest campuses is located in Dania Beach. Known as SeaTech, the campus is a marine and ocean engineering facility. The downtown Fort Lauderdale campus primarily offers graduate programs in the busy city center. A third campus in Broward County is located on Commercial Boulevard. The Harriet L. Wilkes Honors College in Jupiter opened in fall 1999. To the north, the university provides classes and services at its Port St. Lucie campus and offers extension classes in Belle Glade and Okeechobee.

WHERE IT'S AT

The 850-acre Boca Raton campus is located on a former U.S. Army airfield and inhabited by various wildlife, including burrowing owls. The campus was designated as a burrowing owl sanctuary by the Audubon Society in 1971. The FAU–Boca Raton campus is three miles west of the Atlantic Ocean and midway between Palm Beach and Fort Lauderdale. Located off I-95 on Glades Road, the university is 25 miles from both the Palm Beach and Fort Lauderdale international airports. South Florida's climate is subtropical, with an average year-round temperature of 75 degrees. FAU's campuses are within easy driving distance of some of the most beautiful beaches and recreational facilities to be found anywhere.

THE DETAILS

Campus setting:	suburban
Degrees:	bachelor's, master's, doctoral
Calendar:	semesters
Public/Private:	public state
Number of full-time faculty:	733
Student-to-teacher ratio:	18:1

Admissions requirements:
- **Options:** common application, deferred entrance, early admission, electronic application
- **Application fee:** $30
- **Required:** high school transcript, letter of recommendation, SAT and SAT Subject Tests, or ACT
- **Application deadlines:** 6/1 (freshmen), 6/1 (transfer)
- **Early decision:** —
- **Notification:** continuous (freshmen), continuous (transfer)

Average high school GPA:	3.40
Average freshman SAT verbal/math score:	515 / 520
Average freshman ACT score:	21
Number of applicants:	10,435
Number of applicants accepted:	6,835
Percentage of students from out of state:	5%
Total freshman enrollment:	2,215
Total enrollment:	25,383
Percentage of students who live in campus housing:	9%
Total in-state tuition, fees & expenses:	$10,878
Total out-of-state tuition, fees & expenses:	$23,385
Average financial aid package:	$6,845

FLORIDA ATLANTIC UNIVERSITY

MAJORS

- Accounting
- Anthropology
- Architecture
- Art/Art Studies, General
- Biology/Biological Sciences, General
- Business Administration and Management, General
- Chemistry, General
- City/Urban, Community and Regional Planning
- Civil Engineering, General
- Clinical Laboratory Science/Medical Technology/Technologist
- Computer and Information Sciences, General
- Computer Engineering, General
- Criminal Justice/Safety Studies
- Digital Communication and Media/Multimedia
- Drama and Dramatics/Theatre Arts, General
- Economics, General
- Electrical, Electronics and Communications Engineering
- Elementary Education and Teaching
- English/Language Arts Teacher Education
- English Language and Literature, General
- Finance, General
- French Language and Literature
- Geography
- Geology/Earth Science, General
- German Language and Literature
- Health/Health Care Administration/Management
- Health Science
- Health Services/Allied Health/Health Sciences, General
- History, General
- Hospitality Administration/Management, General
- Human Resources Management/Personnel Administration, General
- International Business/Trade/Commerce
- Jewish/Judaic Studies
- Kinesiology and Exercise Science
- Liberal Arts and Sciences, General Studies and Humanities, Other
- Liberal Arts and Sciences/Liberal Studies
- Linguistics
- Management Information Systems, General
- Marketing/Marketing Management, General
- Mathematics, General
- Mathematics Teacher Education
- Mechanical Engineering
- Music, General
- Music Teacher Education
- Nursing/Registered Nurse Training
- Ocean Engineering
- Philosophy
- Physics, General
- Physiological Psychology/Psychobiology
- Political Science and Government, General
- Psychology, General
- Public Administration
- Real Estate
- Science Teacher Education/General Science Teacher Education
- Social Psychology
- Social Sciences, General
- Social Science Teacher Education
- Social Work
- Sociology
- Spanish Language and Literature
- Special Education and Teaching, General
- Speech and Rhetorical Studies

FLORIDA GULF COAST UNIVERSITY

10501 FGCU Boulevard South
Fort Myers, FL 33965

(239) 590-1000
http://www.fgcu.edu/

BIG DEAL

UNIVERSITY 101
Special academic advisors assigned to first-year students; optional first-year residential learning communities; required first-year summer reading; extended orientation program; optional first-year convocation ceremony; upperclassman mentors; required first-year seminar.

BIG FISH

Built during the '90s tech boom, Florida Gulf Coast University fully embraces the digital age.

This tech-savvy campus is known for producing computer-literate grads and incorporating multimedia into classroom teaching methods. Both traditional and distance-learning courses include an online component to acclimate students to the computer systems they'll likely use in future careers. To make sure students have the right equipment for class, the university also provides 323 on-campus computers for student use, as well as a laptop loan program. Students who aren't fluent in geek-speak need not fear: Online tutorials help fill in the gaps in their electronic skills, and tech support is just a phone call away.

FLORIDA GULF COAST UNIVERSITY

WHAT IT IS

Less than a decade old, Florida Gulf Coast University is the tenth school to become a part of the State University System of Florida. Established by the Florida legislature in 1991, FGCU began offering classes in 1997. Since that first year, FGCU has grown quickly and enrollment has nearly doubled. Now students from 32 states and 74 countries attend classes at the institution, creating the traditions that will shape the university's history. An FGCU education is designed to meet the diverse needs of students, with majors in fields like marine science, bioengineering, community health, and criminal forensics, as well as an honors program, distance-learning options, and evening courses. Class sizes are small, and students can count on personal attention from faculty as they learn in labs, classrooms, and libraries outfitted with state-of-the-art technology.

WHERE IT'S AT

Florida Gulf Coast University's ultramodern campus sprawls across 760 acres in Fort Myers. All campus facilities have been recently constructed, and the university boasts the latest in design and technology. Many FGCU buildings are energy efficient, and the WCI Green Building hosts outreach and education programs for the Fort Myers community, spotlighting the importance of creating a sustainable future. Students who live on campus can reside in the school's lakefront apartments, close to on-campus diversions like FGCU's art gallery and black box theater.

THE DETAILS

Campus setting:	suburban
Degrees:	bachelor's, master's
Calendar:	semesters
Public/Private:	public state
Number of full-time faculty:	225
Student-to-teacher ratio:	18:1

Admissions requirements:
- **Options:** deferred entrance, electronic application
- **Application fee:** $30
- **Required:** high school transcript, letter of recommendation, SAT or ACT
- **Application deadlines:** 8/1 (freshmen), 8/1 (transfer)
- **Early decision:** —
- **Notification:** continuous (freshmen), continuous (transfer)

Average high school GPA:	3.53
Average freshman SAT verbal/math score:	527 / 530
Average freshman ACT score:	22
Number of applicants:	2,979
Number of applicants accepted:	2,175
Percentage of students from out of state:	9%
Total freshman enrollment:	896
Total enrollment:	5,955
Percentage of students who live in campus housing:	32%
Total in-state tuition, fees & expenses:	$12,351
Total out-of-state tuition, fees & expenses:	$24,447
Average financial aid package:	$7,123

FLORIDA GULF COAST UNIVERSITY

MAJORS

- Accounting
- Biotechnology
- Business Administration and Management, General
- Computer and Information Sciences, General
- Criminal Justice/Safety Studies
- Early Childhood Education and Teaching
- Elementary Education and Teaching
- Finance, General
- General Studies
- Health Services/Allied Health/Health Sciences, General
- Human Services, General
- Kinesiology and Exercise Science
- Legal Assistant/Paralegal
- Liberal Arts and Sciences/Liberal Studies
- Management Information Systems, General
- Marketing/Marketing Management, General
- Mental Health Counseling/Counselor
- Nursing/Registered Nurse Training
- Occupational Therapy/Therapist
- Political Science and Government, General
- Resort Management
- Special Education and Teaching, General

FLORIDA INSTITUTE OF TECHNOLOGY

150 West University Boulevard (321) 674-8000
Melbourne, FL 32901 http://www.fit.edu/

BIG FISH

UNIVERSITY 101
Required first-year transitional seminar; extended orientation program; required first-year math, English, and chemistry courses; faculty mentors.

Florida Tech was founded as a continuing education school for NASA employees.

Florida Tech is one of the most cutting-edge institutions in the country. With 24 FIT–manned research centers and $9 million in research contracts and grants for 2005, virtual reality labs, eight flight simulators, 30 aircraft, 30 acres of botanic gardens, 70 microcomputers, and the largest telescope in Florida—you'll be hard-pressed to find a better bang for your buck. More than 125 on-campus laboratories allow undergrads to learn by doing through independent and collaborative projects with the help of faculty researchers. Florida Tech grads use their education to become anything from space-shuttle pilots to four-star generals.

FLORIDA INSTITUTE OF TECHNOLOGY

WHAT IT IS

Born in the age of space exploration, Florida Institute of Technology was founded in 1958 to offer continuing education to the scientists, engineers, and technicians working at what is now NASA's Kennedy Space Center. As the only independent technological university in the southeastern United States, the university remains dedicated to providing a high-quality education that enhances knowledge through basic and applied research. In support of this mission, Florida Tech is committed to providing students with a world-class faculty; a hands-on, technology-focused curriculum; a high-quality, highly selective, and culturally diverse student body; and personal and career growth opportunities.

More than 100 student organizations represent the varied interests of Florida Tech's students, including student government; fraternities and sororities; political and religious groups; college-run radio and television; dance, music, science fiction, choral, and theater performance groups; and academic and honor organizations. Panther athletic teams have earned national championships in men's soccer and crew; regional titles in baseball, men's soccer, and women's basketball; and Sunshine State Conference Championships in men's soccer, men's and women's cross-country, men's and women's basketball, and women's rowing. Students can take advantage of the subtropical climate to participate in outdoor activities year-round.

WHERE IT'S AT

Florida Tech is located along the Atlantic coastline of central Florida in Brevard County, better known as the Space Coast. Situated within Florida's high-technology corridor, it is home to the Kennedy Space Center and United Space Alliance. The area's attractive business climate is matched only by its natural resources, including the estuarine habitats of the Indian River Lagoon; the Atlantic Ocean marine ecosystem; area beaches, marshes, and wetlands; thousands of acres of protected wildlife habitats; and various tropical/subtropical Gulf Stream weather phenomena. With the Indian River Lagoon and Atlantic Ocean less than five miles from the campus, water sports such as swimming, sailing, surfing, diving, fishing, and boating are popular year-round activities. Central Florida attractions, such as Walt Disney World, Sea World, and Universal Orlando, are within an hour's drive, and Miami is only three hours south of the campus.

THE DETAILS

Campus setting:	small town
Degrees:	bachelor's, master's, doctoral
Calendar:	semesters
Public/Private:	private nonprofit
Number of full-time faculty:	204
Student-to-teacher ratio:	12:1

Admissions requirements:
- **Options:** common application, deferred entrance, early admission, electronic application
- **Application fee:** $50
- **Required:** high school transcript, SAT or ACT
- **Application deadlines:** continuous (freshmen), continuous (transfer)
- **Early decision:** —
- **Notification:** continuous (freshmen), continuous (transfer)

Average high school GPA:	3.55
Average freshman SAT verbal/math score:	572 / 610
Average freshman ACT score:	23
Number of applicants:	2,481
Number of applicants accepted:	2,044
Percentage of students from out of state:	61%
Total freshman enrollment:	552
Total enrollment:	4,683
Percentage of students who live in campus housing:	52%
Total tuition	$23,730
Total cost with fees & expenses:	$31,550
Average financial aid package:	$20,548

FLORIDA INSTITUTE OF TECHNOLOGY

MAJORS

- Accounting
- Aeronautics/Aviation/Aerospace Science and Technology, General
- Aerospace, Aeronautical and Astronautical Engineering
- Air Transportation, Other
- Analytical Chemistry
- Applied Mathematics
- Aquatic Biology/Limnology
- Astrophysics
- Aviation/Airway Management and Operations
- Biochemistry
- Biological and Physical Sciences
- Biology/Biological Sciences, General
- Biology Teacher Education
- Biomedical Sciences, General
- Business Administration, Management and Operations, Other
- Business Administration and Management, General
- Chemical Engineering
- Chemistry, General
- Chemistry, Other
- Chemistry Teacher Education
- Civil Engineering, General
- Communication Studies/Speech Communication and Rhetoric
- Computer Engineering, General
- Computer Science
- Computer Software Engineering
- Computer Teacher Education
- Ecology
- Electrical, Electronics and Communications Engineering
- Environmental Science
- Forensic Psychology
- Humanities/Humanistic Studies
- Hydrology and Water Resources Science
- Information Science/Studies
- Interdisciplinary Studies
- Management Information Systems, General
- Marine Biology and Biological Oceanography
- Mathematics Teacher Education
- Mechanical Engineering
- Meteorology
- Molecular Biology
- Multi-/Interdisciplinary Studies, Other
- Ocean Engineering
- Oceanography, Chemical and Physical
- Physics, General
- Physics, Other
- Physics Teacher Education
- Psychology, General
- Science Teacher Education/General Science Teacher Education

FLORIDA INTERNATIONAL UNIVERSITY

11200 S.W. 8th Street
Miami, FL 33199

(305) 348-2000
http://www.fiu.edu/

BIG DEAL

UNIVERSITY 101
Upperclassman mentors; extended orientation program; required attendance at the Freshman Convocation Ceremony; optional first-year learning communities; required first-year transitional seminar.

BIG IDEA

Embrace your inner fish.

The tropical studies programs at Florida International University are some of the finest in the world. Three university-run research centers devoted exclusively to examining the climate and creatures of the tropics provide interdisciplinary courses for undergrads and joint faculty-student research opportunities. On any given day, you might find students measuring exotic plant growth at the on-campus tropical garden, assisting faculty members with workshops that debunk the misconceptions about great white sharks for elementary school students, or estimating the damage that tropical storms wreak on human communities. Hands-on fieldwork may take place in the classroom or in the 57,000-square-foot marine biology lab.

FLORIDA INTERNATIONAL UNIVERSITY

WHAT IT IS

Florida International University is Miami's public research university. Major academic divisions are the colleges of Arts and Sciences, Business Administration, Education, Engineering, Health and Urban Affairs, the Honors College, and the College of Law. The Carnegie Foundation classifies FIU as a doctoral/research university—extensive. FIU is a member of Phi Beta Kappa, the country's oldest and most distinguished academic honor society. The university's priorities are to graduate a well-educated, technologically sophisticated, ethnically diverse student body whose members can think critically about a changing world.

FIU has two main sites: University Park in southwest Miami-Dade County, 10 miles west of downtown Miami, and Biscayne Bay campus located on Biscayne Bay in North Miami. In addition, the Pines Center offers services to students in adjacent Broward County. The campuses and the center operate under one central administration. The university currently has more than 300 registered student organizations. Nationally recognized lecturers appear regularly, and concerts and movies are offered. The university offers apartment-style housing for students at both University Park and the Biscayne Bay campus. Most of the residence halls offer a full range of amenities for students, including cable TV, computer connectivity, study rooms, and computer labs, as well as a swimming pool and various recreational areas.

WHERE IT'S AT

Miami and FIU are comparable in their explosive growth, rich ethnic and cultural diversity, and quest for excellence. FIU is a leading institution in one of the most dynamic, artistically expressive, and cosmopolitan cities in the United States. Miami is also the gateway to Latin America and the Caribbean. Walt Disney World, the Everglades, marine and state parks, Seaquarium, Metro Zoo, Fairchild Tropical Gardens, and the Parrot Jungle are popular student attractions. Other favorite year-round activities include swimming, waterskiing, scuba diving, sailing, tennis, golf, and horseback riding. Students can also head south for a weekend in the Florida Keys or the Bahamas.

THE DETAILS

Campus setting:	urban
Degrees:	bachelor's, master's, doctoral
Calendar:	semesters
Public/Private:	public state
Number of full-time faculty:	769
Student-to-teacher ratio:	17:1

Admissions requirements:
- **Options:** common application, deferred entrance, early admission, electronic application
- **Application fee:** $25
- **Required:** high school transcript, letter of recommendation, SAT or ACT
- **Application deadlines:** continuous (freshmen), continuous (transfer)
- **Early decision:** —
- **Notification:** 8/1 (freshmen), 8/1 (transfer)

Average high school GPA:	3.59
Average freshman SAT verbal/math score:	537 / 540
Average freshman ACT score:	21
Number of applicants:	11,692
Number of applicants accepted:	5,689
Percentage of students from out of state:	5%
Total freshman enrollment:	3,315
Total enrollment:	34,865
Percentage of students who live in campus housing:	7%
Total in-state tuition, fees & expenses:	$13,658
Total out-of-state tuition, fees & expenses:	$26,164
Average financial aid package:	$6,140

FLORIDA INTERNATIONAL UNIVERSITY

MAJORS

- Accounting
- Applied Mathematics
- Architecture and Related Services, Other
- Art History, Criticism and Conservation
- Art Teacher Education
- Asian Studies/Civilization
- Biology/Biological Sciences, General
- Biomedical/Medical Engineering
- Broadcast Journalism
- Business Administration and Management, General
- Chemical Engineering
- Chemistry, General
- Civil Engineering, General
- Communication Studies/Speech Communication and Rhetoric
- Computer and Information Sciences, General
- Computer Engineering, General
- Computer Science
- Construction Engineering Technology/Technician
- Criminal Justice/Safety Studies
- Dance, General
- Dietetics/Dietitians
- Drama and Dramatics/Theatre Arts, General
- Economics, General
- Education/Teaching of Individuals with Emotional Disturbances
- Education/Teaching of Individuals with Mental Retardation
- Education/Teaching of Individuals with Specific Learning Disabilities
- Electrical, Electronics and Communications Engineering
- Elementary Education and Teaching
- English/Language Arts Teacher Education
- English Language and Literature, General
- Environmental Control Technologies/Technicians, Other
- Environmental Design/Architecture
- Environmental Studies
- Family and Consumer Sciences/Home Economics Teacher Education
- Finance, General
- Fine/Studio Arts, General
- Foreign Language Teacher Education
- French Language and Literature
- Geography
- Geology/Earth Science, General
- German Language and Literature
- Health/Health Care Administration/Management
- Health Information/Medical Records Administration/Administrator
- Health Science
- Health Services/Allied Health/Health Sciences, General
- Health Teacher Education
- History, General
- Hospitality Administration/Management, General
- Humanities/Humanistic Studies
- Human Resources Management/Personnel Administration, General
- Information Technology
- Insurance
- Interior Design
- International Business/Trade/Commerce
- International Relations and Affairs
- Italian Language and Literature
- Kinesiology and Exercise Science
- Liberal Arts and Sciences/Liberal Studies
- Logistics and Materials Management
- Management Information Systems, General
- Marine Biology and Biological Oceanography
- Marketing/Marketing Management, General
- Mathematics, General
- Mathematics Teacher Education
- Mechanical Engineering
- Music, General
- Music Teacher Education
- Nursing/Registered Nurse Training
- Occupational Therapy/Therapist
- Orthotist/Prosthetist
- Parks, Recreation and Leisure Facilities Management
- Philosophy
- Physical Education Teaching and Coaching
- Physics, General
- Political Science and Government, General
- Portuguese Language and Literature
- Psychology, General
- Public Administration
- Real Estate
- Religion/Religious Studies
- Science Teacher Education/General Science Teacher Education
- Social Science Teacher Education
- Social Work
- Sociology
- Spanish Language and Literature
- Statistics, General
- Systems Engineering
- Tourism and Travel Services Management
- Trade and Industrial Teacher Education
- Urban Studies/Affairs
- Women's Studies

FLORIDA SOUTHERN COLLEGE

111 Lake Hollingsworth Drive
Lakeland, FL 33801

(863) 680-4111
http://www.flsouthern.edu/

BIG FISH

UNIVERSITY 101
Extended orientation program; required first-year seminar; upperclassman mentors; optional first-year residential learning communities.

Get a tan *and* a future at Florida Southern.

Thirty-eight academic majors and 40 minors ranging from general arts and business majors to highly specific programs like recreational turf grass management give students choices when it comes to their education. Florida Southern also offers such academic add-ons as internships, co-ops, and service-learning ventures that enhance classroom instruction. Internationally inclined students can take courses at sites around the world through the college's study abroad programs or the College Consortium for International Study. Bonus: 93 percent of all Florida Southern students receive financial aid to help their bank accounts stay on the plus side of things.

FLORIDA SOUTHERN COLLEGE

WHAT IT IS

Florida Southern College was founded in 1885 by the Methodist Church. Today, Florida Southern is an intentionally interactive, residential college of liberal arts and sciences. Students come to Florida Southern because they want a liberal arts education and believe that a smaller campus is the best place to find it. The atmosphere is relaxed and personal, fostering a close-knit student body and faculty.

All members of the academic community take pride in the campus, a historic landmark and site of the largest collection of buildings designed by renowned architect Frank Lloyd Wright. Annie Pfeiffer Chapel, the first of the Wright buildings to be completed, hosts regular worship services where students of all denominations are welcome. The George Jenkins Field House, which seats 3,000 people, includes a three-court gymnasium and weight and sports equipment rooms. Facilities for tennis, racquetball, dance, swimming, and waterskiing are also available. Branches of five national Greek fraternities and five national Greek sororities are on campus. Student activities include intercollegiate and intramural sports, drama and music groups, publications, and various clubs and organizations related to academic, political, religious, and social interests. Entertainment on campus includes the Fine Arts Series performances in music, the Child of the Sun Jazz Festival, distinguished speakers, and college and business symposiums. In addition, many students are involved in volunteer programs and internships in the surrounding community.

WHERE IT'S AT

Florida Southern's scenic campus consists of approximately 100 acres on the shore of Lake Hollingsworth in Lakeland, a pleasant community of about 120,000 residents in the heart of Florida's citrus belt. Lakeland is just 45 minutes from Tampa and an hour from Orlando. Within an hour's drive from many of the state's major recreational attractions, including Walt Disney World and several major beaches, the college is ideally situated for internships and job opportunities with leading corporations. The Lakeland Center also offers many cultural, recreational, and entertainment opportunities.

THE DETAILS

Campus setting:	suburban
Degrees:	bachelor's, master's
Calendar:	semesters
Public/Private:	private religious
Number of full-time faculty:	109
Student-to-teacher ratio:	14:1

Admissions requirements:
- **Options:** common application, deferred entrance, early admission, early decision, electronic application
- **Application fee:** $30
- **Required:** essay or personal statement, high school transcript, 3 letters of recommendation, SAT or ACT
- **Application deadlines:** 4/1 (freshmen), continuous (transfer)
- **Early decision:** 12/1
- **Notification:** continuous (freshmen), continuous (transfer), 12/15 (early decision)

Average high school GPA:	3.48
Average freshman SAT verbal/math score:	531 / 533
Average freshman ACT score:	23
Number of applicants:	1,808
Number of applicants accepted:	1,361
Percentage of students from out of state:	27%
Total freshman enrollment:	572
Total enrollment:	1,990
Percentage of students who live in campus housing:	67%
Total tuition:	$17,860
Total cost with fees & expenses:	$25,650
Average financial aid package:	$15,998

FLORIDA SOUTHERN COLLEGE

MAJORS

- Accounting
- Advertising
- Agricultural Business and Management, General
- Art/Art Studies, General
- Art Teacher Education
- Athletic Training/Trainer
- Biology/Biological Sciences, General
- Broadcast Journalism
- Business/Commerce, General
- Business Administration and Management, General
- Chemistry, General
- Commercial and Advertising Art
- Communication Studies/Speech Communication and Rhetoric
- Computer Science
- Criminal Justice/Safety Studies
- Drama and Dramatics/Theatre Arts, General
- Economics, General
- Education, General
- Education/Teaching of Individuals with Specific Learning Disabilities
- Elementary Education and Teaching
- English Composition
- English Language and Literature, General
- Environmental Studies
- Finance, General
- Fine/Studio Arts, General
- History, General
- Horticultural Science
- Hotel/Motel Administration/Management
- Humanities/Humanistic Studies
- Human Resources Management/Personnel Administration, General
- International Business/Trade/Commerce
- Journalism
- Kindergarten/Preschool Education and Teaching
- Management Information Systems, General
- Marketing/Marketing Management, General
- Mathematics, General
- Music, General
- Music Management and Merchandising
- Music Teacher Education
- Natural Sciences
- Nursing/Registered Nurse Training
- Operations Management and Supervision
- Ornamental Horticulture
- Physical Education Teaching and Coaching
- Political Science and Government, General
- Pre-Dentistry Studies
- Pre-Medicine/Pre-Medical Studies
- Pre-Veterinary Studies
- Psychology, General
- Public Relations/Image Management
- Religion/Religious Studies
- Religious/Sacred Music
- Religious Education
- Secondary Education and Teaching
- Social Sciences, General
- Sociology
- Spanish Language and Literature

FLORIDA STATE UNIVERSITY

PO Box 5000 (850) 644-2525
Tallahassee, FL 32306 http://www.fsu.edu/

BIG DEAL

UNIVERSITY 101
Special academic advisors assigned to first-year students; optional first-year transitional seminar; upperclassman mentors; optional first-year residential learning communities; extended orientation program.

BIG REP

Florida State's faculty members are known internationally for being top-notch—and they have the awards to prove it.

Guggenheim fellows, Pulitzer Prize winners, and members of the American Academy of Arts and Sciences can all be found teaching here. Future researchers and inventors will find a home in the FSU science programs. Undergrads conduct independent research, participate in joint faculty-student projects, and travel to other institutions, such as Harvard, Notre Dame, and UC Berkeley, to work with scholars from across the globe.

FLORIDA STATE UNIVERSITY

WHAT IT IS

Florida State University takes pride in its ability to offer the personal benefits of a small, liberal-arts college and the vast resources and research opportunities of a major research university. Established in 1851 as the Seminary West of the Suwannee, it became the Florida State College for Women in 1909 and finally, a comprehensive co-educational institution known as Florida State University in 1947.

The Florida State University faculty includes Nobel laureates, Pulitzer Prize winners, National Academy of Sciences members, and recipients of university, state, and national teaching awards. The FSU community offers life outside of the classroom that includes social organizations, athletic events, cultural exposure, and service learning. Students can choose from more than 300 campus organizations through which they can meet others with similar interests or goals. Several Saturdays each fall, students may wish to join 80,000 other fans to support their 'Noles (as the FSU Seminoles are affectionately known). Theater, music, and dance performances and art exhibits expose students to new cultural experiences. In addition, to help them discover the rewards of giving back to the community, the university offers incentives for participating in community service. More than half of the first-year class lives on campus in one of 14 residence halls. FSU has extensive facilities that support student activities and recreation, including a completely equipped University Union, a state-of-the-art Student Recreation Center, and the Seminole Reservation (a lakefront recreation area).

WHERE IT'S AT

FSU's 450-acre main campus is well designed and compact, making it convenient for students to get to and from classes. Florida State University is nestled in the heart of historic Tallahassee, the capital of Florida and home to more than 250,000 residents. Tallahassee is a classic college town and is considered the "other" Florida because of its rolling hills, canopy roads, mild climate, and southern hospitality. The Florida State University Reservation is a 73-acre facility, with 10 active acres, located on beautiful Lake Bradford, four miles from campus. Students can enjoy canoeing, kayaking, picnicking, and swimming there or on the Gulf Coast beaches, which are just 45 minutes away.

THE DETAILS

Campus setting:	suburban
Degrees:	bachelor's, master's, doctoral
Calendar:	semesters
Public/Private:	public state
Number of full-time faculty:	1,104
Student-to-teacher ratio:	22:1

Admissions requirements:
- **Options:** common application, early admission, electronic application
- **Application fee:** $30
- **Required:** high school transcript, SAT or ACT
- **Application deadlines:** 3/1 (freshmen), 7/1 (transfer)
- **Early decision:** —
- **Notification:** 3/15 (freshmen), 7/15 (transfer)

Average high school GPA:	3.74
Average freshman SAT verbal/math score:	584 / 591
Average freshman ACT score:	24
Number of applicants:	22,127
Number of applicants accepted:	14,313
Percentage of students from out of state:	15%
Total freshman enrollment:	6,196
Total enrollment:	38,431
Percentage of students who live in campus housing:	14%
Total in-state tuition, fees & expenses:	$10,996
Total out-of-state tuition, fees & expenses:	$23,502
Average financial aid package:	$8,269

FLORIDA STATE UNIVERSITY

MAJORS

- Accounting
- Acting
- Actuarial Science
- Advertising
- African-American/Black Studies
- American/United States Studies/Civilization
- Anthropology
- Apparel and Textile Marketing Management
- Apparel and Textiles, General
- Applied Economics
- Applied Mathematics
- Art/Art Studies, General
- Art History, Criticism and Conservation
- Art Teacher Education
- Asian Studies/Civilization
- Athletic Training/Trainer
- Atmospheric Sciences and Meteorology, General
- Audiology/Audiologist and Speech-Language Pathology/Pathologist
- Bilingual, Multilingual, and Multicultural Education, Other
- Bilingual and Multilingual Education
- Biochemistry
- Biology/Biological Sciences, General
- Biomathematics and Bioinformatics, Other
- Biomedical/Medical Engineering
- Business/Commerce, General
- Business Administration and Management, General
- Caribbean Studies
- Cell/Cellular and Molecular Biology
- Central/Middle and Eastern European Studies
- Chemical Engineering
- Chemistry, General
- Chemistry, Other
- Child Development
- Cinematography and Film/Video Production
- Civil Engineering, General
- Classics and Languages, Literatures and Linguistics, General
- Commercial and Advertising Art
- Communication and Media Studies, Other
- Communication Studies/Speech Communication and Rhetoric
- Community Health Services/Liaison/Counseling
- Computer and Information Sciences, General
- Computer Engineering, General
- Computer Programming/Programmer, General
- Computer Science
- Computer Software and Media Applications, Other
- Computer Software Engineering
- Creative Writing
- Criminal Justice/Safety Studies
- Criminology
- Dance, General
- Dietetics/Dietitians
- Drama and Dramatics/Theatre Arts, General
- Early Childhood Education and Teaching
- Ecology
- Economics, General
- Education/Teaching of Individuals with Emotional Disturbances
- Education/Teaching of Individuals with Mental Retardation
- Education/Teaching of Individuals with Specific Learning Disabilities
- Education/Teaching of Individuals with Vision Impairments, Including Blindness
- Electrical, Electronics and Communications Engineering
- Elementary Education and Teaching
- English/Language Arts Teacher Education
- English Language and Literature, General
- Entrepreneurial and Small Business Operations, Other
- Environmental/Environmental Health Engineering
- Environmental Biology
- Environmental Studies
- Evolutionary Biology
- Family and Consumer Economics and Related Services, Other
- Family and Consumer Sciences/Home Economics Teacher Education
- Family and Consumer Sciences/Human Sciences, General
- Fashion/Apparel Design
- Fashion Merchandising
- Film/Cinema Studies
- Finance, General
- Fine/Studio Arts, General
- Foods, Nutrition, and Wellness Studies, General
- Foreign Language Teacher Education
- French Language and Literature
- Geography
- Geology/Earth Science, General
- German Language and Literature
- Gerontology
- Graphic Design
- Health Teacher Education
- History, General
- Hospitality Administration/Management, General
- Hospitality Administration/Management, Other
- Housing and Human Environments, General
- Human Development and Family Studies, General
- Humanities/Humanistic Studies
- Human Resources Management/Personnel Administration, General
- Industrial Engineering
- Information Science/Studies
- Insurance
- Interior Design
- International Business/Trade/Commerce
- International Relations and Affairs
- Italian Language and Literature
- Jazz/Jazz Studies
- Junior High/Intermediate/Middle School Education and Teaching
- Kindergarten/Preschool Education and Teaching
- Kinesiology and Exercise Science
- Latin American Studies
- Latin Language and Literature
- Literature
- Management Information Systems, General
- Marine Biology and Biological Oceanography
- Marketing/Marketing Management, General

FLORIDA STATE UNIVERSITY

- Mass Communication/Media Studies
- Materials Engineering
- Mathematics, General
- Mathematics Teacher Education
- Mechanical Engineering
- Meteorology
- Modern Greek Language and Literature
- Multicultural Education
- Music, General
- Music History, Literature, and Theory
- Music Pedagogy
- Music Performance, General
- Music Teacher Education
- Music Theory and Composition
- Music Therapy/Therapist
- Neurobiology and Neurophysiology
- Nursing/Registered Nurse Training
- Nutrition Sciences
- Parks, Recreation and Leisure Facilities Management
- Philosophy
- Physical Education Teaching and Coaching
- Physical Sciences
- Physical Sciences, Other
- Physics, General
- Piano and Organ
- Plant Physiology
- Political Science and Government, General
- Pre-Dentistry Studies
- Pre-Law Studies
- Pre-Medicine/Pre-Medical Studies
- Pre-Pharmacy Studies
- Pre-Theology/Pre-Ministerial Studies
- Pre-Veterinary Studies
- Psychology, General
- Public Relations/Image Management
- Radio, Television, and Digital Communication, Other
- Radio and Television
- Real Estate
- Religion/Religious Studies
- Russian Language and Literature
- Russian Studies
- Sales, Distribution and Marketing Operations, General
- Science Teacher Education/General Science Teacher Education
- Secondary Education and Teaching
- Social Sciences, General
- Social Science Teacher Education
- Social Work
- Sociology
- Spanish Language and Literature
- Sport and Fitness Administration/Management
- Statistics, General
- Technical and Business Writing
- Technical Theatre/Theatre Design and Technology
- Textile Science
- Violin, Viola, Guitar and Other Stringed Instruments
- Vocational Rehabilitation Counseling/Counselor
- Voice and Opera
- Wind and Percussion Instruments
- Women's Studies
- Zoology/Animal Biology

JACKSONVILLE UNIVERSITY

2800 University Boulevard North
Jacksonville, FL 32211

(904) 256-8000
http://www.ju.edu/

BIG FISH

UNIVERSITY 101
Extended orientation program; faculty mentors; optional first-year transitional seminar.

"Boredom schmoredom" appears to be the unofficial motto for Jacksonville students.

The university recognizes that the collegiate experience extends beyond academics, and it provides a wealth of organizations, recreational centers, and facilities exclusively for student use. Instead of succumbing to term-paper burnout and study-session ennui, students get involved in 37 on-campus professional clubs, 16 honor societies, 13 Greek organizations, 18 intramural sports, the Student Government Association, 16 NCAA Division I sports teams, and 107.1 The Mixx, Jacksonville U's student-run radio station. Students can also participate in art exhibitions, theater productions, and musical performances or join the staff of *The Navigator*, the school's newspaper. Student organizations converge at JU's Davis Student Commons, which serves as a hub for student activities and provides space for club meetings.

JACKSONVILLE UNIVERSITY

WHAT IT IS

Jacksonville University was originally founded in 1934 as a junior college that served local commuter students for the first 28 years of its existence. In the 1950s, the institution moved to its current location and expanded its course and degree offerings. With this change, the institution became Jacksonville University.

The students who attend classes on campus come from 46 states and more than 50 countries. JU accommodates more than 1,000 students in its residence facilities, which include traditional residence halls and apartments with kitchenettes. Campus facilities include a gymnasium, a football stadium, tennis courts, a baseball stadium, intramural fields, a football/soccer/track complex, and handball/racquetball courts. Beaches are only minutes away by car. Students pursue their creative talents and special interests by participating in such co-curricular activities as student publications, chorus, orchestra, band, dance, and theatrical productions. Six sororities and seven fraternities, as well as numerous academic, service, and social organizations, are active on campus.

WHERE IT'S AT

The university occupies a 260-acre, suburban, riverfront campus across the St. Johns River from downtown Jacksonville and 12 miles from the Atlantic Ocean beaches. With an area population of more than 1 million, the city of Jacksonville has numerous public parks hosting organized recreational programs, a major national jazz festival, and a zoo. Jacksonville is also the home of a professional symphony orchestra, a performing arts center, theaters, art museums and galleries, the Jacksonville Jaguars (NFL), and minor-league baseball, soccer, and ice hockey teams. The Jacksonville Landing riverfront festival marketplace and two major shopping malls are within a short drive of the campus. Major airlines serve the Jacksonville International Airport. The region's year-round climate is mild and pleasant, permitting outdoor activities throughout the year.

THE DETAILS

Campus setting:	suburban
Degrees:	bachelor's, master's
Calendar:	semesters
Public/Private:	private nonprofit
Number of full-time faculty:	121
Student-to-teacher ratio:	15:1

Admissions requirements:
- **Options:** common application, deferred entrance, early admission, electronic application
- **Application fee:** $30
- **Required:** essay or personal statement, high school transcript, letter of recommendation, SAT or ACT
- **Application deadlines:** continuous (freshmen), continuous (transfer)
- **Early decision:** —
- **Notification:** continuous (freshmen), continuous (transfer)

Average high school GPA:	—
Average freshman SAT verbal/math score:	513 / 523
Average freshman ACT score:	22
Number of applicants:	1,902
Number of applicants accepted:	1,372
Percentage of students from out of state:	37%
Total freshman enrollment:	462
Total enrollment:	2,948
Percentage of students who live in campus housing:	59%
Total tuition:	$19,970
Total cost with fees & expenses:	$27,030
Average financial aid package:	$15,853

JACKSONVILLE UNIVERSITY

MAJORS

- Accounting
- Airline/Commercial/Professional Pilot and Flight Crew
- Art/Art Studies, General
- Art History, Criticism and Conservation
- Aviation/Airway Management and Operations
- Biology/Biological Sciences, General
- Business/Commerce, General
- Business Administration and Management, General
- Chemistry, General
- Communication Studies/Speech Communication and Rhetoric
- Computer and Information Sciences, General
- Dance, General
- Design and Visual Communications, General
- Drama and Dance Teacher Education
- Drama and Dramatics/Theatre Arts, General
- Economics, General
- Electrical, Electronics and Communications Engineering
- Elementary Education and Teaching
- Engineering Physics
- English Language and Literature, General
- Environmental Studies
- Finance, General
- Fine/Studio Arts, General
- French Language and Literature
- Geography
- History, General
- Humanities/Humanistic Studies
- Interdisciplinary Studies
- International Business/Trade/Commerce
- International Relations and Affairs
- Kinesiology and Exercise Science
- Liberal Arts and Sciences/Liberal Studies
- Management Information Systems, General
- Marine Science/Merchant Marine Officer
- Marketing/Marketing Management, General
- Mathematics, General
- Mechanical Engineering
- Music, General
- Music Management and Merchandising
- Music Performance, General
- Music Teacher Education
- Music Theory and Composition
- Nursing/Registered Nurse Training
- Philosophy
- Physical Education Teaching and Coaching
- Physics, General
- Political Science and Government, General
- Pre-Dentistry Studies
- Pre-Law Studies
- Pre-Medicine/Pre-Medical Studies
- Pre-Veterinary Studies
- Psychology, General
- Secondary Education and Teaching
- Sociology
- Spanish Language and Literature
- Special Education and Teaching, General
- Visual and Performing Arts, General
- Voice and Opera

LYNN UNIVERSITY

3601 North Military Trail
Boca Raton, FL 33431

(561) 237-7000
http://www.lynn.edu/

BIG FISH

UNIVERSITY 101
Extended orientation program; required first-year transitional seminar; required first-year Academic Adventure; special academic advisors assigned to first-years.

BIG IDEA

Passports, please.

Lynn University believes that travel is key to understanding the issues that face our ever-shrinking world. All Lynn students are not just encouraged but required to complete at least one international studies program to graduate. The globe trekking begins with the First-Year Experience program, a two-semester course during which first-years take part in the university's annual Academic Adventure. In past years, the school-sponsored adventure has included swimming with stingrays and snorkeling over coral reefs as part of a cruise to the western Caribbean. Because the Academic Adventure is a required part of the Lynn University curriculum, the cost is included in tuition. While you work on your tan and listen to steel-drum music, you can thank Lynn University for the field trip of a lifetime.

LYNN UNIVERSITY

WHAT IT IS

Founded in 1962, Lynn University, small by design, provides an environment within and outside of the classroom in which a community of learners can discover and nurture their personal strengths and pursue academic excellence. Faculty, staff members, and students contribute to an atmosphere that nurtures creativity, fosters achievement, and values diversity. Lynn leads the country in offering majors in many of the world's fastest-growing professions.

Lynn is a residential institution with five air-conditioned residence halls. These halls include study and computer lounges and recreation areas, as well as health and fitness facilities that offer free weights, exercise machines, and cardiovascular equipment. The Lynn Student Center, the "living room" of the university, houses the dining room and the auditorium. Students study or relax outside on the patio or on comfortable sofas in the lounge. Also in the student center is the Knights' Court, a popular snacking spot for students, faculty, and staff. University life is designed to provide a learning situation through which students are guided toward responsible decision-making and leadership. Students may choose from a variety of campus organizations and activities, including student government, the newspaper or yearbook, co-curricular clubs, such leadership groups as the Knights of the Roundtable, a fraternity, and a sorority. In the NCAA Division II and Sunshine State Conference, Lynn has won 17 national championship titles and 14 conference championships.

WHERE IT'S AT

Lynn University is located in Boca Raton, Florida, only 50 minutes from Miami, 30 minutes from West Palm Beach, and 30 minutes from Fort Lauderdale. Boca Raton is one of the most vibrant communities in the state. Its location provides a variety of cultural and recreational opportunities to students. A progressive community with tremendous economic potential, Boca Raton is quickly becoming one of the nation's leading centers of commerce. The picturesque 123-acre campus is only three miles from the Atlantic Ocean and two miles from the heart of Boca Raton. Lynn is set among seven freshwater lakes, palms, and lush tropical foliage, providing the peace and quiet needed to concentrate on academics.

THE DETAILS

Campus setting:	suburban
Degrees:	bachelor's, master's, doctoral
Calendar:	semesters, plus 3 summer sessions
Public/Private:	private nonprofit
Number of full-time faculty:	72
Student-to-teacher ratio:	17:1

Admissions requirements:
- **Options:** common application, deferred entrance, early admission, electronic application
- **Application fee:** $35
- **Required:** essay or personal statement, high school transcript, letter of recommendation, SAT or ACT
- **Application deadlines:** continuous (freshmen), continuous (transfer)
- **Early decision:** —
- **Notification:** continuous (freshmen), continuous (transfer)

Average high school GPA:	2.59
Average freshman SAT verbal/math score:	458 / 460
Average freshman ACT score:	18
Number of applicants:	2,361
Number of applicants accepted:	1,875
Percentage of students from out of state:	56%
Total freshman enrollment:	587
Total enrollment:	2,510
Percentage of students who live in campus housing:	45%
Total tuition:	$24,700
Total cost with fees & expenses:	$35,950
Average financial aid package:	$19,332

LYNN UNIVERSITY

MAJORS

- Accounting
- Adult and Continuing Education and Teaching
- Airline/Commercial/Professional Pilot and Flight Crew
- Aviation/Airway Management and Operations
- Business Administration and Management, General
- Commercial and Advertising Art
- Drafting and Design Technology/Technician, General
- Education, General
- Elementary Education and Teaching
- English Language and Literature, General
- Environmental Studies
- Fashion/Apparel Design
- Fashion Merchandising
- Gerontology
- Health/Health Care Administration/Management
- History, General
- Hotel/Motel Administration/Management
- Humanities/Humanistic Studies
- International Business/Trade/Commerce
- Junior High/Intermediate/Middle School Education and Teaching
- Kindergarten/Preschool Education and Teaching
- Liberal Arts and Sciences/Liberal Studies
- Marketing/Marketing Management, General
- Mass Communication/Media Studies
- Music, General
- Natural Sciences
- Nursing/Registered Nurse Training
- Parks, Recreation and Leisure Facilities Management
- Political Science and Government, General
- Pre-Law Studies
- Pre-Medicine/Pre-Medical Studies
- Psychology, General
- Secondary Education and Teaching
- Social Sciences, General
- Special Products Marketing Operations
- Sport and Fitness Administration/Management
- Tourism and Travel Services Management

NEW COLLEGE OF FLORIDA

5700 North Tamiami Trail
Sarasota, FL 34243

(941) 359-4700
http://www.ncf.edu/

BIG DEAL

UNIVERSITY 101
Extended orientation program.

BIG IDEA

Be careful what you wish for . . .

At New College of Florida, there are no traditional grades, but this doesn't mean an easy four years of the old slack-then-cram routine. Students work just as hard—if not harder—for their professors' written performance evaluations. All New College students plan individualized programs of study in consultation with their faculty advisors. These academic contracts may incorporate internships, co-ops, fieldwork, study abroad programs, independent research, and student exchanges, alongside courses taken both on and off campus. Students also complete the required senior thesis project, a summation of their college accomplishments. While most students leave their schools with a brief transcript of letter or number grades, New College students graduate with a portfolio and written critique of their performance.

NEW COLLEGE OF FLORIDA

WHAT IT IS

Throughout the history of New College, four principles have defined its educational philosophy: Each student is ultimately responsible for his or her education; the best education demands a joint search for knowledge by exciting teachers and able-minded students; students' progress should be based on demonstrated competence and real mastery, rather than on the accumulation of credits and grades; and from the outset, students should have opportunities to explore, in depth, areas of interest to them. New College was founded in 1960 as a private institution with a devotion to the values implicit in a liberal arts education and dedicated to creating an innovative academic community of talented scholars and outstanding faculty members.

First- and second-years must live on campus, but many continuing students also choose to live there. The 131-room, three-court Pei residence halls provide rooms with individual entrances, private baths, central air-conditioning, and various combinations of large picture windows, sliding glass doors, and balconies. New College student life is informal. Activities are largely student initiated and include academic, artistic, religious, political, and recreational athletic pursuits. The college's 144-acre bayfront location on the Gulf of Mexico contains basketball, racquetball, and tennis courts; a multipurpose field; a running path; a volleyball pit; a 25-meter swimming pool; and a fitness center. Sailboats, sailboards, and canoes are available for use on Sarasota Bay.

WHERE IT'S AT

Situated on Sarasota Bay, New College serves as the northern gateway to Sarasota, a city of more than 50,000 located 50 miles south of Tampa on the west coast of Florida. Noted as a cultural and recreational center, Sarasota's beautiful public beaches and professional theater, art, and music, attract visitors and new residents from throughout the world. The climate is semitropical, consisting of long, warm autumns and springs and mild winters. Many major airlines serve Sarasota, and within the city, buses link the campus to downtown, shopping malls, parks, and beaches. New College is in a residential neighborhood; mass transit is available, but bicycles are a favored means of transportation among students.

THE DETAILS

Campus setting:	suburban
Degrees:	bachelor's
Calendar:	4-1-4
Public/Private:	public state
Number of full-time faculty:	66
Student-to-teacher ratio:	10:1

Admissions requirements:
- **Options:** common application, deferred entrance, early admission, electronic application
- **Application fee:** $30
- **Required:** essay or personal statement, high school transcript, letter of recommendation, SAT or ACT
- **Application deadlines:** 5/1 (freshman), 5/1 (transfer)
- **Early decision:** —
- **Notification:** 5/1 (freshmen), 5/1 (transfer)

Average high school GPA:	3.95
Average freshman SAT verbal/math score:	675 / 638
Average freshman ACT score:	26
Number of applicants:	716
Number of applicants accepted:	383
Percentage of students from out of state:	19%
Total freshman enrollment:	189
Total enrollment:	692
Percentage of students who live in campus housing:	68%
Total in-state tuition, fees & expenses:	$10,248
Total out-of-state tuition, fees & expenses:	$25,308
Average financial aid package:	$10,858

NEW COLLEGE OF FLORIDA

MAJORS

- Anthropology
- Art History, Criticism and Conservation
- Biology/Biological Sciences, General
- Chemistry, General
- Classics and Classical Languages, Literatures, and Linguistics, Other
- Comparative Literature
- Economics, General
- English Language and Literature, General
- Environmental Studies
- Fine/Studio Arts, General
- Foreign Languages and Literatures, General
- French Language and Literature
- French Studies
- General Studies
- Germanic Languages, Literatures, and Linguistics, General
- German Language and Literature
- History, General
- Humanities/Humanistic Studies
- International/Global Studies
- Liberal Arts and Sciences/Liberal Studies
- Literature
- Marine Biology and Biological Oceanography
- Mathematics, General
- Medieval and Renaissance Studies
- Music, General
- Music History, Literature, and Theory
- Natural Sciences
- Neurobiology and Neurophysiology
- Philosophy
- Physics, General
- Political Science and Government, General
- Psychology, General
- Public Policy Analysis
- Religion/Religious Studies
- Russian Language and Literature
- Social Sciences, General
- Sociology
- Spanish Language and Literature
- Urban Studies/Affairs

NOVA SOUTHEASTERN UNIVERSITY

3301 College Avenue
Fort Lauderdale, FL 33314

(954) 262-7300
http://www.nova.edu/

BIG FISH

UNIVERSITY 101
Extended orientation program.

How about getting a BS and an MD, JD, or PhD?

If graduate or professional school is part of your post-college plans, then Nova Southeastern's got a cool program for you. The school's many dual-admission programs allow qualified students to apply to Nova Southeastern's undergraduate and graduate/professional colleges at the same time. Students enrolled in joint degrees will make a seamless transition into graduate or professional school, and some will even have the chance to knock out some higher-level coursework prior to finishing up their undergrad degrees. By the time that graduate, law, medical, or dental school rolls around, dual-admission students have already secured a spot in one of the university's competitive colleges. Savvy students who plan ahead can save more than a few bucks on tuition.

NOVA SOUTHEASTERN UNIVERSITY

WHAT IT IS

Founded in 1964, Nova Southeastern University has enjoyed tremendous growth and success, which continues to this day. Students are now enrolled on both the main campus and at NSU locations in 24 states and nine countries. NSU is a not-for-profit university accredited by the Commission on Colleges of the Southern Association of Colleges and Schools. NSU is a university for all ages: The University School for children, numerous undergraduate and graduate degree programs in a variety of fields, and nondegree continuing education programs are all available.

With students from all 50 states and 42 countries, NSU is a university of national and international scope. Student activities include more than 25 faculty-sponsored clubs; events sponsored by the student government; NCAA Division II sports, such as baseball, basketball, cross-country, golf, soccer, softball, and volleyball; a newspaper; a radio station; intramurals; five national fraternities and seven national sororities; and a variety of sport clubs.

WHERE IT'S AT

NSU's 300-acre main campus in sunny South Florida is a place of impressive new buildings, palm trees, ponds, and fountains. The weather is near perfect, with an average temperature of 77 degrees (25 degrees Celsius) and 3,000 hours of sunshine a year. When students need a study break, they're just 15 minutes from miles of some of the cleanest and most beautiful beaches in the United States. Students are also only a few minutes from the center of Fort Lauderdale, one of the nation's seven fastest-growing cities, which offers endless activities, sports, and entertainment. Laced with 300 miles of waterways and 40,000 resident yachts, greater Fort Lauderdale is also known as the "Venice of America." The area features innumerable holes of golf, miles of wilderness trails for hiking and biking, and great snorkeling, diving, and deep-sea fishing. Students also enjoy world-class concerts, sports, museums, and ballet.

THE DETAILS

Campus setting:	suburban
Degrees:	bachelor's, master's, doctoral
Calendar:	trimesters
Public/Private:	private nonprofit
Number of full-time faculty:	542
Student-to-teacher ratio:	12:1

Admissions requirements:
- **Options:** common application, deferred entrance, early admission, electronic application
- **Application fee:** $50
- **Required:** high school transcript, letter of recommendation, SAT or ACT
- **Application deadlines:** continuous (freshmen), continuous (transfer)
- **Early decision:** —
- **Notification:** continuous (freshmen), continuous (transfer)

Average high school GPA:	3.60
Average freshman SAT verbal/math score:	503 / 512
Average freshman ACT score:	20
Number of applicants:	1,915
Number of applicants accepted:	1,177
Percentage of students from out of state:	37%
Total freshman enrollment:	383
Total enrollment:	25,430
Percentage of students who live in campus housing:	9%
Total tuition:	$15,600
Total cost with fees & expenses:	$25,087
Average financial aid package:	$14,653

NOVA SOUTHEASTERN UNIVERSITY

MAJORS

- Accounting
- Athletic Training/Trainer
- Biology/Biological Sciences, General
- Business Administration and Management, General
- Computer and Information Sciences, General
- Computer Science
- Elementary Education and Teaching
- English Language and Literature, General
- Environmental Science
- Environmental Studies
- Finance, General
- Health Services/Allied Health/Health Sciences, General
- History, General
- Humanities/Humanistic Studies
- Interdisciplinary Studies
- Legal Assistant/Paralegal
- Liberal Arts and Sciences/Liberal Studies
- Management Science, General
- Marine Biology and Biological Oceanography
- Multi-/Interdisciplinary Studies, Other
- Nursing/Registered Nurse Training
- Physician Assistant
- Pre-Dentistry Studies
- Pre-Law Studies
- Pre-Medicine/Pre-Medical Studies
- Psychology, General
- Special Education and Teaching, General
- Sport and Fitness Administration/Management

PALM BEACH ATLANTIC UNIVERSITY

901 South Flagler Drive, PO Box 24708
West Palm Beach, FL 33416

(561) 803-2000
http://www.pba.edu/

BIG FISH

UNIVERSITY 101
Required first-year transitional seminar; required first-year extracurricular activities; special academic advisors assigned to first-year students.

In homeless shelters, refugee camps in Israel, and small villages in India, Palm Beach Atlantic students learn to put their principles into practice.

Workship, PBA's credited service-learning program, provides domestic and international community service projects for students. The Workship program includes hundreds of volunteer opportunities that may be incorporated into classroom or student club requirements. By building, teaching, cooking, and mentoring together, students get to know one another and their professors while exploring global issues firsthand. Work assignments vary greatly in terms of time commitment, group size, and type of project, so there's something to fit every interest and ability level.

PALM BEACH ATLANTIC UNIVERSITY

WHAT IT IS

Palm Beach Atlantic University was founded in 1968 by concerned Palm Beach County residents who felt the need for a distinctive institution of higher learning that would stress not only academic quality, but also character development and spiritual maturity. Chartered as a Christian liberal arts college, PBA offers a high-quality education for students of all faiths.

For both undergraduate and graduate students, Palm Beach Atlantic seeks to promote intellectual, moral, and spiritual growth. Undergraduates have a variety of ways to get involved in college life, including service and leadership organizations, intercollegiate and intramural sports, fine arts, religious groups, and professionally oriented organizations, such as Kappa Delta Epsilon and Phi Beta Lambda. In 2002, the university dedicated an additional 250,000 square feet of campus facilities as part of its comprehensive campus growth plan. The DeSantis Family Chapel hosts multiple weekly chapel services on the PBA campus. Oceanview Residence Hall and Dixie Garage offer additional first-year housing and convenient access to the university's educational and cultural programs. Vera Lea Rinker Hall houses PBA's School of Music.

WHERE IT'S AT

Palm Beach Atlantic University occupies nearly 26 acres in the heart of West Palm Beach on the Intracoastal Waterway across from Palm Beach, approximately one mile from the Atlantic Ocean. Palm Beach County provides a broad spectrum of cultural activities, such as Broadway plays, operas, concerts, and lectures by national and world leaders. Only a few blocks from the campus, the Kravis Center for the Performing Arts brings world-renowned performers to Palm Beach County. Students may also use the facilities of the famed Norton Gallery, Flagler Museum, Society of the Four Arts, and Science Museum and Planetarium of Palm Beach County. The cosmopolitan area of the Palm Beaches, with its shopping, recreation, and service opportunities, is at the university's doorstep.

THE DETAILS

Campus setting:	urban
Degrees:	bachelor's, master's
Calendar:	semesters
Public/Private:	private religious
Number of full-time faculty:	140
Student-to-teacher ratio:	12:1

Admissions requirements:
- **Options:** common application, deferred entrance, early admission, early action, electronic application
- **Application fee:** $25
- **Required:** essay or personal statement, high school transcript, 2 letters of recommendation, SAT or ACT
- **Application deadlines:** continuous (freshmen)
- **Early action:** —
- **Notification:** continuous (freshmen), — (early action)

Average high school GPA:	3.49
Average freshman SAT verbal/math score:	552 / 541
Average freshman ACT score:	23
Number of applicants:	1,825
Number of applicants accepted:	863
Percentage of students from out of state:	26%
Total freshman enrollment:	439
Total enrollment:	3,066
Percentage of students who live in campus housing:	45%
Total tuition:	$17,130
Total cost with fees & expenses:	$24,648
Average financial aid package:	$11,999

PALM BEACH ATLANTIC UNIVERSITY

MAJORS

- Accounting and Finance
- Acting
- Art Teacher Education
- Bible/Biblical Studies
- Biology/Biological Sciences, General
- Broadcast Journalism
- Business Administration, Management and Operations, Other
- Business Administration and Management, General
- Communication Studies/Speech Communication and Rhetoric
- Computer and Information Sciences, General
- Dance, General
- Drama and Dramatics/Theatre Arts, General
- Education, General
- Elementary Education and Teaching
- English Language and Literature, General
- Entrepreneurship/Entrepreneurial Studies
- Fine/Studio Arts, General
- General Studies
- Graphic Design
- History, General
- Human Resources Management/Personnel Administration, General
- International Business/Trade/Commerce
- Journalism
- Marketing/Marketing Management, General
- Mathematics, General
- Music, General
- Music Performance, General
- Music Teacher Education
- Music Theory and Composition
- Nursing/Registered Nurse Training
- Organizational Communication, General
- Philosophy
- Physical Education Teaching and Coaching
- Piano and Organ
- Playwriting and Screenwriting
- Political Science and Government, General
- Pre-Law Studies
- Psychology, General
- Radio and Television
- Religion/Religious Studies
- Religious/Sacred Music
- Secondary Education and Teaching
- Theological and Ministerial Studies, Other
- Voice and Opera
- Wind and Percussion Instruments

ROLLINS COLLEGE

1000 Holt Avenue
Winter Park, FL 32789

(407) 646-2000
http://www.rollins.edu/

BIG IDEA

UNIVERSITY 101
Extended orientation program; required first-year community service projects; upperclassman mentors; special academic advisors assigned to first-years; required first-year transitional seminar.

BIG FISH

From start to finish, Rollins is the epitome of a liberal arts education.

In the Rollins College Conference program, first-years get a taste of Rollins in small, dynamic, discussion-based seminars with titles like History of Comic Books and Microbes, Disease, and Humans. These courses are taught by faculty advisors, and students are also mentored by upperclassman peers. Beyond their first year, many students take advantage of the college's extensive off-campus learning opportunities and study abroad courses. Field study options lead students to the heart of the Big Apple to examine art in a metropolitan context, the rural towns of Puerto Rico to construct houses for impoverished families, and into the rainforests of Oregon to learn about sustainable living. Internships with local businesses (more than 120 of which have recruiting sessions on campus every year) and international organizations set students up for bright careers.

WHAT IT IS

Rollins College, which was founded in 1885, occupies a 70-acre campus noted for its beautiful grounds and traditional Spanish-Mediterranean architecture. Although most traditional-age undergraduate students pursue their studies in the four-year, residential College of Arts and Sciences, Rollins also offers the master's of business administration degree in the Crummer Graduate School of Business and undergraduate and graduate degrees in the Hamilton Holt School. The College of Arts and Sciences enrolls students from most states and more than 40 other countries.

A campaign concluded in 2001 raised more than $160 million for financial aid, endowed faculty chairs, programming, and facilities, including the Harold & Ted Alfond Sports Center, the Cornell Campus Center, the Olin Electronic Research and Information Center, and the Marshall and Vera Lea Rinker Building. A $93 million bequest from alumnus George Cornell, the largest gift in Rollins' history, provided additional resources for scholarships, faculty development, and innovative initiatives.

WHERE IT'S AT

Winter Park is considered one of the nation's most beautiful residential communities and enjoys the benefits of a bustling metropolis while maintaining a small-town atmosphere. Nationally renowned events, such as the annual Bach Festival, Winter Park Autumn Art Festival, and Winter Park Sidewalk Art Festival, have helped to make Winter Park a center of cultural attraction.

The town is adjacent to Orlando, one of the nation's fastest-growing and most popular metropolitan areas and an important center of business, science, and technology. Located 50 miles from the Atlantic Ocean and 90 miles from the Gulf of Mexico, the Rollins campus is bounded by Lake Virginia to the east and south.

THE DETAILS

Campus setting:	suburban
Degrees:	bachelor's, master's
Calendar:	semesters
Public/Private:	private nonprofit
Number of full-time faculty:	179
Student-to-teacher ratio:	11:1

Admissions requirements:
- **Options:** common application, deferred entrance, early admission, early decision, electronic application
- **Application fee:** $40
- **Required:** essay or personal statement, high school transcript, letter of recommendation, SAT or ACT
- **Application deadlines:** 2/15 (freshmen), 4/15 (transfer)
- **Early decision:** 11/15
- **Notification:** 4/1 (freshmen), continuous (transfer), 12/15 (early decision)

Average high school GPA:	3.40
Average freshman SAT verbal/math score:	594 / 591
Average freshman ACT score:	24
Number of applicants:	2,598
Number of applicants accepted:	1,544
Percentage of students from out of state:	51%
Total freshman enrollment:	486
Total enrollment:	2,571
Percentage of students who live in campus housing:	66%
Total tuition:	$26,910
Total cost with fees & expenses:	$36,820
Average financial aid package:	$26,666

ROLLINS COLLEGE

MAJORS

- Anthropology
- Art History, Criticism and Conservation
- Biochemistry
- Biology/Biological Sciences, General
- Chemistry, General
- Classics and Languages, Literatures and Linguistics, General
- Computer Science
- Drama and Dramatics/Theatre Arts, General
- Economics, General
- Education, General
- English Language and Literature, General
- Environmental Studies
- European Studies/Civilization
- Fine/Studio Arts, General
- French Language and Literature
- History, General
- Interdisciplinary Studies
- International Business/Trade/Commerce
- International Relations and Affairs
- Latin American Studies
- Mathematics, General
- Music, General
- Philosophy
- Physics, General
- Political Science and Government, General
- Pre-Dentistry Studies
- Pre-Law Studies
- Pre-Medicine/Pre-Medical Studies
- Psychology, General
- Religion/Religious Studies
- Sociology
- Spanish Language and Literature

SAINT LEO UNIVERSITY

PO Box 6665
Saint Leo, FL 33574

(352) 588-8200
http://www.saintleo.edu/

BIG FISH

UNIVERSITY 101
Extended orientation program; optional first-year leadership program for students who do not yet meet admissions requirements; required first-year transitional seminar; required first-year religion course; upperclassman mentors.

Student council members, yearbook editors, and team captains aren't the only students with leadership qualities.

Everyone has them, and the PEAK Leadership program at Saint Leo University is designed to help all students discover theirs. This optional four-year program teaches students communication and teamwork skills that will serve them far beyond college. Beginning their first year, students take leadership courses and develop and execute community service projects. Participants in the PEAK program are expected to make an active contribution to Saint Leo by volunteering for Campus Community Service Day and coordinating student activities that promote the school.

SAINT LEO UNIVERSITY

WHAT IT IS

Saint Leo University is affiliated with the Catholic Church. Founded in 1889 by the Order of Saint Benedict, today Saint Leo has students enrolled both on the main campus and in extension programs located on 11 military bases stretching from Virginia to Key West. Saint Leo is committed to giving its students an education that prepares them for the future. The goal of the university is to develop the whole student, both academically and personally, by providing a values-based education in the Benedictine tradition.

Students can participate in the nationally recognized honors program and the more than 40 clubs and organizations on campus, including national fraternities and sororities. On campus are racquetball and tennis courts; soccer, baseball, and softball fields; a weight room; and an outdoor swimming pool. A 154-acre lake and an 18-hole golf course are adjacent to the campus. The university also hosts a variety of events that are open to the university community and residents of the surrounding area, including art exhibits and musical concerts. In addition, the Student Government Union and various campus organizations sponsor movies, lectures, dances, and special events throughout the academic year.

WHERE IT'S AT

The Saint Leo University campus occupies 170 acres of rolling hills and wooded grounds. The rural setting is conducive to academic success, but the university is also located near metropolitan areas, which give the students numerous social and professional options. Saint Leo's location in west-central Florida offers easy access to Interstate 75, the gateway to a wide range of entertainment, shopping, dining, and recreational opportunities in several large metropolitan areas, including Tampa and Orlando, which are 25 miles and 65 miles away, respectively. Tampa is home to Ybor City, a National Historic Landmark District that's considered the "nightlife capital" of Florida's west coast. This growing and vibrant city also boasts fantastic ethnic restaurants, fine arts, professional sports teams, and concert venues.

THE DETAILS

Campus setting:	rural
Degrees:	bachelor's, master's
Calendar:	semesters
Public/Private:	private religious
Number of full-time faculty:	63
Student-to-teacher ratio:	15:1

Admissions requirements:
- **Options:** common application, deferred entrance, early admission, electronic application
- **Application fee:** $35
- **Required:** essay or personal statement, high school transcript, letter of recommendation, SAT or ACT
- **Application deadlines:** 8/15 (freshmen), 8/1 (transfer)
- **Early decision:** —
- **Notification:** continuous (freshmen), continuous (transfer)

Average high school GPA:	3.1
Average freshman SAT verbal/math score:	511 / 511
Average freshman ACT score:	21
Number of applicants:	2,466
Number of applicants accepted:	1,246
Percentage of students from out of state:	31%
Total freshman enrollment:	394
Total enrollment:	1,825
Percentage of students who live in campus housing:	68%
Total tuition:	$13,650
Total cost with fees & expenses:	$22,540
Average financial aid package:	$15,130

SAINT LEO UNIVERSITY

MAJORS

- Accounting
- Biology/Biological Sciences, General
- Business Administration and Management, General
- Clinical Laboratory Science/Medical Technology/Technologist
- Community Organization and Advocacy
- Creative Writing
- Criminal Justice/Safety Studies
- Elementary Education and Teaching
- English Language and Literature, General
- English Language and Literature/Letters, Other
- Environmental Studies
- Health/Health Care Administration/Management
- History, General
- Hospital and Health Care Facilities Administration/Management
- Hospitality Administration/Management, General
- Hospitality Administration/Management, Other
- Human Resources Management/Personnel Administration, General
- Human Services, General
- International Business/Trade/Commerce
- International Relations and Affairs
- Liberal Arts and Sciences/Liberal Studies
- Literature
- Management Information Systems, General
- Marketing/Marketing Management, General
- Operations Management and Supervision
- Political Science and Government, General
- Psychology, General
- Social Work
- Sociology
- Sport and Fitness Administration/Management
- Theology/Theological Studies

SOUTHEASTERN UNIVERSITY

1000 Longfellow Boulevard
Lakeland, FL 33801

(863) 667-5000
www.seuniversity.edu

BIG FISH

UNIVERSITY 101
Extended orientation program; special academic advisors assigned to first-years.

Discover the academic side of faith.

Spirituality is a vital part of a Southeastern University education. All students are required to take biblical studies courses and convene three times a week for chapel services. In addition, each academic department coordinates ministry and spiritual outreach programs that combine students' areas of study with service-learning activities. For instance, psychology majors may be partnered with local counseling agencies, and accounting students might provide tax help to low-income families. Five pastoral majors, each focusing on a different aspect of ministry, along with degree programs in sacred music and biblical studies, give students a wealth of opportunities.

SOUTHEASTERN UNIVERSITY

WHAT IT IS

For students looking for a school at which they can combine a desire to pursue higher education with their religious faith, Southeastern University may be just the place. Founded in 1935 as a Bible institute to train pastors and missionaries, Southeastern has grown into a small but comprehensive liberal arts college. However, although the offerings of the college have expanded beyond its original ministerial focus to include programs in journalism, social work, and recreation management, the school, which is affiliated with the Assemblies of God Church, remains rooted in its commitment to Christ-centered living in all aspects of the college experience. Southeastern requires all students to take 20 hours of religion courses and attend chapel three days a week. A focus on community service is another important part of the Southeastern education, and traditional classroom learning is often combined with outreach activities. Southeastern also offers services to meet the needs of married or engaged students, including couples' social events and premarital counseling.

WHERE IT'S AT

Students looking for a scenic, relaxing campus environment should be right at home at Southeastern, located in the town of Lakeland in west-central Florida. They'll find themselves studying among palm trees and orange groves, with beautiful Gulf Coast beaches within a short drive. Tampa and Orlando are both less than 40 miles away, and students can entertain themselves at such area attractions as Walt Disney World, Orlando Magic basketball games, and the Salvador Dalí Museum. While at school, students reside on a Mediterranean-style campus that occupies about 68 acres between two lakes. Southeastern has made several campus improvements in recent years, such as building a fitness center, swimming pool, and student union. Dorms are pleasant and modern, and all have recently been renovated or newly built.

THE DETAILS

Campus setting:	suburban
Degrees:	bachelor's
Calendar:	semesters
Public/Private:	private religious
Number of full-time faculty:	48
Student-to-teacher ratio:	21:1

Admissions requirements:
- **Options:** deferred entrance, early admission, electronic application
- **Application fee:** $40
- **Required:** high school transcript, 2 letters of recommendation
- **Application deadlines:** 8/1 (freshmen), 8/1 (transfer)
- **Early decision:** —
- **Notification:** 8/1 (freshmen), 8/1 (transfer)

Average high school GPA:	3.40
Average freshman SAT verbal/math score:	—/—
Average freshman ACT score:	—
Number of applicants:	509
Number of applicants accepted:	436
Percentage of students from out of state:	40%
Total freshman enrollment:	—
Total enrollment:	1,964
Percentage of students who live in campus housing:	60%
Total tuition:	$9,900
Total cost with fees & expenses:	$16,410
Average financial aid package:	$7,027

SOUTHEASTERN UNIVERSITY

MAJORS

- Accounting
- Bible/Biblical Studies
- Biology/Biological Sciences, General
- Business, Management, Marketing, and Related Support Services, Other
- Communication Studies/Speech Communication and Rhetoric
- Drama and Dramatics/Theatre Arts, General
- Elementary Education and Teaching
- English/Language Arts Teacher Education
- English Language and Literature, General
- Interdisciplinary Studies
- Marketing/Marketing Management, General
- Mathematics Teacher Education
- Missions/Missionary Studies and Missiology
- Music Performance, General
- Music Teacher Education
- Pastoral Studies/Counseling
- Pre-Medicine/Pre-Medical Studies
- Psychology, General
- Religious/Sacred Music
- Science Teacher Education/General Science Teacher Education
- Social Studies Teacher Education
- Social Work
- Theological and Ministerial Studies, Other

STETSON UNIVERSITY

421 North Woodland Boulevard
DeLand, FL 32723

(386) 822-7000
http://www.stetson.edu/

BIG FISH

UNIVERSITY 101
Extended orientation program; optional first-year residential learning communities.

The spirit of innovation is old hat at Stetson.

Stetson University is Florida's first private university, boasts the state's first theatrical company, pioneered its first School of Music and College of Law, and has the first basketball team in the state to win 1,000 victories. The school also gives students the freedom to plan their courses of study, create off-campus learning opportunities, and do in-depth explorations of the subjects they choose. The Stetson Undergraduate Research Experience provides research grants for undergrads who conduct and present their studies on Undergraduate Scholarship Day. Humanities students construct unique interdisciplinary majors, with concentrations in the three academic departments of their choice, and students enrolled in the Roland George Program collaboratively manage a stock portfolio worth more than $2.5 million.

STETSON UNIVERSITY

WHAT IT IS

A challenging academic environment and commitment to values characterize the Stetson University experience. Stetson is Florida's first private university and since 1883 has offered something for everyone in its undergraduate degrees in the arts and sciences, business, and music.

With more than 100 organizations, students can explore interests in other cultures, join one of 14 Greek social organizations, or expand on their classroom interests in an academic or honorary organization. The university provides 22 residence halls, Greek housing, and special interest facilities. Student services available on campus include the Commons and Hat Rack, food court–style dining options that include an Einstein Bros. Bagels and Freshens Smoothie Company; a bookstore; a post office; a health clinic; a counseling center; an academic support office; an ATM; and a coffee kiosk. The Hollis Center houses a fitness room, group exercise classes, an outdoor pool, a game room, a lobby, and a gymnasium. Throughout the year, Stetson offers its students and surrounding community numerous cultural opportunities, including lectures, concerts in Elizabeth Hall, performances in historic Stover Theatre, and exhibitions at the Duncan Gallery of Art and Gillespie Museum of Minerals. Past lecturers include journalist and author Bill Moyers and scientist and conservationist Jane Goodall.

WHERE IT'S AT

Stetson's 165-acre DeLand campus is listed on the National Register of Historic Places and filled with turn-of-the-century buildings that have been modernized and updated without losing their charm. Stetson University appeals to students looking for an intimate college experience while being close to the action in the Orlando area and on Daytona Beach. The campus is located in DeLand, a city of 24,000 people surrounded by a larger community of 65,000 residents. Downtown DeLand is within walking distance of the university and offers a variety of coffeehouses, restaurants, and unique shops in a hometown atmosphere. Students can also appreciate some of Florida's natural wonders at nearby Blue Spring State Park and along the St. Johns River.

THE DETAILS

Campus setting:	small town
Degrees:	bachelor's, master's
Calendar:	semesters
Public/Private:	private nonprofit
Number of full-time faculty:	183
Student-to-teacher ratio:	12:1

Admissions requirements:
- **Options:** common application, deferred entrance, early admission, early decision, electronic application
- **Application fee:** $40
- **Required:** essay or personal statement, high school transcript, letter of recommendation, SAT or ACT
- **Application deadlines:** 3/15 (freshmen), continuous (transfer)
- **Early decision:** 11/1
- **Notification:** — (freshmen), continuous (transfer), 11/15 (early decision)

Average high school GPA:	3.69
Average freshman SAT verbal/math score:	575 / 566
Average freshman ACT score:	23
Number of applicants:	2,513
Number of applicants accepted:	1,858
Percentage of students from out of state:	20%
Total freshman enrollment:	598
Total enrollment:	3,577
Percentage of students who live in campus housing:	67%
Total tuition:	$22,730
Total cost with fees & expenses:	$31,995
Average financial aid package:	$20,853

STETSON UNIVERSITY

MAJORS

- Accounting
- American/United States Studies/Civilization
- Aquatic Biology/Limnology
- Art/Art Studies, General
- Biochemistry
- Biology/Biological Sciences, General
- Business/Managerial Economics
- Business Administration and Management, General
- Chemistry, General
- Clinical Laboratory Science/Medical Technology/Technologist
- Communication Studies/Speech Communication and Rhetoric
- Computer Science
- Drama and Dramatics/Theatre Arts, General
- E-Commerce/Electronic Commerce
- Economics, General
- Education, General
- Elementary Education and Teaching
- English Language and Literature, General
- Environmental Studies
- Finance, General
- French Language and Literature
- Geography
- German Language and Literature
- Health Services/Allied Health/Health Sciences, General
- History, General
- Humanities/Humanistic Studies
- International Business/Trade/Commerce
- International Relations and Affairs
- Kinesiology and Exercise Science
- Latin American Studies
- Management Science, General
- Marketing/Marketing Management, General
- Mathematics, General
- Molecular Biology
- Music, General
- Music Performance, General
- Music Teacher Education
- Music Theory and Composition
- Philosophy
- Physics, General
- Piano and Organ
- Political Science and Government, General
- Pre-Dentistry Studies
- Pre-Law Studies
- Pre-Medicine/Pre-Medical Studies
- Pre-Veterinary Studies
- Psychology, General
- Religion/Religious Studies
- Russian Studies
- Secondary Education and Teaching
- Social Sciences, General
- Social Science Teacher Education
- Sociology
- Spanish Language and Literature
- Sport and Fitness Administration/Management
- Violin, Viola, Guitar and Other Stringed Instruments
- Visual and Performing Arts, Other
- Voice and Opera
- Web Page, Digital/Multimedia and Information Resources Design

ST. THOMAS UNIVERSITY

16401 Northwest 37th Avenue
Miami Gardens, FL 33054

(305) 625-6000
http://www.stu.edu/

BIG FISH

UNIVERSITY 101
Upperclassman mentors; optional first-year leadership program.

St. Thomas is dedicated to teaching students how to be leaders in social justice.

The school's global leadership major is one of the only academic programs in the country that requires students to critique America's core values. The interdisciplinary program examines the economic, ecological, and sociological perspectives of conscious leadership in the modern world. Students who choose this accelerated three-year program take summer courses together and spend at least one semester break interning in New York City, Europe, or Latin America through Pax Romana, the International Catholic Movement for Intellectual and Social Affairs. When the program is over, students may choose to move directly into the working world or complete a second major on campus.

WHAT IT IS

St. Thomas University was founded in 1961 by the Augustinian Order of Villanova, Pennsylvania, at the invitation of the late Most Reverend Coleman F. Carroll, the Archbishop of Miami. It has grown from an institution with an initial enrollment of 45 students to become one of Florida's most comprehensive Catholic universities.

The undergraduate student population represents 28 states, the District of Columbia, Puerto Rico, the Virgin Islands, and 65 countries. More than half of the undergraduates are women. On campus, the Student Center contains a student lounge, a bookstore, the rathskeller, and other facilities. Adjacent to the university's two dormitories are the dining hall and the University Inn. Sports facilities include six tennis courts, a recreational swimming pool, two basketball courts, four baseball fields, a soccer field, and two football fields. The university offers a full range of cultural, governmental, and social activities, including publications and clubs. The Office of Campus Ministry provides liturgical celebrations in the university chapel and sponsors social justice and community service activities.

WHERE IT'S AT

The university is located in northwest Miami on a 140-acre campus with 15 major buildings. Midway between Fort Lauderdale and downtown Miami, the university is near numerous cultural and recreational facilities. In fact, St. Thomas is located less than two miles south of Pro Player Stadium, which is home to the Miami Dolphins. The area's subtropical climate allows students to enjoy the nearby Atlantic Ocean beaches and many other natural attractions, such as the Florida Keys, Everglades National Park, and state and county parks, throughout the year. A short drive from campus are Key Biscayne, Bal Harbour, Miami Beach, Fort Lauderdale, and other cities of Florida's Gold Coast. Miami and surrounding Dade County, known as the "Gateway to South America," house an international banking and trade center and offer a truly cosmopolitan atmosphere.

THE DETAILS

Campus setting:	suburban
Degrees:	bachelor's, master's
Calendar:	semesters
Public/Private:	private religious
Number of full-time faculty:	92
Student-to-teacher ratio:	11:1

Admissions requirements:
- **Options:** common application, deferred entrance, early admission, electronic application
- **Application fee:** $40
- **Required:** high school transcript, letter of recommendation, SAT and SAT Subject Tests, or ACT
- **Application deadlines:** continuous (freshmen), continuous (transfer)
- **Early decision:** —
- **Notification:** continuous (freshmen), continuous (transfer)

Average high school GPA:	2.96
Average freshman SAT verbal/math score:	463 / 445
Average freshman ACT score:	18
Number of applicants:	903
Number of applicants accepted:	249
Percentage of students from out of state:	7%
Total freshman enrollment:	191
Total enrollment:	2,630
Percentage of students who live in campus housing:	10%
Total tuition:	$17,010
Total cost with fees & expenses:	$28,730
Average financial aid package:	$11,270

ST. THOMAS UNIVERSITY

MAJORS

- Accounting
- Biology/Biological Sciences, General
- Business Administration and Management, General
- Chemistry, General
- Computer Science
- Criminal Justice/Law Enforcement Administration
- Elementary Education and Teaching
- English Language and Literature, General
- Finance, General
- History, General
- Hotel/Motel Administration/Management
- Information Science/Studies
- International Business/Trade/Commerce
- Liberal Arts and Sciences/Liberal Studies
- Marketing/Marketing Management, General
- Mass Communication/Media Studies
- Pastoral Studies/Counseling
- Political Science and Government, General
- Pre-Dentistry Studies
- Pre-Law Studies
- Pre-Medicine/Pre-Medical Studies
- Psychology, General
- Public Administration
- Religion/Religious Studies
- Secondary Education and Teaching
- Sociology
- Sport and Fitness Administration/Management
- Tourism and Travel Services Management

UNIVERSITY OF CENTRAL FLORIDA

4000 Central Florida Boulevard
Orlando, FL 32816

(407) 823-2000
http://www.ucf.edu/

BIG DEAL

UNIVERSITY 101
Office of First-Year Advising to help answer questions and solve problems; special academic advisors assigned to first-year students; extended orientation program; required first-year seminar; upperclassman mentors; optional first-year leadership program; optional first-year residential learning communities.

BIG FISH

The fight to stop global warming is on at the University of Central Florida.

The Florida Solar Energy Center, located on campus, is the largest state-supported energy research facility in the United States and conducts more than $8 million worth of studies on solar technology each year. The Solar Center is just one of UCF's research centers and institutes. Seven other university-operated facilities—including the Nanoscience Technology Center, the Florida Space Institute, and the Biomolecular Science Center—give undergrads a chance to do cutting-edge work with faculty members who are active players in the scientific community.

UNIVERSITY OF CENTRAL FLORIDA

WHAT IT IS

The University of Central Florida is one of the nation's fastest-growing universities. UCF enrolls a diverse student body representing 50 states and more than 120 countries. The university offers educational and research programs that complement the economy, with strong components in aerospace engineering, business, education, film, health, hospitality management, nursing, and social sciences. UCF's programs in communication and the fine arts help to meet the cultural and recreational needs of a growing metropolitan area.

UCF has established extensive partnerships with businesses and industries in central Florida that provide students with exceptional research and learning experiences. These partnerships bring practical learning environments to UCF students through co-op and internship programs. Joint curriculum development strategies include BE2020, which is a widely modeled business curriculum incorporating classes taught by local business and industry executives.

The on-campus and campus-affiliated housing facilities include traditional residence halls, apartment-style options, and Greek housing. Students participate in more than 300 organizations, including special interest clubs, multicultural associations, fraternities and sororities, honor societies, and academic and preprofessional organizations. The Office of Student Involvement and Office of Student Activities schedule a wide array of extracurricular programs, including concerts, movies, and guest speakers.

WHERE IT'S AT

The University of Central Florida occupies approximately 1,415 acres of east-central Florida habitat, and some of the last elevated land before the St. Johns River, lying between the campus and the coast. The scenic campus includes patches of wetlands, canals, exotic plants, and the Arboretum of the University of Central Florida. The university is 13 miles east of downtown Orlando, one of the most dynamic metropolitan areas in the United States; 45 miles from the Atlantic Ocean and Cape Canaveral; and 100 miles from Tampa and the Gulf of Mexico. The area boasts world-class shopping and dining, lakes, golf courses, jogging trails, nature preserves, and theme parks. Regional campuses are located in Daytona Beach, Cocoa, and South Lake.

THE DETAILS

Campus setting:	suburban
Degrees:	bachelor's, master's, doctoral
Calendar:	semesters
Public/Private:	public state
Number of full-time faculty:	1,152
Student-to-teacher ratio:	25:1
Admissions requirements:	
• **Options:** common application, early admission, electronic application	
• **Application fee:** $30	
• **Required:** high school transcript, SAT or ACT	
• **Application deadlines:** 5/1 (freshmen), 5/1 (transfer)	
• **Early decision:** —	
• **Notification:** 10/1 (freshmen), continuous (transfer)	

Average high school GPA:	3.80
Average freshman SAT verbal/math score:	575 / 586
Average freshman ACT score:	24
Number of applicants:	22,367
Number of applicants accepted:	12,388
Percentage of students from out of state:	3%
Total freshman enrollment:	5,761
Total enrollment:	42,568
Percentage of students who live in campus housing:	20%
Total in-state tuition, fees & expenses:	$11,212
Total out-of-state tuition, fees & expenses:	$23,718
Average financial aid package:	$5,397

UNIVERSITY OF CENTRAL FLORIDA

MAJORS

- Accounting
- Actuarial Science
- Advertising
- Aerospace, Aeronautical and Astronautical Engineering
- Anthropology
- Art/Art Studies, General
- Art Teacher Education
- Audiology/Audiologist and Speech-Language Pathology/Pathologist
- Biology/Biological Sciences, General
- Business/Commerce, General
- Business/Managerial Economics
- Business Administration and Management, General
- Business Teacher Education
- Chemistry, General
- Cinematography and Film/Video Production
- Civil Engineering, General
- Clinical Laboratory Science/Medical Technology/Technologist
- Computer and Information Sciences, General
- Computer Engineering, General
- Computer Technology/Computer Systems Technology
- Criminal Justice/Safety Studies
- Drama and Dramatics/Theatre Arts, General
- Early Childhood Education and Teaching
- Economics, General
- Electrical, Electronic and Communications Engineering Technology/Technician
- Electrical, Electronics and Communications Engineering
- Elementary Education and Teaching
- Engineering Technology, General
- English/Language Arts Teacher Education
- English Language and Literature, General
- Environmental/Environmental Health Engineering
- Finance, General
- Fine/Studio Arts, General
- Foreign Languages and Literatures, General
- Foreign Language Teacher Education
- Forensic Science and Technology
- French Language and Literature
- Health/Health Care Administration/Management
- Health Information/Medical Records Administration/Administrator
- Health Science
- Health Services/Allied Health/Health Sciences, General
- History, General
- Hospitality Administration/Management, General
- Humanities/Humanistic Studies
- Industrial Engineering
- Information Technology
- Intermedia/Multimedia
- Journalism
- Legal Assistant/Paralegal
- Liberal Arts and Sciences/Liberal Studies
- Management Information Systems, General
- Marketing/Marketing Management, General
- Mass Communication/Media Studies
- Mathematics, General
- Mathematics Teacher Education
- Mechanical Engineering
- Mechanical Engineering Related Technologies/Technicians, Other
- Medical Microbiology and Bacteriology
- Medical Radiologic Technology, Science/Radiation Therapist
- Music Performance, General
- Music Teacher Education
- Nursing/Registered Nurse Training
- Philosophy
- Photography
- Physical Education Teaching and Coaching
- Physics, General
- Political Science and Government, General
- Psychology, General
- Public Administration
- Radio and Television
- Respiratory Care Therapy/Therapist
- Science Teacher Education/General Science Teacher Education
- Social Sciences, General
- Social Science Teacher Education
- Social Work
- Sociology
- Spanish Language and Literature
- Special Education and Teaching, General
- Speech and Rhetorical Studies
- Statistics, General
- Trade and Industrial Teacher Education

UNIVERSITY OF FLORIDA

PO Box 114000
Gainesville, FL 32611

(352) 392-3261
http://www.ufl.edu/

BIG REP

UNIVERSITY 101
Extended orientation program; optional first-year transitional seminar; optional first-year residential learning communities; upperclassman mentors.

BIG DEAL

Gatorade! Just one of the many famous discoveries at the University of Florida.

The university's 16 colleges include more than 100 research and resource centers that serve both faculty and students. The University Scholars Program pairs undergrads of all majors with faculty mentors for collaborative research projects. Students get a hands-on introduction to the school's facilities, one-on-one instruction, and a $2,500 stipend for their work. They also gain an opportunity to present and publish their studies in the university-produced *Journal of Undergraduate Research*. The University of Florida has one of the largest research programs in the country and brings in more than $470 million in sponsored contracts each year.

UNIVERSITY OF FLORIDA

WHAT IT IS

With approximately 48,000 students, the University of Florida is one of the largest universities in the United States. The school is also the oldest and most comprehensive institution of higher education in Florida. Founded in 1853 and settling in its current location in Gainesville in 1905, the University of Florida offers its students a full plate of educational options, including a choice of more than 100 undergraduate majors, a popular honors program, and the University Scholars Program, which gives undergrads the opportunity to work closely with faculty on research projects. Future UF student-researchers might even have a hand in creating something as well known as Gatorade. The popular sports drink was developed at the university, and royalties from sales of the beverage help fund research in a variety of areas. Students who would rather make their mark in the media and entertainment industries gravitate toward the College of Journalism and Communication, where they can gain practical experience working at one of four radio or two television stations on campus. Students also attend more than 2,000 on-campus events each year, including concerts, plays, sporting events, and guest lectures.

WHERE IT'S AT

The University of Florida occupies a 2,000-acre campus in Gainesville. The city has a population of nearly 100,000 and a thriving local music scene—punk bands like Less Than Jake and Hot Water Music hail from the city. The UF campus is made up of more than 900 buildings, some of which are listed on the National Register of Historic Places. The university has been engaged in numerous improvement and expansion projects in recent years, including the opening of the McKnight Brain Institute and the new Public Health and Health Professions, Nursing and Pharmacy Building. The UF Honors Residential College at Hume Hall is the first such building specifically designed to house honors students in the country. Other campus landmarks include the largest natural history museum in the Southeast and Lake Alice, an alligator and bird sanctuary.

THE DETAILS

Campus setting:	suburban
Degrees:	bachelor's, master's, doctoral
Calendar:	semesters
Public/Private:	public state
Number of full-time faculty:	1,622
Student-to-teacher ratio:	23:1

Admissions requirements:
- **Options:** common application, early admission, early decision, electronic application
- **Application fee:** $30
- **Required:** high school transcript, SAT or ACT
- **Application deadlines:** 1/12 (freshmen)
- **Early decision:** 10/1
- **Notification:** continuous (freshmen), 12/1 (early decision)

Average high school GPA:	3.8
Average freshman SAT verbal/math score:	615 / 633
Average freshman ACT score:	25
Number of applicants:	22,973
Number of applicants accepted:	12,029
Percentage of students from out of state:	4%
Total freshman enrollment:	6,524
Total enrollment:	47,858
Percentage of students who live in campus housing:	21%
Total in-state tuition, fees & expenses:	$9,785
Total out-of-state tuition, fees & expenses:	$22,657
Average financial aid package:	$10,004

UNIVERSITY OF FLORIDA

MAJORS

- Accounting
- Advertising
- Aerospace, Aeronautical and Astronautical Engineering
- Agricultural/Biological Engineering and Bioengineering
- Agricultural and Food Products Processing
- Agricultural Economics
- Agricultural Teacher Education
- Agronomy and Crop Science
- American/United States Studies/Civilization
- Animal Sciences, General
- Anthropology
- Architecture
- Art History, Criticism and Conservation
- Art Teacher Education
- Asian Studies/Civilization
- Astronomy
- Audiology/Audiologist and Speech-Language Pathology/Pathologist
- Botany/Plant Biology
- Business Administration and Management, General
- Chemical Engineering
- Chemistry, General
- Civil Engineering, General
- Classics and Languages, Literatures and Linguistics, General
- Community Health Services/Liaison/Counseling
- Computer and Information Sciences, General
- Computer Engineering, General
- Construction Engineering Technology/Technician
- Criminology
- Dairy Science
- Dance, General
- Drama and Dramatics/Theatre Arts, General
- East Asian Languages, Literatures, and Linguistics, Other
- Economics, General
- Electrical, Electronics and Communications Engineering
- Elementary Education and Teaching
- Engineering Science
- English Language and Literature, General
- Entomology
- Environmental/Environmental Health Engineering
- Environmental Science
- Family and Community Services
- Finance, General
- Fine/Studio Arts, General
- Fire Science/Firefighting
- Food Science
- Forestry, General
- French Language and Literature
- Geography
- Geology/Earth Science, General
- German Language and Literature
- Graphic Design
- Health Services/Allied Health/Health Sciences, General
- Health Teacher Education
- History, General
- Horticultural Science
- Industrial Engineering
- Insurance
- Interior Design
- Intermedia/Multimedia
- Jewish/Judaic Studies
- Journalism
- Junior High/Intermediate/Middle School Education and Teaching
- Kinesiology and Exercise Science
- Landscape Architecture
- Linguistics
- Management Science, General
- Marketing/Marketing Management, General
- Materials Engineering
- Mathematics, General
- Mechanical Engineering
- Medical Microbiology and Bacteriology
- Multi-/Interdisciplinary Studies, Other
- Music, General
- Music Teacher Education
- Nuclear Engineering
- Nursing/Registered Nurse Training
- Parks, Recreation and Leisure Facilities Management
- Philosophy
- Physics, General
- Plant Pathology/Phytopathology
- Plant Sciences, General
- Political Science and Government, General
- Portuguese Language and Literature
- Poultry Science
- Psychology, General
- Public Relations/Image Management
- Radio and Television
- Real Estate
- Religion/Religious Studies
- Russian Language and Literature
- Sociology
- Soil Science and Agronomy, General
- Spanish Language and Literature
- Special Education and Teaching, General
- Statistics, General
- Survey Technology/Surveying
- Systems Engineering
- Zoology/Animal Biology

UNIVERSITY OF MIAMI

PO Box 248025　　　　　　　　　　　　　　　　(305) 284-2211
Coral Gables, FL 33124　　　　　　　　　　　　http://www.miami.edu/

BIG REP

UNIVERSITY 101
Extended orientation program; optional first-year service-learning projects; optional first-year seminars.

The University of Miami offers students more choices than any other school in the state.

The school has more than 300 degree programs, over 250 student organizations, and $270 million in sponsored research projects. Students have to be bright, driven, and creative to keep up with faculty members armed with awards from institutions like the National Science Foundation and American Academy for Arts and Sciences. Close to two-thirds of all entering first-years ranked in the top 10 percent of their graduating class. If you're one of the 15,000 lucky enough to make it through the admissions process, expect a long road of challenges ahead.

UNIVERSITY OF MIAMI

WHAT IT IS

In 1925, when the young town of Coral Gables, Florida, was growing rapidly, community leaders decided that a world-class university would benefit the development of their town. Since then, the University of Miami has matured into a nationally recognized institution of higher education and one of the largest private universities in the region. Miami offers more than 180 undergraduate concentrations in eight schools and colleges, including programs in psychology, marine science, and pre-law. Specialized programs and centers include the Sue and Leonard Miller Center for Contemporary Judaic Studies, one of the only academic teaching and research centers in the country dedicated to the study of twentieth-century Jewish culture and history.

At the University of Miami, there's a place for everyone—students can choose from an honors program, undergraduate research opportunities, and numerous clubs and activities. The institution's popular extracurricular activities include its award-winning, student-produced news program, the Sunsations dance team, and the Miami cheerleaders, who, in addition to providing school spirit at games, are active in community service. Hurricane sports teams are also top-notch, having won more than 20 national championships.

WHERE IT'S AT

The University of Miami's main campus in the town of Coral Gables is just a short drive from beautiful Atlantic coast beaches and Miami's thriving social and cultural scenes, as well as nature sites like John Pennekamp Coral Reef State Park and the Everglades. The 230-acre campus is home to the Lowe Art Museum, Cosford Cinema, Gusman Concert Hall, and John C. Gifford Arboretum. Sports facilities include the Convocation Center, a 7,000-plus-seat multipurpose arena that hosts UM's basketball teams, and an Olympic-size pool in the center of the University Center patio.

THE DETAILS

Campus setting:	suburban
Degrees:	bachelor's, master's, doctoral
Calendar:	semesters
Public/Private:	private nonprofit
Number of full-time faculty:	877
Student-to-teacher ratio:	13:1

Admissions requirements:
- **Options:** common application, deferred entrance, early admission, early decision, early action, electronic application
- **Application fee:** $65
- **Required:** essay or personal statement, high school transcript, SAT or ACT
- **Application deadlines:** 2/1 (freshmen), 3/1 (transfer), 11/1 (early action)
- **Early decision:** 11/1
- **Notification:** 4/15 (freshmen), 4/15 (transfer), 12/20 (early decision), 2/1 (early action)

Average high school GPA:	—
Average freshman SAT verbal/math score:	621 / 639
Average freshman ACT score:	26
Number of applicants:	18,507
Number of applicants accepted:	7,784
Percentage of students from out of state:	45%
Total freshman enrollment:	2,025
Total enrollment:	15,250
Percentage of students who live in campus housing:	42%
Total tuition:	$27,384
Total cost with fees & expenses:	$37,250
Average financial aid package:	$22,711

MAJORS

- Accounting
- Advertising
- Aerospace, Aeronautical and Astronautical Engineering
- African-American/Black Studies
- American/United States Studies/Civilization
- Anthropology
- Architectural Engineering
- Architecture
- Art/Art Studies, General
- Art History, Criticism and Conservation
- Athletic Training/Trainer
- Atmospheric Sciences and Meteorology, General
- Biochemistry
- Biology/Biological Sciences, General
- Biomedical/Medical Engineering
- Biophysics
- Broadcast Journalism
- Business/Managerial Economics
- Business Administration, Management and Operations, Other
- Business Administration and Management, General
- Ceramic Arts and Ceramics
- Chemistry, General
- Chemistry, Other
- Cinematography and Film/Video Production
- Civil Engineering, General
- Commercial and Advertising Art
- Communication, Journalism and Related Programs, Other
- Communication Studies/Speech Communication and Rhetoric
- Computer and Information Sciences, General
- Computer Engineering, General
- Computer Science
- Computer Systems Analysis/Analyst
- Conducting
- Creative Writing
- Criminology
- Dance, General
- Drama and Dramatics/Theatre Arts, General
- Education, General
- Electrical, Electronics and Communications Engineering
- Elementary Education and Teaching
- Engineering Science
- English Language and Literature, General
- English Literature (British and Commonwealth)
- Entrepreneurial and Small Business Operations, Other
- Entrepreneurship/Entrepreneurial Studies
- Environmental/Environmental Health Engineering
- Environmental Studies
- Family and Community Services
- Film/Cinema Studies
- Finance, General
- Fine/Studio Arts, General
- French Language and Literature
- General Studies
- Geography
- Geological and Earth Sciences/Geosciences, Other
- Geology/Earth Science, General
- German Language and Literature
- Health/Medical Preparatory Programs, Other
- Health and Medical Administrative Services, Other
- Health Professions and Related Clinical Sciences, Other
- History, General
- Human Resources Management/Personnel Administration, General
- Industrial Engineering
- Information Science/Studies
- International Business/Trade/Commerce
- International Relations and Affairs
- Italian Language and Literature
- Jewish/Judaic Studies
- Journalism
- Kinesiology and Exercise Science
- Latin American Studies
- Liberal Arts and Sciences/Liberal Studies
- Marine Biology and Biological Oceanography
- Marketing/Marketing Management, General
- Mass Communication/Media Studies
- Mathematics, General
- Mathematics and Statistics, Other
- Mechanical Engineering
- Medical Microbiology and Bacteriology
- Music, General
- Music, Other
- Music Management and Merchandising
- Musicology and Ethnomusicology
- Music Performance, General
- Music Teacher Education
- Music Theory and Composition
- Music Therapy/Therapist
- Natural Resources and Conservation, Other
- Natural Resources Management and Policy
- Neurobiology and Neurophysiology
- Neuroscience
- Nursing/Registered Nurse Training
- Oceanography, Chemical and Physical
- Painting
- Philosophy
- Photography
- Physics, General
- Physics, Other
- Physiological Psychology/Psychobiology
- Piano and Organ
- Political Science and Government, General
- Pre-Pharmacy Studies
- Printmaking
- Psychology, General
- Public Relations/Image Management
- Radio and Television
- Religion/Religious Studies
- Sculpture
- Secondary Education and Teaching
- Sociology
- Spanish Language and Literature
- Special Education and Teaching, General
- Visual and Performing Arts, General
- Voice and Opera
- Wildlife and Wildlands Science and Management
- Women's Studies

UNIVERSITY OF NORTH FLORIDA

4567 St. Johns Bluff Road South
Jacksonville, FL 32224

(904) 620-1000
http://www.unf.edu/

BIG DEAL

UNIVERSITY 101
Optional first-year residential learning communities; required first-year humanities seminars.

BIG FISH

Home to the only anatomy lab in the area, this school brings in more than $3.2 million in health-related research grants each year.

Beyond the basic health studies, nutrition, and health administration majors, this university offers highly specified programs of study in areas like athletic training and community health. College of Health faculty members are recognized routinely as the best in their field. When they're not learning from the best, health students also have the opportunity to network with current caregiving professionals in the school's eight alumni and wellness honor societies.

UNIVERSITY OF NORTH FLORIDA

WHAT IT IS

Founded in 1972, UNF has grown into a comprehensive state university that attracts both talented students and professors. Most faculty members have PhDs or other terminal degrees in their field, and many are actively involved in research and study both globally and in the local community. Prestigious visiting instructors are not unusual either—in 2003, Archbishop Desmond Tutu taught at the university. A UNF education is focused on fulfilling students' educational needs in addition to providing them with practical, real-world experience, and the university offers 50 undergraduate degree programs with 115 areas of concentration. Sports are another source of UNF pride. The UNF Ospreys compete in basketball, soccer, and track/cross-country, among other sports, and the women's tennis and men's golf teams have won national championships.

WHERE IT'S AT

Home of the University of North Florida, Jacksonville is the largest city in the lower 48 states in land area. This northeast Florida metropolis has a population of more than 800,000 and the largest urban park system in the United States. Area attractions, all within a short drive of UNF, include St. Augustine, the nation's oldest city; Kennedy Space Center; and Daytona Beach. Major tourist attractions like Walt Disney World and Universal Studios are about two hours away. The campus itself sits on 1,300 acres in a southeastern suburb of Jacksonville and is a designated bird sanctuary with 12 miles of nature trails. New facilities at the university include the Science and Engineering Building and the Thomas G. Carpenter Library.

THE DETAILS

Campus setting:	urban
Degrees:	bachelor's, master's, doctoral
Calendar:	semesters
Public/Private:	public state
Number of full-time faculty:	421
Student-to-teacher ratio:	23:1

Admissions requirements:
- **Options:** common application, deferred entrance, early admission, early action, electronic application
- **Application fee:** $30
- **Required:** high school transcript, letter of recommendation, SAT or ACT
- **Application deadlines:** 7/2 (freshmen), 7/2 (transfer)
- **Early action:** 11/15
- **Notification:** continuous (freshmen), continuous (transfer), 12/2 (early action)

Average high school GPA:	3.51
Average freshman SAT verbal/math score:	557 / 557
Average freshman ACT score:	22
Number of applicants:	8,307
Number of applicants accepted:	5,752
Percentage of students from out of state:	5%
Total freshman enrollment:	2,223
Total enrollment:	14,534
Percentage of students who live in campus housing:	17%
Total in-state tuition, fees & expenses:	$10,179
Total out-of-state tuition, fees & expenses:	$21,929
Average financial aid package:	$2,286

UNIVERSITY OF NORTH FLORIDA

MAJORS

- Accounting
- Anthropology
- Art/Art Studies, General
- Art Teacher Education
- Banking and Financial Support Services
- Biological and Physical Sciences
- Biology/Biological Sciences, General
- Business/Managerial Economics
- Business Administration and Management, General
- Chemistry, General
- Civil Engineering, General
- Communication Studies/Speech Communication and Rhetoric
- Computer and Information Sciences, General
- Construction Engineering Technology/Technician
- Criminal Justice/Safety Studies
- Economics, General
- Electrical, Electronics and Communications Engineering
- Elementary Education and Teaching
- English Language and Literature, General
- Finance, General
- Fine/Studio Arts, General
- Health Services/Allied Health/Health Sciences, General
- History, General
- International Business/Trade/Commerce
- International Relations and Affairs
- Jazz/Jazz Studies
- Junior High/Intermediate/Middle School Education and Teaching
- Liberal Arts and Sciences/Liberal Studies
- Marketing/Marketing Management, General
- Mathematics, General
- Mathematics Teacher Education
- Mechanical Engineering
- Music, General
- Music Performance, General
- Music Teacher Education
- Nursing/Registered Nurse Training
- Philosophy
- Physical Education Teaching and Coaching
- Physics, General
- Political Science and Government, General
- Psychology, General
- Science Teacher Education/General Science Teacher Education
- Secondary Education and Teaching
- Sociology
- Spanish Language and Literature
- Special Education and Teaching, General
- Statistics, General
- Trade and Industrial Teacher Education
- Transportation/Transportation Management

UNIVERSITY OF SOUTH FLORIDA

4202 East Fowler Avenue
Tampa, FL 33620

(813) 974-2011
http://www.usf.edu

BIG DEAL

UNIVERSITY 101
Optional first-year transitional seminar; extended orientation program; upperclassman mentors; optional first-year residential learning communities; optional first-year college preparation program before each semester.

My how USF has grown.

The second-largest university in the Southeast and among the top 20 largest in the nation, USF has a place for everyone. The Tampa Bay campus hosts more than 40,000 students from all 50 states and 116 countries. The university offers more than 200 degree programs and work-placement programs with 800 companies worldwide. A cool $250 million in sponsored research grants and contracts, brought in by on-campus researchers every year, only adds to the number of learning opportunities available to undergrads. The student body is just as diverse as its academic offerings—nearly one-third of students are ethnic minorities.

UNIVERSITY OF SOUTH FLORIDA

WHAT IT IS

Founded in 1956, the University of South Florida is among the nation's largest and most dynamic national research universities. As the principal university in the Tampa Bay region, USF serves the community and offers degrees at several campuses: Tampa, St. Petersburg, Lakeland, and Sarasota, with additional centers in Pinellas, Pasco, and Hernando counties and downtown Tampa. USF's national stature as an academic institution was acknowledged by the Carnegie Foundation for the Advancement of Teaching, which ranked the university in the top tier of American colleges and universities as doctoral/research-extensive.

USF's student body is as diverse as its academic program profile. Students come from 52 states and U.S. territories and 116 other countries. African Americans, Hispanics, and students from other minority groups comprise 27 percent of the student body. Traditional dorms, suites, apartments, fraternities and sororities, and married and family student housing is available. There are more than 300 student clubs and organizations at USF, and the university has 17 national fraternities and 13 national sororities. The Campus Activities Board and the Offices of Student Activities and Residence Services schedule a wide array of extracurricular programs, including concerts, movies, and a lecture series. The Tampa campus features an 18-hole championship golf course, four swimming pools, sand volleyball and tennis courts, a state-of-the-art recreation center, indoor and outdoor racquetball courts, and a private riverfront park.

WHERE IT'S AT

USF is located on 1,700 acres in northeast Tampa, a thriving urban setting just north of downtown businesses in one of the fastest-growing areas in Tampa Bay. With 2.5 million residents, the Tampa Bay area boasts a booming employment rate, year-round festivals and activities, and a consistently pleasant and sunny climate. The campus is across the street from the Busch Gardens Theme Park. Other attractions include the Lowry Park Zoo, Florida Aquarium, Museum of Science and Industry, Tampa Bay Performing Arts Center, Tampa Museum of Art, and historic Ybor City area. Regional campuses are located in St. Petersburg on the historic Bayboro Harbor; Lakeland on the I-4 High Technology Corridor; and Sarasota, which touches the Gulf of Mexico.

THE DETAILS

Campus setting:	urban
Degrees:	bachelor's, master's, doctoral
Calendar:	semesters
Public/Private:	public state
Number of full-time faculty:	1,641
Student-to-teacher ratio:	16:1

Admissions requirements:
- **Options:** common application, early admission, electronic application
- **Application fee:** $30
- **Required:** high school transcript, letter of recommendation, SAT or ACT
- **Application deadlines:** 4/15 (freshmen), 4/15 (transfer)
- **Early decision:** —
- **Notification:** continuous (freshmen), continuous (transfer)

Average high school GPA:	3.7
Average freshman SAT verbal/math score:	556 / 559
Average freshman ACT score:	23
Number of applicants:	16,985
Number of applicants accepted:	8,652
Percentage of students from out of state:	4%
Total freshman enrollment:	4,190
Total enrollment:	42,238
Percentage of students who live in campus housing:	13%
Total in-state tuition, fees & expenses:	$10,694
Total out-of-state tuition, fees & expenses:	$23,564
Average financial aid package:	$9,439

MAJORS

- Accounting
- African-American/Black Studies
- American/United States Studies/Civilization
- Anthropology
- Art/Art Studies, General
- Art Teacher Education
- Athletic Training/Trainer
- Audiology/Audiologist and Speech-Language Pathology/Pathologist
- Biological and Physical Sciences
- Biology/Biological Sciences, General
- Business/Commerce, General
- Business/Managerial Economics
- Business Administration and Management, General
- Business Teacher Education
- Chemical Engineering
- Chemistry, General
- Civil Engineering, General
- Classics and Languages, Literatures and Linguistics, General
- Clinical Laboratory Science/Medical Technology/Technologist
- Communication Studies/Speech Communication and Rhetoric
- Computer/Information Technology Services Administration and Management, Other
- Computer and Information Sciences, General
- Computer Engineering, General
- Criminal Justice/Safety Studies
- Dance, General
- Drama and Dance Teacher Education
- Drama and Dramatics/Theatre Arts, General
- Economics, General
- Education, General
- Education/Teaching of Individuals with Emotional Disturbances
- Education/Teaching of Individuals with Mental Retardation
- Education/Teaching of Individuals with Specific Learning Disabilities
- Electrical, Electronics and Communications Engineering
- Elementary Education and Teaching
- Engineering, General
- English/Language Arts Teacher Education
- English Language and Literature, General
- Environmental Studies
- Finance, General
- Foreign Language Teacher Education
- French Language and Literature
- General Studies
- Geography
- Geology/Earth Science, General
- German Language and Literature
- Gerontology
- History, General
- Hospitality Administration/Management, General
- Humanities/Humanistic Studies
- Industrial Engineering
- Information Science/Studies
- International Business/Trade/Commerce
- International Relations and Affairs
- Italian Language and Literature
- Kindergarten/Preschool Education and Teaching
- Liberal Arts and Sciences/Liberal Studies
- Management Information Systems, General
- Management Science, General
- Marketing/Marketing Management, General
- Mathematics, General
- Mathematics Teacher Education
- Mechanical Engineering
- Medical Microbiology and Bacteriology
- Modern Languages
- Music Performance, General
- Music Teacher Education
- Nursing/Registered Nurse Training
- Philosophy
- Physical Education Teaching and Coaching
- Physics, General
- Political Science and Government, General
- Psychology, General
- Religion/Religious Studies
- Russian Language and Literature
- Science Teacher Education/General Science Teacher Education
- Social Sciences, General
- Social Science Teacher Education
- Social Work
- Sociology
- Spanish Language and Literature
- Special Education and Teaching, General
- Speech and Rhetorical Studies
- Trade and Industrial Teacher Education
- Women's Studies

UNIVERSITY OF TAMPA

401 West Kennedy Boulevard
Tampa, FL 33606

(813) 253-3333
http://www.utampa.edu/

BIG FISH

UNIVERSITY 101
Extended orientation program; required first-year transitional seminar; upperclassman mentors; special academic advisors assigned to first-year students; required first-year English and global issues courses; optional first-year leadership program.

UT's got great programs on campus, but its off-campus programs are truly incredible.

The University of Tampa's off-campus programs put students in the studio, dugout, and West Wing. The university operates one of the most expansive internship networks in the United States and has affiliations with the nation's top commercial, government, and nonprofit agencies. Local internships are available at area radio stations, advertising companies, television studios, research centers, and government offices and allow students to work and maintain a full schedule of classes. Students may also bid campus a temporary adieu while they spend a semester interning outside of the Tampa area. Undergrads who envision working for the White House, Congress, the World Bank, the Center for Marine Conservation, the New York Yankees, the CIA, the American Red Cross, Merrill Lynch, or PricewaterhouseCoopers can get both feet in the door while earning credit.

FLORIDA

UNIVERSITY OF TAMPA

WHAT IT IS

The University of Tampa offers challenging learning experiences in two colleges: the College of Liberal Arts and Sciences and the John H. Sykes College of Business. In both colleges, students work with experts in their fields, and there is a shared belief in the value of a liberal arts–centered education, practical work experience, and the ability to communicate effectively, all of which are trademarks of a University of Tampa education.

At the center of campus is Plant Hall, once a luxurious 511-room hotel for the rich and famous. Its ornate Victorian gingerbread and Moorish minarets, domes, and cupolas still remain a symbol of the city and one of the finest examples of Moorish architecture in the Western Hemisphere. Eighty percent of all residence hall space is new and built since 1998.

The environment outside the classroom is supportive, stimulating, and fun. Students choose from more than 115 student organizations, including honor societies, social clubs, fraternities, and sororities. The University of Tampa has one of the best NCAA Division II sports programs in the nation. Spartan athletes have won nine national championships, including three in baseball and three in men's soccer. Students attend concerts, art exhibitions, theater productions, dance performances, and special lectures on campus and nearby.

WHERE IT'S AT

Situated on a beautiful, parklike campus on the Hillsborough River, the university is just two blocks from downtown Tampa. There is much more to Tampa's location than beautiful beaches and pleasant year-round temperatures. Home to 2.3 million people, Tampa Bay is one of the fastest-growing areas in the United States. The city is the commercial and cultural center of Florida's west coast. Nearby are the Museum of Art, the St. Pete Times Forum, the Performing Arts Center, the Gallery of Photographic Art, the Convention Center, the Aquarium, and the Lowry Park Zoo. Busch Gardens is just a few miles from campus. Within one hour are Walt Disney World and Universal Studios in Orlando. Tampa International Airport is just 15 minutes from campus.

THE DETAILS

Campus setting:	urban
Degrees:	bachelor's, master's
Calendar:	semesters
Public/Private:	private nonprofit
Number of full-time faculty:	201
Student-to-teacher ratio:	17:1

Admissions requirements:
- **Options:** common application, deferred entrance, early admission, electronic application
- **Application fee:** $35
- **Required:** essay or personal statement, high school transcript, letter of recommendation, SAT or ACT
- **Application deadlines:** continuous (freshmen), continuous (transfer)
- **Early decision:** —
- **Notification:** — (freshmen), continuous (transfer)

Average high school GPA:	3.28
Average freshman SAT verbal/math score:	546 / 546
Average freshman ACT score:	23
Number of applicants:	5,306
Number of applicants accepted:	2,821
Percentage of students from out of state:	53%
Total freshman enrollment:	956
Total enrollment:	4,879
Percentage of students who live in campus housing:	59%
Total tuition:	$17,250
Total cost with fees & expenses:	$25,681
Average financial aid package:	$14,398

UNIVERSITY OF TAMPA

MAJORS

- Accounting
- Art/Art Studies, General
- Biochemistry
- Biology/Biological Sciences, General
- Business Administration and Management, General
- Chemistry, General
- Computer Graphics
- Computer Programming/Programmer, General
- Creative Writing
- Criminology
- Drama and Dramatics/Theatre Arts, General
- Economics, General
- Elementary Education and Teaching
- English Language and Literature, General
- Environmental Biology
- Environmental Studies
- Finance, General
- History, General
- Information Science/Studies
- International Business/Trade/Commerce
- International Relations and Affairs
- Kinesiology and Exercise Science
- Liberal Arts and Sciences/Liberal Studies
- Marine Science/Merchant Marine Officer
- Marketing/Marketing Management, General
- Mass Communication/Media Studies
- Mathematics, General
- Music, General
- Nursing/Registered Nurse Training
- Physical Education Teaching and Coaching
- Political Science and Government, General
- Pre-Dentistry Studies
- Pre-Law Studies
- Pre-Medicine/Pre-Medical Studies
- Pre-Veterinary Studies
- Psychology, General
- Secondary Education and Teaching
- Social Sciences, General
- Sociology
- Spanish Language and Literature
- Teacher Education, Multiple Levels
- Urban Studies/Affairs
- Visual and Performing Arts, General

UNIVERSITY OF WEST FLORIDA

11000 University Parkway
Pensacola, FL 32514

(850) 474-2000
http://uwf.edu/

BIG DEAL

UNIVERSITY 101 Extended orientation program; required first-year transitional seminar; upperclassman mentors.

BIG IDEA

Despite its size (nearly 10,000 students on campus), the University of West Florida provides a surprisingly personal education.

Ninety-eight percent of all classes are faculty-taught, and more than 80 percent of all professors have their terminal degrees. For a large state-supported school, West Florida also boasts an unusually low average class size and faculty-student ratio. The university also retains all the positive aspects of being a large university: 100-plus student-run clubs; more than 45 degree programs and 80 specializations; a diverse student body (49 states and 94 countries are represented on campus); one gigantic library (more than 2.3 million volumes are available); and a varied selection of courses.

UNIVERSITY OF WEST FLORIDA

WHAT IT IS

One of the 11 state universities of Florida, the University of West Florida enrolls students in its colleges of Arts and Sciences, Business, and Professional Studies. The university's facilities, which are valued at more than $81 million, have been designed to complement the natural beauty of the site. Since the University of West Florida opened in fall 1967, students and professors have enjoyed a close relationship that is more common at a small, private college.

UWF operates centers in downtown Pensacola and at Eglin Air Force Base, a branch campus in Fort Walton Beach (in conjunction with a local community college), and a Navy program office at Naval Air Station Pensacola. In addition, UWF owns 152 acres of beachfront property on nearby Santa Rosa Island, adjacent to the Gulf Islands National Seashore. Available for both recreation and research, this property provides special opportunities for students pursuing degrees in marine biology, maritime studies, and coastal-zone studies. UWF hosts six national sororities and five national fraternities, and 110 professional, academic, and religious organizations are open to UWF students. Varsity soccer fields, tennis courts, handball and racquetball courts, baseball and softball fields, a lighted track, jogging trails, picnic areas, and sites for canoeing are available on campus. Sailing and waterskiing facilities are nearby, and campus nature trails attract thousands of visitors annually.

WHERE IT'S AT

The University of West Florida is located on a 1,600-acre nature preserve 10 miles north of downtown Pensacola. Students and visitors alike delight in the beauty of the campus, which is nestled in the rolling hills with massive moss-draped oaks and spacious lawns that capture the traditional charm and grace of the South. Only minutes from the campus gate are the waters and beaches of the Gulf of Mexico and the Gulf Islands National Seashore, one of the nation's most beautiful beaches. The Pensacola area attracts vacationers from around the country to its historic Seville Square, golf tournaments, sailing regattas, restaurants on the bay, and various art and music festivals. UWF is less than four hours from New Orleans, Louisiana; one hour from Mobile, Alabama; three hours from Tallahassee; and five hours from Atlanta, Georgia.

THE DETAILS

Campus setting:	suburban
Degrees:	bachelor's, master's, doctoral
Calendar:	semesters
Public/Private:	public state
Number of full-time faculty:	257
Student-to-teacher ratio:	20:1

Admissions requirements:
- **Options:** deferred entrance, early admission, electronic application
- **Application fee:** $30
- **Required:** high school transcript, SAT or ACT
- **Application deadlines:** 6/30 (freshmen), 6/30 (transfer)
- **Early decision:** —
- **Notification:** continuous (freshmen), continuous (transfer)

Average high school GPA:	3.43
Average freshman SAT verbal/math score:	567 / 556
Average freshman ACT score:	23
Number of applicants:	3,583
Number of applicants accepted:	2,358
Percentage of students from out of state:	13%
Total freshman enrollment:	868
Total enrollment:	9,518
Percentage of students who live in campus housing:	18%
Total in-state tuition, fees & expenses:	$10,133
Total out-of-state tuition, fees & expenses:	$22,640
Average financial aid package:	—

MAJORS

- Accounting
- Anthropology
- Art/Art Studies, General
- Art History, Criticism and Conservation
- Art Teacher Education
- Biological and Physical Sciences
- Biology/Biological Sciences, General
- Business/Managerial Economics
- Business Administration and Management, General
- Chemistry, General
- Clinical Laboratory Science/Medical Technology/Technologist
- Communication Studies/Speech Communication and Rhetoric
- Community Health Services/Liaison/Counseling
- Computer and Information Sciences, General
- Computer Engineering, General
- Criminal Justice/Safety Studies
- Drama and Dramatics/Theatre Arts, General
- Early Childhood Education and Teaching
- Education/Teaching of Individuals with Mental Retardation
- Electrical, Electronics and Communications Engineering
- Elementary Education and Teaching
- Engineering Technology, General
- English/Language Arts Teacher Education
- English Language and Literature, General
- Environmental Studies
- Finance, General
- Fine/Studio Arts, General
- Foreign Language Teacher Education
- Health and Physical Education, General
- History, General
- Hospitality Administration/Management, General
- Humanities/Humanistic Studies
- International Relations and Affairs
- Junior High/Intermediate/Middle School Education and Teaching
- Management Information Systems, General
- Marine Biology and Biological Oceanography
- Marketing/Marketing Management, General
- Mathematics, General
- Mathematics Teacher Education
- Music Performance, General
- Music Teacher Education
- Nursing/Registered Nurse Training
- Philosophy
- Physics, General
- Political Science and Government, General
- Psychology, General
- Religion/Religious Studies
- Science Teacher Education/General Science Teacher Education
- Social Sciences, General
- Social Sciences, Other
- Social Science Teacher Education
- Social Work
- Sociology
- Special Education and Teaching, General
- Trade and Industrial Teacher Education

COOLEST CLASSROOMS EVER

Classrooms can be so much more than a blackboard
and a bunch of folding desks.

Rollins Ruminant Research Center: Berry College
Make sure you pet the cows on your way to class. This 560-acre, 150-cow research barn is the ultimate place to hone your veterinary skills and fine-tune your milking technique.

Roland George Program: Stetson University
See bull and bear markets firsthand in the school's simulated stock-trading room. Stetson students can buy and sell their way to a good grade using state-of-the-art research and trading equipment.

Underwater Technologies Lab: Florida Institute of Technology
Want to get up close and personal with the deep blue sea? Take a spin on one of the "autonomous underwater vehicles" (aka robotic submarines) housed in this lab. Robotic submarines!

Interactive Realities Laboratory: University of Central Florida
This virtual reality laboratory lets you see, hear, feel, and smell a whole new world. Slip on your CyberGrasp glove, strap on your ScentAir olfactory device, grab your three-dimensional Spaceball controller, and get in the game.

GEORGIA

AGNES SCOTT COLLEGE

141 East College Avenue
Decatur, GA 30030

(404) 471-6000
http://www.agnesscott.edu/

BIG IDEA

UNIVERSITY 101
Required first-year seminars; extended orientation program.

BIG FISH

Where in the world is the Agnes Scott student?

She's studying astronomy in Poland, participating in AIDS research in South Africa, meeting politicians and pundits in Washington, D.C., or interning at the Carter Center in Atlanta. For attendees of this women's liberal arts college, off-campus learning experiences are just as important as on-campus academics, and an array of programs encourage them to find out firsthand what's happening beyond the quad. Students intern for nonprofits, corporations, or government agencies; direct their own research; take classes at any of the 18 schools in the Atlanta Regional Consortium for Higher Education; or study abroad through 123 institutions (spanning 33 countries) affiliated with the International Student Exchange Program. Study abroad options are so popular that more than one-third of ASC students wind up packing their bags.

AGNES SCOTT COLLEGE

WHAT IT IS

For more than a century, minds have sparked minds at Agnes Scott College, a highly selective liberal arts college for women, located in metropolitan Atlanta. Agnes Scott College educates women to think deeply, live honorably, and engage the intellectual and social challenges of their times.

Founded in 1889 by Presbyterians, Agnes Scott College is a diverse and growing residential community of scholars, with one of the largest endowments per student of any college or university in the United States. Agnes Scott was the first accredited college or university in Georgia, and the college's Phi Beta Kappa chapter is the second-oldest in the state.

Students may pursue special interests in the arts (music, dance, and theater); with clubs for international cultures, politics, cultural awareness, religious affiliations, and foreign languages; and through student publications, sports, and volunteer community service. The Social Council plans dances, mixers, and parties with neighboring colleges. Traditional annual highlights are Black Cat (the culmination of first-year-student orientation), Senior Investiture, and Sophomore Family Weekend. The college sponsors a variety of events, including lectures by noted authorities and concerts by world-famous artists. Each spring, the Writers' Festival brings well-known authors and poets to the campus for readings and informal meetings with students.

WHERE IT'S AT

The 100-acre wooded campus is located in metropolitan Atlanta and the historic residential community of Decatur. Six miles away is downtown Atlanta, accessible by a rapid-transit rail station two blocks from campus. A cosmopolitan city, Atlanta offers a multitude of opportunities for personal contact with most of the world's cultures and for study through internships and volunteer work with art, business, educational, and political organizations. Atlanta is the cultural center of the South, offering entertainment and cultural events and facilities. Rock concerts or performances by the Atlanta Symphony Orchestra, local theater or touring Broadway shows, recreational parks or major-league sports—there's something here for everyone.

THE DETAILS

Campus setting:	urban
Degrees:	bachelor's, master's
Calendar:	semesters
Public/Private:	private religious
Number of full-time faculty:	74
Student-to-teacher ratio:	11:1

Admissions requirements:
- **Options:** common application, deferred entrance, early admission, early decision, electronic application
- **Application fee:** $35
- **Required:** essay or personal statement, high school transcript, 2 letters of recommendation, SAT or ACT
- **Application deadlines:** 3/1 (freshmen), 3/1 (transfer)
- **Early decision:** 11/15
- **Notification:** 5/1 (freshmen), continuous (transfer), 12/15 (early decision)

Average high school GPA:	3.62
Average freshman SAT verbal/math score:	615 / 570
Average freshman ACT score:	24
Number of applicants:	1,252
Number of applicants accepted:	741
Percentage of students from out of state:	46%
Total freshman enrollment:	256
Total enrollment:	1,002
Percentage of students who live in campus housing:	87%
Total tuition:	$22,050
Total cost with fees & expenses:	$31,110
Average financial aid package:	$23,111

AGNES SCOTT COLLEGE

MAJORS

- Anthropology
- Art/Art Studies, General
- Astrophysics
- Biochemistry
- Biology/Biological Sciences, General
- Chemistry, General
- Classics and Languages, Literatures and Linguistics, General
- Creative Writing
- Drama and Dramatics/Theatre Arts, General
- Economics, General
- English Language and Literature, General
- French Language and Literature
- German Language and Literature
- History, General
- Interdisciplinary Studies
- International Relations and Affairs
- Literature
- Mathematics, General
- Music, General
- Philosophy
- Physics, General
- Political Science and Government, General
- Psychology, General
- Religion/Religious Studies
- Sociology
- Spanish Language and Literature
- Women's Studies

ALBANY STATE UNIVERSITY

504 College Drive
Albany, GA 31705

(229) 430-4600
http://www.asurams.edu/

BIG DEAL

UNIVERSITY 101
Extended orientation program; required first-year transitional seminar; first-year lecture series; first-year tutors for general-education courses.

BIG FISH

Watching all three versions of *CSI* won't make you a forensics expert.

Albany State's forensic science major, on the other hand, will give you the education you need to land a job at any of the 320 crime labs across the United States. This interdisciplinary major combines chemistry, biology, anatomy, and physics to prepare students for a wide range of lucrative careers as DNA specialists, toxicologists, firearms examiners, drug analysts, and staff photographers. Besides lab science, students learn how to craft arguments to become expert witnesses for trials. Hands-on learning is a crucial part of this major. During their senior year, future investigators either perform their own on-campus research or take two off-campus internships. Albany State is currently the only school in Georgia to offer a degree program in forensic science.

ALBANY STATE UNIVERSITY

WHAT IT IS

An historically black institution, Albany State University was established in 1903 to provide religious and vocational training to black youth in southwest Georgia. Since then, this small, public university has matured into a comprehensive institution that serves an increasingly diverse student population, making a special effort to reach out to underprivileged populations in the region. The school offers seven undergraduate degree programs and has excellent programs in nursing, education, public administration, and the sciences. All students graduate with a strong foundation in the liberal arts, and the most popular majors include criminal justice, biology, computer science, and nursing.

The university remains dedicated to promoting and preserving black history and culture through initiatives like the Center for the African American Male, which uses education, research, and service programs to improve the quality of life of black men.

WHERE IT'S AT

Albany is located on the banks of the Flint River and has a population of 100,000, making it one of the largest communities in southwest Georgia. Albany State University occupies a 204-acre campus that has undergone significant expansion and renovation in recent years. After a flood devastated the campus and the surrounding area in 1994, the university community focused its energy on rebuilding and improving campus facilities. There are six dorms on campus, and the school has plans to further expand student housing by building two apartment- and suite-style residences. Albany is about three hours from Atlanta and two hours from Tallahassee, Florida.

THE DETAILS

Campus setting:	urban
Degrees:	bachelor's, master's
Calendar:	semesters
Public/Private:	public state
Number of full-time faculty:	142
Student-to-teacher ratio:	16:1
Admissions requirements:	

- **Options:** deferred entrance, early admission
- **Application fee:** $20
- **Required:** high school transcript, SAT or ACT
- **Application deadlines:** 7/1 (freshmen), 7/1 (transfer)
- **Early decision:** —
- **Notification:** —

Average high school GPA:	2.96
Average freshman SAT verbal/math score:	474 / 474
Average freshman ACT score:	12
Number of applicants:	1,777
Number of applicants accepted:	1,610
Percentage of students from out of state:	—
Total freshman enrollment:	594
Total enrollment:	3,668
Percentage of students who live in campus housing:	35%
Total in-state tuition, fees & expenses:	$6,586
Total out-of-state tuition, fees & expenses:	$13,554
Average financial aid package:	$7,057

ALBANY STATE UNIVERSITY

MAJORS

- Accounting
- Administrative Assistant and Secretarial Science, General
- Art/Art Studies, General
- Biology/Biological Sciences, General
- Business Administration and Management, General
- Business Teacher Education
- Chemistry, General
- Computer and Information Sciences, General
- Criminal Justice/Safety Studies
- Education, Other
- English Language and Literature, General
- French Language and Literature
- Health Professions and Related Clinical Sciences, Other
- History, General
- Junior High/Intermediate/Middle School Education and Teaching
- Kindergarten/Preschool Education and Teaching
- Marketing/Marketing Management, General
- Mathematics, General
- Music, General
- Nursing/Registered Nurse Training
- Physical Education Teaching and Coaching
- Political Science and Government, General
- Psychology, General
- Science Teacher Education/General Science Teacher Education
- Social Work
- Sociology
- Spanish Language and Literature
- Special Education and Teaching, General
- Speech and Rhetorical Studies

ATLANTA COLLEGE OF ART

1280 Peachtree Street, NE
Atlanta, GA 30309

(404) 733-5001
http://www.aca.edu/

BIG FISH

UNIVERSITY 101
Extended orientation program; required first-year foundational drawing and visual studies courses.

Artists and designers from around the world converge on this urban campus to cultivate their talents.

Students at Atlanta College of Art train in the 121,000-square-foot Woodruff Arts Center. Housing a digital media center, several computer labs, video editing rooms, private painting studios, darkrooms, and a two-story library, the center is an art student's dream come true. Other facilities include a sculpture studio, a covered courtyard for larger projects, and two college-run galleries to display student work. All professors are not only teachers but also practicing artists and scholars.

ATLANTA COLLEGE OF ART

WHAT IT IS

Atlanta College of Art provides an educational environment for the career-minded student with a talent and passion for art or design. Founded in 1905, the college is an accredited institutional member of the National Association of Schools of Art and Design and the Commission on Colleges of the Southern Association of Colleges and Schools. Students from across the United States and abroad compose a highly charged, creative community that nurtures the development of educated, effective, and successful professionals in the visual arts.

Atlanta College of Art is a founding member of the Woodruff Arts Center, the focus of the cultural life of the region. As the only art college in the United States that shares its campus with three other arts organizations—the High Museum of Art, the Alliance Theater, and the Atlanta Symphony Orchestra—the college is able to offer students access to a variety of art forms and resources on a working, thriving campus. The student Affairs Office provides career-planning services and coordinates an internship program for students wishing to gain professional work experience to complement their academic and studio training. Recent internship sponsors have included the American Museum of Papermaking, CNN Headline News, Coca-Cola, Georgia Pacific Corporation, IBM, Museum of Modern Art, Turner Publishing, and Zoo Atlanta. Students are encouraged to become involved in the extracurricular life of the college. Various clubs and organizations are recognized and funded by the college to give students opportunities for enrichment beyond the classroom.

WHERE IT'S AT

Atlanta College of Art is located in Midtown, the cultural heart of the city and a neighborhood where skyscrapers soar above tree-lined streets filled with restored older residences, some dating from the Victorian era. Atlanta has a flourishing grassroots art scene—an optimal environment for the emerging artist or designer. Atlanta also has scores of galleries and alternative spaces that exhibit a broad variety of artwork. It also offers a ballet and opera; numerous movie houses showing new releases and foreign and classic films; a growing number of theater companies, large and small; and many opportunities for rock, jazz, avant-garde music, and outdoor performances. In addition, Atlanta has myriad natural areas and parks, restaurants and coffeehouses of every description, and four professional sports teams.

THE DETAILS

Campus setting:	urban
Degrees:	bachelor's
Calendar:	semesters
Public/Private:	private nonprofit
Number of full-time faculty:	24
Student-to-teacher ratio:	10:1

Admissions requirements:
- **Options:** deferred entrance, electronic application
- **Application fee:** $30
- **Required:** essay or personal statement, high school transcript, letter of recommendation, SAT or ACT
- **Application deadlines:** continuous (freshmen), continuous (transfer)
- **Early decision:** —
- **Notification:** continuous (freshmen), continuous (transfer)

Average high school GPA:	3.03
Average freshman SAT verbal/math score:	522 / 493
Average freshman ACT score:	20
Number of applicants:	222
Number of applicants accepted:	155
Percentage of students from out of state:	31%
Total freshman enrollment:	72
Total enrollment:	330
Percentage of students who live in campus housing:	43%
Total tuition:	$16,900
Total cost with fees & expenses:	$18,400
Average financial aid package:	$11,981

ATLANTA COLLEGE OF ART

MAJORS
- Cinematography and Film/Video Production
- Commercial and Advertising Art
- Computer Graphics
- Design and Visual Communications, General
- Drawing
- Fine/Studio Arts, General
- Illustration
- Painting
- Photography
- Printmaking
- Sculpture
- Web Page, Digital/Multimedia and Information Resources Design

BERRY COLLEGE

PO Box 490159
Mount Berry, GA 30149

(706) 232-5374
http://www.berry.edu/

BIG FISH

UNIVERSITY 101
Extended orientation program; upperclassman mentors; required first-year transitional seminar; first year–only extracurricular and social activities; required first-year adventure experience; optional first-year service day; special academic advisors assigned to first-years.

Berry College is all about choice.

The school offers internship opportunities, long- and short-term study abroad trips, discussion-based seminars, design-your-own-major options, combined degree programs, preprofessional degree tracks, faculty-mentored projects, guest speaker lecture series, and a comprehensive first-year experience program to help you get started. If it seems a little overwhelming at first, don't sweat. With a low student-faculty ratio, Berry's accessible professors double as academic mentors to help you find precisely what you need. If you can't find exactly what you're looking for, Berry faculty members are known for creating collaborative projects alongside undergraduate students.

BERRY COLLEGE

WHAT IT IS

Berry College is a comprehensive liberal arts school dedicated to providing students with a challenging education, practical experience, and Christian values. Founded by Martha Berry in 1902, the college was created to give rural Georgia residents opportunities at a time when there were few public schools in the area.

Today, Berry offers more than 30 undergraduate majors, as well as preprofessional programs in such areas as veterinary medicine, pharmacy, and dentistry. Dual-degree programs in nursing and engineering are offered in conjunction with Emory and the Georgia Institute of Technology. More than 90 percent of faculty members have PhDs or other terminal degrees in their field, and classes are small, ensuring individual attention.

WHERE IT'S AT

Berry College abuts Rome, a city of about 35,000 located in northwest Georgia and approximately 65 miles from both Atlanta and Chattanooga, Tennessee. Although the student population is small, Berry's 28,000-acre campus is one of the largest in the world. More than 35 major buildings are situated among the college's forests, fields, lakes, and mountains. The Oak Hill Gardens add to the scenic beauty of the campus. Additionally, the college plans to build a new athletic and recreation center, which will be constructed next to the existing student center.

THE DETAILS

Campus setting:	suburban
Degrees:	bachelor's, master's
Calendar:	semesters
Public/Private:	private religious
Number of full-time faculty:	133
Student-to-teacher ratio:	13:1

Admissions requirements:
- **Options:** common application, deferred entrance, early admission, electronic application
- **Application fee:** $50
- **Required:** high school transcript, SAT or ACT
- **Application deadlines:** 7/22 (freshmen), 7/22 (transfer)
- **Early decision:** —
- **Notification:** continuous (freshmen), continuous (transfer)

Average high school GPA:	3.66
Average freshman SAT verbal/math score:	592 / 583
Average freshman ACT score:	25
Number of applicants:	1,864
Number of applicants accepted:	1,416
Percentage of students from out of state:	18%
Total freshman enrollment:	514
Total enrollment:	2,008
Percentage of students who live in campus housing:	72%
Total tuition:	$16,240
Total cost with fees & expenses:	$23,490
Average financial aid package:	$14,480

BERRY COLLEGE

MAJORS

- Accounting
- Animal Sciences, General
- Anthropology
- Art/Art Studies, General
- Biochemistry
- Biology/Biological Sciences, General
- Business Administration and Management, General
- Chemistry, General
- Communication, Journalism and Related Programs, Other
- Computer Science
- Early Childhood Education and Teaching
- Economics, General
- Engineering Technology, General
- English Language and Literature, General
- Environmental Science
- Finance, General
- French Language and Literature
- German Language and Literature
- History, General
- International Relations and Affairs
- Junior High/Intermediate/Middle School Education and Teaching
- Marketing/Marketing Management, General
- Mathematics, General
- Multi-/Interdisciplinary Studies, Other
- Music, General
- Music Management and Merchandising
- Music Teacher Education
- Nursing/Registered Nurse Training
- Philosophy and Religious Studies, Other
- Physical Education Teaching and Coaching
- Physics, General
- Political Science and Government, General
- Psychology, General
- Social Sciences, General
- Sociology
- Spanish Language and Literature

BRENAU UNIVERSITY

500 Washington Street SE
Gainesville, GA 30501

(770) 534-6299
http://www.brenau.edu/

BIG IDEA

UNIVERSITY 101 Extended orientation program (women's college only); required first-year transitional seminar (women's college and evening college only).

BIG FISH

Why settle for one school when you can have four?

Brenau is a women's residential day college, a co-ed evening and weekend school, an online university, and a preparatory academy for young women—all rolled into one. Brenau's four-schools-in-one status makes it one of the most diverse institutions in the United States, with students hailing from all walks of life and corners of the globe. Brenau specializes in career-oriented degree programs with an emphasis on leadership. A commitment to excellence in teaching and a low student-faculty ratio are features of all four schools.

BRENAU UNIVERSITY

WHAT IT IS

The Women's College of Brenau University is a liberal arts college for women. The name Brenau, derived from German and Latin, means "refined gold." A constantly evolving educational program combines a broad base in the liberal arts with career-oriented majors for women of all ages. The Women's College student is provided with opportunities to learn through participation. Many degree plans emphasize hands-on activities, laboratory experiences, and internships. The university's Evening and Weekend College offers undergraduate and graduate instruction, both on and off campus.

Leadership experiences are plentiful in more than 40 campus organizations, including seven national sororities, special interest groups, and professional and honorary societies. Brenau is the center of much of the activity of the local community. Examples of this are a version of *Meet the Press* called the *Brenau News Forum*, a weekly feature on the college's own WBCX-FM and area cable television; nationally recognized artists and performers showcased in Pearce Auditorium (a European-style opera theater) and the new John S. Burd Center for the Performing Arts; and a wide variety of events featuring award-winning students and faculty. Special guests include current newsmakers, national leaders, writers, and scholars. These people bring a real-life perspective and in-depth knowledge to augment the faculty's academic preparation and extensive practical experience.

WHERE IT'S AT

Brenau is located 50 miles northeast of Atlanta in the foothills of the Blue Ridge Mountains, in Gainesville, Georgia. With a population of 100,000, the metropolitan area is a cultural and economic center of northeast Georgia. Recreation activities abound in a geographic area rich in natural resources. There are plenty of outdoor activities nearby, such as hiking on the Appalachian Trail, camping, horseback riding, boating, swimming, water- and snow skiing, golf, and tennis. Gainesville is bordered by Lake Sidney Lanier, the largest freshwater lake in Georgia. Sky Valley, a modern snow-skiing resort, is only an hour's drive from the campus. There are six colleges and universities within an hour's drive.

THE DETAILS

Campus setting:	small town
Degrees:	bachelor's, master's
Calendar:	semesters
Public/Private:	private nonprofit
Number of full-time faculty:	70
Student-to-teacher ratio:	10:1

Admissions requirements:
- **Options:** common application, deferred entrance, early admission, electronic application
- **Application fee:** $35
- **Required:** essay or personal statement, high school transcript, letter of recommendation, SAT or ACT
- **Application deadlines:** continuous (freshmen), continuous (transfer)
- **Early decision:** —
- **Notification:** continuous (freshmen), continuous (transfer)

Average high school GPA:	—
Average freshman SAT verbal/math score:	519 / 494
Average freshman ACT score:	20
Number of applicants:	1,286
Number of applicants accepted:	641
Percentage of students from out of state:	8%
Total freshman enrollment:	196
Total enrollment:	696
Percentage of students who live in campus housing:	55%
Total tuition:	$14,610
Total cost with fees & expenses:	$23,620
Average financial aid package:	$15,452

BRENAU UNIVERSITY

MAJORS

- Accounting
- Arts Management
- Art Teacher Education
- Biology/Biological Sciences, General
- Business/Corporate Communications
- Business Administration and Management, General
- Commercial and Advertising Art
- Dance, General
- Drama and Dance Teacher Education
- Drama and Dramatics/Theatre Arts, General
- Education, General
- English Language and Literature, General
- Environmental Studies
- Fashion Merchandising
- Fine/Studio Arts, General
- General Studies
- History, General
- Interior Design
- International Relations and Affairs
- Junior High/Intermediate/Middle School Education and Teaching
- Kindergarten/Preschool Education and Teaching
- Legal Professions and Studies, Other
- Marketing/Marketing Management, General
- Mass Communication/Media Studies
- Music, General
- Music, Other
- Music Teacher Education
- Nursing/Registered Nurse Training
- Occupational Therapy/Therapist
- Piano and Organ
- Political Science and Government, General
- Pre-Law Studies
- Psychology, General
- Special Education and Teaching, General
- Voice and Opera

CLARK ATLANTA UNIVERSITY

223 James P. Brawley Drive, SW
Atlanta, GA 30314

(404) 880-8000
http://www.cau.edu/

BIG FISH

UNIVERSITY 101
Required first-year transitional seminars; upperclassman mentors; special academic advisors assigned to first-year students; extended orientation program.

Home to some of the most advanced computer labs and facilities on the East Coast.

All students are required to take computer-literacy courses as part of the general-education curriculum, and professors are encouraged to incorporate the latest technology into their lectures. In addition to its extensive microcomputer centers, CAU has a multimedia library, a full television broadcast production facility, and 18 sponsored research programs. The school's Research Center for Science and Technology houses ongoing interdisciplinary projects funded by big-name agencies, including the Department of Defense, National Institute of Health, and National Science Foundation.

CLARK ATLANTA UNIVERSITY

WHAT IT IS

Incorporated in 1988, Clark Atlanta University is a predominantly African American institution that has inherited the historical missions and achievements of its parent institutions, Atlanta University, founded in 1865, and Clark College, founded in 1869. Although one of only two private, comprehensive, and historically black universities in the nation that offer degrees from the bachelor's to the doctorate, CAU is one of six institutions that make up the Atlanta University Center, the largest consortium of historically black educational institutions in the country.

The faculty are known for their warm and dedicated spirit. They provide the quality of instruction necessary to ensure that their students become productive, creative, and socially responsible citizens. The family spirit at CAU is enhanced by the many traditions that are celebrated each year on campus, including the induction services for first-years, the United Negro College Fund Drive, Homecoming, Consolidation Day, and the Spring Arts Festival. There are more than 60 chartered student organizations, special interest clubs, and academic honor societies on campus.

WHERE IT'S AT

One mile east of the Clark Atlanta University campus are the mirrored skyscrapers and modern expressways of Atlanta, capital of the Sun Belt. The city's highlights include the World Congress Center, the Civic Center, the Arts Alliance Center (home of the Atlanta Symphony Orchestra and the Atlanta Ballet Company), the Martin Luther King Jr. Center for Nonviolent Social Change, Turner Field (home of the Atlanta Braves baseball team), the Georgia Dome (home of the Atlanta Falcons football team), the Jimmy Carter Presidential Library, and outstanding entertainment features, such as Underground Atlanta, Stone Mountain Park, and Six Flags Over Georgia amusement park.

THE DETAILS

Campus setting:	urban
Degrees:	bachelor's, master's, doctoral
Calendar:	semesters
Public/Private:	private religious
Number of full-time faculty:	260
Student-to-teacher ratio:	13:1

Admissions requirements:
- **Options:** common application, deferred entrance, early admission, electronic application
- **Application fee:** $35
- **Required:** essay or personal statement, high school transcript, 2 letters of recommendation, SAT or ACT
- **Application deadlines:** 7/1 (freshmen), 7/1 (transfer)
- **Early decision:** —
- **Notification:** continuous (freshmen), continuous (transfer)

Average high school GPA:	2.99
Average freshman SAT verbal/math score:	—/—
Average freshman ACT score:	—
Number of applicants:	5,181
Number of applicants accepted:	3,127
Percentage of students from out of state:	61%
Total freshman enrollment:	804
Total enrollment:	4,598
Percentage of students who live in campus housing:	37%
Total tuition:	$12,936
Total cost with fees & expenses:	$21,302
Average financial aid package:	$10,935

CLARK ATLANTA UNIVERSITY

MAJORS

- Accounting
- Art/Art Studies, General
- Art Teacher Education
- Biology/Biological Sciences, General
- Business Administration and Management, General
- Business Teacher Education
- Chemistry, General
- Computer and Information Sciences, General
- Computer Science
- Criminal Justice/Law Enforcement Administration
- Developmental and Child Psychology
- Drama and Dramatics/Theatre Arts, General
- Early Childhood Education and Teaching
- Economics, General
- Education, General
- Elementary Education and Teaching
- Engineering, General
- English Language and Literature, General
- Fashion/Apparel Design
- French Language and Literature
- Health Information/Medical Records Administration/Administrator
- Health Teacher Education
- History, General
- History Teacher Education
- Information Science/Studies
- Interdisciplinary Studies
- Junior High/Intermediate/Middle School Education and Teaching
- Kindergarten/Preschool Education and Teaching
- Marketing, Other
- Mass Communication/Media Studies
- Mathematics, General
- Medical Illustration/Medical Illustrator
- Music, General
- Music Teacher Education
- Philosophy
- Physical Education Teaching and Coaching
- Physics, General
- Political Science and Government, General
- Psychology, General
- Religion/Religious Studies
- Science Teacher Education/General Science Teacher Education
- Secondary Education and Teaching
- Social Sciences, General
- Social Work
- Sociology
- Spanish Language and Literature
- Speech and Rhetorical Studies

COLUMBUS STATE UNIVERSITY

4225 University Avenue
Columbus, GA 31907

(706) 568-2001
http://www.colstate.edu/

BIG DEAL

BIG FISH

UNIVERSITY 101
Optional first-year convocation ceremony; required first-year transitional seminar; optional first-year nonresidential learning communities; upperclassman mentors; optional first-year leadership program; first-year extracurricular and social activities; extended orientation program.

"Bond. James Bond."

If you can see yourself as the next 007, check out Columbus State, which produces approximately 70 percent of the area's law enforcement. The Department of Criminal Justice offers three degree programs, all designed to prepare students for positions ranging from local traffic cop to Secret Service agent. If you prefer your drama in the medical field, the Department of Nursing offers two degree tracks that prepare students to take the Registered Nurse Licensing Exam and move quickly into a growing industry. Both departments offer honor societies to help students make professional connections.

COLUMBUS STATE UNIVERSITY

WHAT IT IS

Established in 1958 as a junior college, Columbus State University has operated as a comprehensive, four-year university since 1965. The school currently offers more than 50 undergraduate major programs and prides itself on providing learning opportunities that go beyond the traditional classroom experience. Students often take part in internships, clinical experiences, and field research. The university also offers its students special programs, such as the Servant Leadership Program, which trains them to become community leaders; various study abroad opportunities; and an honors program. Columbus State offers numerous extracurricular activities through these organizations, some of which have been nationally recognized for their excellence. The cheerleading team has won many conference championships, and the dance team has been awarded several conference titles. Columbus State's golf team has won the NCAA Division II national championship six times.

WHERE IT'S AT

The university's home is in Columbus, Georgia, about 100 miles southwest of Atlanta in the scenic Chattahoochee River Valley. Columbus State's 132-acre campus is located near the center of town on the site of an old dairy farm. In addition to the main campus, the school operates four off-campus centers: the Oxbow Meadows Environmental Learning Center, the Coca-Cola Space Science Center, the Rankin Arts Centers, and RiverCenter, a new performing arts facility in downtown Columbus. The school also owns a facility in the United Kingdom: Spencer House neighbors the renowned Oxford University and provides valuable study abroad opportunities to Columbus State students.

THE DETAILS

Campus setting:	suburban
Degrees:	bachelor's, master's
Calendar:	semesters
Public/Private:	public state
Number of full-time faculty:	202
Student-to-teacher ratio:	19:1

Admissions requirements:
- **Options:** common application, deferred entrance, early admission, electronic application
- **Application fee:** $25
- **Required:** high school transcript, SAT or ACT
- **Application deadlines:** 7/28 (freshmen), 7/28 (transfer)
- **Early decision:** —
- **Notification:** continuous (freshmen), continuous (transfer)

Average high school GPA:	3.00
Average freshman SAT verbal/math score:	503 / 494
Average freshman ACT score:	20
Number of applicants:	2,616
Number of applicants accepted:	1,771
Percentage of students from out of state:	13%
Total freshman enrollment:	942
Total enrollment:	7,224
Percentage of students who live in campus housing:	14%
Total in-state tuition, fees & expenses:	$9,158
Total out-of-state tuition, fees & expenses:	$16,126
Average financial aid package:	$4,015

COLUMBUS STATE UNIVERSITY

MAJORS

- Accounting
- Applied Mathematics
- Art/Art Studies, General
- Art Teacher Education
- Athletic Training/Trainer
- Biology/Biological Sciences, General
- Biology Teacher Education
- Business/Commerce, General
- Business/Managerial Economics
- Business Administration and Management, General
- Chemistry, General
- Chemistry Teacher Education
- Computer/Information Technology Services Administration and Management, Other
- Computer Science
- Creative Writing
- Criminal Justice/Law Enforcement Administration
- Drama and Dance Teacher Education
- Drama and Dramatics/Theatre Arts, General
- Early Childhood Education and Teaching
- Engineering, General
- English/Language Arts Teacher Education
- English Language and Literature, General
- Finance, General
- Forest Engineering
- Forestry, General
- French Language Teacher Education
- Geology/Earth Science, General
- Health Science
- Health Services/Allied Health/Health Sciences, General
- Health Teacher Education
- History, General
- History Teacher Education
- Information Science/Studies
- Junior High/Intermediate/Middle School Education and Teaching
- Kinesiology and Exercise Science
- Liberal Arts and Sciences/Liberal Studies
- Literature
- Marketing/Marketing Management, General
- Mass Communication/Media Studies
- Mathematics, General
- Mathematics Teacher Education
- Medical Radiologic Technology, Science/Radiation Therapist
- Music, General
- Music Pedagogy
- Music Teacher Education
- Nursing/Registered Nurse Training
- Physical Education Teaching and Coaching
- Piano and Organ
- Political Science and Government, General
- Pre-Dentistry Studies
- Pre-Engineering
- Pre-Law Studies
- Pre-Medicine/Pre-Medical Studies
- Pre-Pharmacy Studies
- Pre-Veterinary Studies
- Psychology, General
- Public Relations/Image Management
- Science Teacher Education/General Science Teacher Education
- Secondary Education and Teaching
- Social Science Teacher Education
- Sociology
- Spanish Language Teacher Education
- Special Education and Teaching, General
- Speech and Theater Education
- Teacher Education, Multiple Levels
- Violin, Viola, Guitar and Other Stringed Instruments
- Voice and Opera
- Wind and Percussion Instruments

COVENANT COLLEGE

14049 Scenic Highway
Lookout Mountain, GA 30750

(706) 820-1560
http://www.covenant.edu/

BIG FISH

UNIVERSITY 101
Extended orientation program.

Covenant College majors in passion.

The school's ultimate goal is to direct students toward Christianity by developing their analytical abilities. Covenant's biblical and theological studies major is one of the strongest of its kind in the South. With minors available in missions work and youth ministry, Covenant College has one of the best pre-seminary programs available. Campus ministries programs allow students to further their spiritual education through international mission trips, small group Bible studies, religious music groups, guest lecture workshops, and chapel services.

COVENANT COLLEGE

WHAT IT IS

Covenant College has come a long way—literally—since it was founded in Pasadena, California, in 1955. The college made its home in St. Louis, Missouri, before it finally found a permanent home in northwest Georgia in 1964. The education is first-rate at this Presbyterian-affiliated school, where both learning and student life are deeply rooted in the Christian faith. English, business, history, psychology, and education are all popular majors, and all programs prepare students for lives dedicated to areas of service. Special programs include the Chalmers Center for Economic Development, a research and training initiative with a focus on community economic development. Students at this small college are part of a lively and close-knit community. Residence halls are at the center of campus life, with all students except seniors required to live in dorms. Bible studies, hall prayer times, and dorm service projects are regular events. In addition, 85 percent of Covenant students participate in intramural sports.

WHERE IT'S AT

The Covenant College campus is located at the peak of Lookout Mountain on a parcel of land that was once a pioneer homestead and a plush resort. The former Lookout Mountain Hotel, built in 1927, is a major campus landmark. Once known for having the largest ballroom in the South and hosting one of Elizabeth Taylor's honeymoons, the building now serves as a residence hall and houses offices, the dining hall, and the college bookstore. The city of Lookout Mountain has a population of about 1,600, and the campus is about 50 miles west of Chattanooga, Tennessee. The area surrounding the campus is scenic, and the mountain itself was the site of several important battles during the Civil War.

THE DETAILS

Campus setting:	suburban
Degrees:	bachelor's, master's
Calendar:	semesters
Public/Private:	private religious
Number of full-time faculty:	60
Student-to-teacher ratio:	15:1

Admissions requirements:
- **Options:** deferred entrance, early admission, electronic application
- **Application fee:** $35
- **Required:** essay or personal statement, high school transcript, 2 letters of recommendation, SAT or ACT, ACT (recommended)
- **Application deadlines:** continuous (freshmen), continuous (transfer)
- **Early decision:** —
- **Notification:** continuous (freshmen), — (transfer)

Average high school GPA:	3.61
Average freshman SAT verbal/math score:	604 / 567
Average freshman ACT score:	24
Number of applicants:	667
Number of applicants accepted:	438
Percentage of students from out of state:	75%
Total freshman enrollment:	247
Total enrollment:	974
Percentage of students who live in campus housing:	86%
Total tuition:	$18,750
Total cost with fees & expenses:	$25,930
Average financial aid package:	$15,903

MAJORS

- Art/Art Studies, General
- Bible/Biblical Studies
- Biology/Biological Sciences, General
- Business Administration and Management, General
- Chemistry, General
- Computer Science
- Economics, General
- Elementary Education and Teaching
- English Language and Literature, General
- Foreign Languages and Literatures, General
- History, General
- Interdisciplinary Studies
- Junior High/Intermediate/Middle School Education and Teaching
- Mathematics, General
- Music, General
- Natural Sciences
- Nursing/Registered Nurse Training
- Philosophy
- Physics, General
- Pre-Law Studies
- Pre-Medicine/Pre-Medical Studies
- Pre-Nursing Studies
- Psychology, General
- Sociology

EMORY UNIVERSITY

1380 South Oxford Road
Atlanta, GA 30322

(404) 727-6123
http://www.emory.edu/

BIG REP

UNIVERSITY 101
Special academic advisors assigned to first-years; upperclassman mentors; faculty mentors; first year–only extracurricular and social activities; extended orientation program; first year–only online forums; optional first-year pre-orientation outdoor adventure trip.

Before they were mainstays on CNN, U.S. presidents, and groundbreaking authors, they taught at Emory University.

Emory students have to be quick-witted, intuitive, and motivated to survive the school's demanding regimen of on- and off-campus programs. Emory commands more sponsored research dollars than any other school in the state, money that goes in part to fund the school's extensive summer and yearlong undergraduate research programs. The university's emphasis on superb faculty and facilities serves its students well. The school's alumni include U.S. senators, Pulitzer Prize–winning historians, world-renowned clothing designers, and Grammy Award–winning recording artists. There's no easy A here.

EMORY UNIVERSITY

WHAT IT IS

Founded by the Methodist Church in 1836 as a college in Oxford, Georgia, Emory University received its university charter in 1915 and in the same year moved to the present campus in northeast Atlanta. The original campus is now Oxford College of Emory University, a two-year liberal arts division. Emory offers a stimulating intellectual environment in one of America's most exciting cities. The undergraduate college provides the advantages of a small college and the resources of a major university. Selective and innovative, with an emphasis on excellent teaching, Emory offers a rewarding environment for students with serious intellectual and professional interests.

The university recently completed building nine new facilities (totaling $250 million), including a performing arts center, physics facility, and an apartment-style, residence hall complex. Nearly 75 percent of the students live on campus in residence halls, fraternity houses, or sorority lodges. Extracurricular activities are plentiful and include lectures, concerts, movies, musical groups, theater, journalism, debate, volunteer groups, intramural sports, club sport teams, and intercollegiate athletics. Emory has finished second in the Sears Director's Cup standings, which ranks the best overall athletic programs in the country out of more than 400 Division III colleges and universities. Seventy percent of the students participate in intramural, club, and recreational sports.

WHERE IT'S AT

Emory's wooded main campus occupies 631 acres in the rolling hills of Atlanta. The original structures are of Italian Renaissance design and have red-tiled roofs and marble facades. The university is in an attractive residential neighborhood called Druid Hills. Adjacent to the campus is Emory Village, a small, neighborhood complex of shops and restaurants. Easily accessible by rapid transit from Emory, downtown Atlanta provides an exciting, progressive atmosphere in which students can enjoy many recreational and cultural activities. In addition, Atlanta is just a few hours from the mountains of north Georgia and the Carolinas and from the beaches of Georgia and Florida.

THE DETAILS

Campus setting:	suburban
Degrees:	bachelor's, master's, doctoral
Calendar:	semesters
Public/Private:	private religious
Number of full-time faculty:	2,451
Student-to-teacher ratio:	7:1

Admissions requirements:
- **Options:** common application, deferred entrance, early admission, early decision, electronic application
- **Application fee:** $40
- **Required:** essay or personal statement, high school transcript, letter of recommendation, SAT or ACT, SAT Subject Tests (recommended)
- **Application deadlines:** 1/15 (freshmen), 6/1 (transfer)
- **Early decision:** 11/1
- **Notification:** 4/1 (freshmen), continuous (transfer), 12/15 (early decision)

Average high school GPA:	3.80
Average freshman SAT verbal/math score:	680 / 696
Average freshman ACT score:	27
Number of applicants:	11,218
Number of applicants accepted:	4,330
Percentage of students from out of state:	83%
Total freshman enrollment:	1,588
Total enrollment:	11,781
Percentage of students who live in campus housing:	70%
Total tuition:	$28,940
Total cost with fees & expenses:	$39,972
Average financial aid package:	$26,373

EMORY UNIVERSITY

MAJORS

- Accounting
- African-American/Black Studies
- African Studies
- Anthropology
- Art History, Criticism and Conservation
- Asian Studies/Civilization
- Biology/Biological Sciences, General
- Biomedical Sciences, General
- Business/Managerial Economics
- Business Administration and Management, General
- Central/Middle and Eastern European Studies
- Chemistry, General
- Chinese Language and Literature
- Classics and Languages, Literatures and Linguistics, General
- Comparative Literature
- Computer Science
- Creative Writing
- Dance, General
- Drama and Dramatics/Theatre Arts, General
- Economics, General
- Education, General
- Elementary Education and Teaching
- English Language and Literature, General
- Film/Cinema Studies
- Finance, General
- French Language and Literature
- German Language and Literature
- History, General
- Human Ecology
- International Relations and Affairs
- Italian Language and Literature
- Japanese Language and Literature
- Jewish/Judaic Studies
- Latin American Studies
- Latin Language and Literature
- Liberal Arts and Sciences/Liberal Studies
- Literature
- Marketing/Marketing Management, General
- Mathematics, General
- Medieval and Renaissance Studies
- Modern Greek Language and Literature
- Music, General
- Neuroscience
- Nursing/Registered Nurse Training
- Philosophy
- Physics, General
- Political Science and Government, General
- Psychology, General
- Religion/Religious Studies
- Russian Language and Literature
- Secondary Education and Teaching
- Sociology
- Spanish Language and Literature
- Women's Studies

FORT VALLEY STATE UNIVERSITY

1005 State University Drive
Fort Valley, GA 31030

(478) 825-6211
http://www.fvsu.edu/

BIG DEAL

UNIVERSITY 101
Required first-year transitional seminar; extended orientation program; special academic advisors assigned to first-years.

BIG FISH

Fort Valley State packs big-school benefits into a fairly small package.

The undergraduate students who attend Fort Valley develop their analytical and creative abilities through small, discussion-based classes and one-on-one mentoring from faculty members. Fort Valley's Cooperative Developmental Energy Program actively works to increase the number of minorities working in the energy industry. The program provides several dual-degree programs (in conjunction with Georgia Tech, the University of Texas-Austin, the University of Nevada, and the University of Oklahoma). Additionally, energy program students receive full scholarships and summer internships that pay up to $3,500 per month with such companies as the Exxon Mobil Corporation, the BP Corporation, Texaco, and the U.S. Environmental Protection Agency.

FORT VALLEY STATE UNIVERSITY

WHAT IT IS

Founded in 1895, Fort Valley State University is a unit of the University System of Georgia. Since its founding, the university has developed a comprehensive and stimulating curriculum that offers educational experiences in the liberal arts, education, and sciences, as well as in selected vocational and technical fields.

There are 73 approved organizations on campus through which students are able to make practical application of knowledge gained in the classroom or pursue a personal interest. Opportunities for travel, interaction with students from other colleges and universities, and participation in community affairs provide valuable experiences. The university also offers the Cooperative Developmental Energy Program. CDEP is the only program of its kind in the nation, partnering the university with the nation's energy industry. The biology program leads the state system in preparing African American students for medical and health professions, and FVSU has the only certified veterinary technology program in the state. Departmental organizations, service organizations, hometown organizations, scholastic honoraries, social fraternities and sororities, special interest organizations, religious organizations, and varsity athletics are among the areas of involvement provided for students.

WHERE IT'S AT

Fort Valley University's 1,365-acre campus is the second-largest (in acreage) public university in the state. The university's physical facilities range from older buildings constructed by students in the early 1900s to the modern buildings constructed in the 1990s. The university is located in the town of Fort Valley in Peach County, the original site of the nation's peach industry. Fort Valley is located in central Georgia, due east of Columbus on Highway 96, and 12 miles west of I-75, between Macon and Perry. The area is known throughout the world for its camellias, peaches, and pecan industry.

THE DETAILS

Campus setting:	small town
Degrees:	bachelor's, master's, doctoral
Calendar:	semesters
Public/Private:	public state
Number of full-time faculty:	105
Student-to-teacher ratio:	22:1

Admissions requirements:
- **Options:** common application, deferred entrance, early admission, electronic application
- **Application fee:** $20
- **Required:** high school transcript, SAT or ACT
- **Application deadlines:** 8/1 (freshmen), 8/1 (transfer)
- **Early decision:** —
- **Notification:** 8/10 (freshmen), 8/10 (transfer)

Average high school GPA:	2.76
Average freshman SAT verbal/math score:	473 / 456
Average freshman ACT score:	—
Number of applicants:	1,863
Number of applicants accepted:	814
Percentage of students from out of state:	6%
Total freshman enrollment:	301
Total enrollment:	2,558
Percentage of students who live in campus housing:	59%
Total in-state tuition, fees & expenses:	$9,096
Total out-of-state tuition, fees & expenses:	$16,064
Average financial aid package:	$7,200

FORT VALLEY STATE UNIVERSITY

MAJORS

- Accounting
- Administrative Assistant and Secretarial Science, General
- Agricultural/Biological Engineering and Bioengineering
- Agricultural Economics
- Agronomy and Crop Science
- Animal Sciences, General
- Biology/Biological Sciences, General
- Botany/Plant Biology
- Business Administration and Management, General
- Chemistry, General
- Computer Science
- Criminal Justice/Law Enforcement Administration
- Developmental and Child Psychology
- Economics, General
- Electrical, Electronic and Communications Engineering Technology/Technician
- Family and Consumer Sciences/Home Economics Teacher Education
- Foods, Nutrition, and Wellness Studies, General
- French Language and Literature
- Health Teacher Education
- Kindergarten/Preschool Education and Teaching
- Marketing/Marketing Management, General
- Mass Communication/Media Studies
- Mathematics, General
- Ornamental Horticulture
- Physical Education Teaching and Coaching
- Political Science and Government, General
- Psychology, General
- Social Sciences, General
- Social Work
- Sociology
- Zoology/Animal Biology

GEORGIA COLLEGE AND STATE UNIVERSITY

Hancock Street
Milledgeville, GA 31061

(478) 445-5004
http://www.gcsu.edu/

BIG DEAL

BIG REP

UNIVERSITY 101
First year–only extracurricular and social events; optional first-year Convocation ceremony; required first-year transitional seminar; special academic advisors assigned to first-year students; first-year nonresidential learning communities (required for undeclared majors); Center for Student Success to help answer questions and solve problems; optional first-year residential learning communities; first-year residential mentors and tutors (learning community students only).

Education knows no bounds at Georgia College and State University.

The Office of Experiential Learning has practical programs designed to fit all types of academic interests. In addition to a full load of on-campus courses, Georgia College students also intern at major private and nonprofit organizations; step up to leadership roles in on-campus clubs; give back through service-learning projects; complete their own undergraduate research; design their own artistic projects; and travel to Namibia, Chile, and everywhere in between for rad study abroad programs. The Experiential Transcript reflects all learning opportunities that transcend the traditional classroom so future employers or grad school admissions committees will know just how motivated you actually are.

GEORGIA COLLEGE AND STATE UNIVERSITY

WHAT IT IS

Since Georgia College and State University began as a state-run normal and industrial college in 1889, the university has matured into a small public school dedicated to educating students from Georgia and around the world. Most students are Georgians by birth, but the institution also attracts enrollees from around the United States and more than 61 countries. The university's enrollment is fewer than 5,000 students, but that doesn't hinder this school from having resources on par with that of a larger institution. The holdings of Russell Library, for example, include the Flannery O'Connor Collection, the papers of late Senator Paul Coverdell, and the Horology Collection (horology is the study of timekeeping devices). Many students are active on campus, participating in debate, theater and musical groups, or student media; others opt to join one of 14 fraternities or sororities. The college's Bobcat cheerleading squad has won three National Cheerleading Association titles in recent years and loyally supports the school's sports teams.

WHERE IT'S AT

Georgia College and State University's 43-acre main campus is located in Milledgeville. An additional 500-acre West campus is home to athletic facilities and student housing. Many college buildings are made of red brick and feature architectural details like white Corinthian columns, giving this southern campus a classic college environment. The Governor's Mansion is a prominent campus landmark; the building, which is on the National Register of Historic Places, serves as a museum and educational center. Milledgeville, which has a population of around 20,000, is a striking antebellum city located almost exactly in the center of the state. The city is 30 miles from Macon and about 100 miles from Atlanta.

THE DETAILS

Campus setting:	small town
Degrees:	bachelor's, master's
Calendar:	semesters
Public/Private:	public state
Number of full-time faculty:	268
Student-to-teacher ratio:	14:1

Admissions requirements:
- **Options:** deferred entrance, early admission, early action, electronic application
- **Application fee:** $25
- **Required:** essay or personal statement, high school transcript, SAT or ACT
- **Application deadlines:** 4/1 (freshmen), 7/1 (transfer)
- **Early action:** 11/1
- **Notification:** continuous (freshmen), continuous (transfer), 12/1 (early action)

Average high school GPA:	3.2
Average freshman SAT verbal/math score:	565 / 565
Average freshman ACT score:	22
Number of applicants:	2,986
Number of applicants accepted:	1,304
Percentage of students from out of state:	1%
Total freshman enrollment:	911
Total enrollment:	5,531
Percentage of students who live in campus housing:	36%
Total in-state tuition, fees & expenses:	$10,944
Total out-of-state tuition, fees & expenses:	$20,400
Average financial aid package:	$5,167

GEORGIA COLLEGE AND STATE UNIVERSITY

MAJORS

- Accounting
- Art/Art Studies, General
- Arts Management
- Biology/Biological Sciences, General
- Business/Commerce, General
- Business/Managerial Economics
- Business Administration and Management, General
- Chemistry, General
- Computer and Information Sciences, General
- Creative Writing
- Criminal Justice/Law Enforcement Administration
- Drama and Dramatics/Theatre Arts, General
- Early Childhood Education and Teaching
- English Language and Literature, General
- Environmental Studies
- French Language and Literature
- Health Teacher Education
- History, General
- International Business/Trade/Commerce
- Journalism
- Junior High/Intermediate/Middle School Education and Teaching
- Logistics and Materials Management
- Management Sciences and Quantitative Methods, Other
- Marketing/Marketing Management, General
- Mathematics, General
- Music, General
- Music Teacher Education
- Music Therapy/Therapist
- Nursing/Registered Nurse Training
- Office Management and Supervision
- Parks, Recreation and Leisure Studies
- Physical Education Teaching and Coaching
- Political Science and Government, General
- Psychology, General
- Sociology
- Spanish Language and Literature
- Special Education and Teaching, General
- Speech and Rhetorical Studies

GEORGIA INSTITUTE OF TECHNOLOGY

225 North Avenue, NW
Atlanta, GA 30332

(404) 894-2000
http://www.gatech.edu/

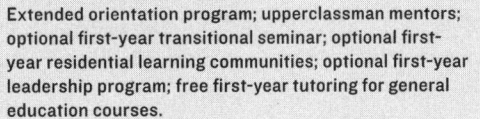

BIG REP

UNIVERSITY 101
Extended orientation program; upperclassman mentors; optional first-year transitional seminar; optional first-year residential learning communities; optional first-year leadership program; free first-year tutoring for general education courses.

BIG DEAL

Flying robots onto Mars is only one example of the research projects going on at Georgia Tech.

This university consistently earns a spot on top-10 research universities lists and, in 2004, brought in more than $300 million in research awards. Georgia Tech is best known for its engineering programs and produces more undergrad engineering degrees than any other institution in the country. The school offers 11 undergrad engineering majors and research opportunities both for pay and credit through the 80 university-run research centers. Students may conduct their own work under the guidance of faculty mentors or jump into studies already underway.

GEORGIA INSTITUTE OF TECHNOLOGY

WHAT IT IS

The Georgia Institute of Technology—Georgia Tech for short—is one of the country's leading public universities. Founded in 1885 as a trade school, in 1960 Georgia Tech became the first university in the Deep South to voluntarily admit black students. Georgia Tech has since developed a tradition of producing successful black graduates, especially in fields like engineering. The sciences and technology are the main focus of undergraduate education, and professors are active researchers and recognized experts in their fields. Many students have an opportunity to learn outside of the classroom as well, with more than 50 percent participating in an internship before graduation. Although the academic environment is intense at Georgia Tech, students still find time for fun, and many of the school's traditions are legendary.

WHERE IT'S AT

Georgia Tech is situated in the heart of Atlanta, one of the fastest-growing cities in the South. Atlanta is a bustling community, with skyscrapers, pro sports teams, historic neighborhoods, and tree-lined streets. A popular destination for Tech students is the Varsity, a fast-food joint founded by a university graduate. This Atlanta institution is the world's largest drive-in, seating more than 800 and serving 10,000 people each day. The Georgia Tech campus occupies 400 acres and includes Technology Square, the heart of a new high-tech corridor in central Atlanta. Several campus buildings were originally built for the 1996 Olympic Games, including the campus recreation center and the West campus residence hall.

THE DETAILS

Campus setting:	urban
Degrees:	bachelor's, master's, doctoral
Calendar:	semesters
Public/Private:	public state
Number of full-time faculty:	801
Student-to-teacher ratio:	14:1

Admissions requirements:
- **Options:** common application, early admission, electronic application
- **Application fee:** $50
- **Required:** essay or personal statement, high school transcript, SAT or ACT, SAT (recommended)
- **Application deadlines:** 1/15 (freshmen), 2/1 (transfer)
- **Early decision:** —
- **Notification:** 3/15 (freshmen), continuous (transfer)

Average high school GPA:	3.7
Average freshman SAT verbal/math score:	648 / 691
Average freshman ACT score:	—
Number of applicants:	8,561
Number of applicants accepted:	6,005
Percentage of students from out of state:	31%
Total freshman enrollment:	2,572
Total enrollment:	16,841
Percentage of students who live in campus housing:	53%
Total in-state tuition, fees & expenses:	$10,804
Total out-of-state tuition, fees & expenses:	$24,084
Average financial aid package:	$8,566

GEORGIA INSTITUTE OF TECHNOLOGY

MAJORS

- Aerospace, Aeronautical and Astronautical Engineering
- Applied Mathematics, Other
- Architecture
- Architecture and Related Services, Other
- Atmospheric Sciences and Meteorology, General
- Biology/Biological Sciences, General
- Biomedical/Medical Engineering
- Business/Managerial Economics
- Business Administration and Management, General
- Chemical Engineering
- Chemistry, General
- Chemistry, Other
- Civil Engineering, General
- Computer and Information Sciences, General
- Computer Engineering, General
- Electrical, Electronics and Communications Engineering
- Geological and Earth Sciences/Geosciences, Other
- History and Philosophy of Science and Technology
- Industrial and Organizational Psychology
- Industrial Design
- Industrial Engineering
- International Economics
- International Relations and Affairs
- Management Science, General
- Materials Engineering
- Mathematics, General
- Mechanical Engineering
- Metallurgical Engineering
- Modern Languages
- Multi-/Interdisciplinary Studies, Other
- Nuclear Engineering
- Operations Management and Supervision
- Physics, General
- Polymer Chemistry
- Public Policy Analysis
- Science, Technology and Society
- Textile Sciences and Engineering

GEORGIA SOUTHWESTERN STATE UNIVERSITY

800 Wheatley Street
Americus, GA 31709

(229) 928-1279
http://www.gsw.edu/

BIG DEAL

UNIVERSITY 101
First-year transitional seminar (required for learning community students); first-year residential learning communities; residential academic advisors assigned to first-years; optional first-year academic skills course; residential first-year tutors.

BIG FISH

Alumni Jimmy and Rosalynn Carter fell in love with Georgia Southwestern, and so will you.

Georgia Southwestern is home to 60-plus student clubs, nationally known sports teams, one of the state's best honors programs, and 11 centers and institutes. A credited service-learning course, UNIV 4000, is undoubtedly the coolest class offered at Georgia Southwestern. Fifteen students are selected to spend the first portion of the semester raising money and the second half working with Habitat for Humanity in Costa Rica to build houses for impoverished families.

GEORGIA SOUTHWESTERN STATE UNIVERSITY

WHAT IT IS

Georgia Southwestern State University was founded in 1906 and began offering four-year degrees in the 1960s. The university is home to several unique institutes and programs, including the Southwest Georgia Writing Project, Center for Asian Studies, Association for Third World Studies, and Rosalynn Carter Institute for Caregiving. Georgia Southwestern offers its diverse student body more than 30 majors, ranging from geology to nursing, and the university's art department has one of only 70 glassblowing studios in the country. The university also provides students with more than 70 campus organizations, such as an arts and literary magazine, a student-run television station, and fraternities and sororities. The university encourages students to become active in at least two groups or activities, ensuring that all undergraduates have an active role in the college community.

WHERE IT'S AT

Georgia Southwestern State University is located in Americus, a small city with a population of about 17,000. Former president and Nobel Peace Prize–winner Jimmy Carter grew up in the area and attended the university; the Jimmy Carter National Historic Site is in the nearby town of Plains. Americus is also home to the international headquarters of Habitat for Humanity. Every year, President Carter and his wife, Rosalynn, volunteer a week of their time to help build homes and raise awareness of the need for affordable housing. On campus, the Marshall Student Center is a hub of activity, with a dining hall, post office, bookstore, weight room, student activities offices, and an ATM.

THE DETAILS

Campus setting:	small town
Degrees:	bachelor's, master's
Calendar:	semesters
Public/Private:	public state
Number of full-time faculty:	92
Student-to-teacher ratio:	16:1

Admissions requirements:
- **Options:** common application, early admission, early decision, electronic application
- **Application fee:** $20
- **Required:** high school transcript, SAT or ACT
- **Application deadlines:** continuous (freshmen), continuous (transfer)
- **Early decision:** 12/15
- **Notification:** 8/1 (freshmen), 8/1 (transfer), 1/15 (early decision)

Average high school GPA:	3.20
Average freshman SAT verbal/math score:	502 / 497
Average freshman ACT score:	19
Number of applicants:	1,105
Number of applicants accepted:	834
Percentage of students from out of state:	2%
Total freshman enrollment:	360
Total enrollment:	2,323
Percentage of students who live in campus housing:	27%
Total in-state tuition, fees & expenses:	$8,248
Total out-of-state tuition, fees & expenses:	$15,216
Average financial aid package:	$6,002

GEORGIA SOUTHWESTERN STATE UNIVERSITY

MAJORS

- Accounting
- Art/Art Studies, General
- Biology/Biological Sciences, General
- Business Administration and Management, General
- Chemistry, General
- Clinical Laboratory Science/Medical Technology/Technologist
- Computer and Information Sciences, General
- Computer Engineering Technology/Technician
- Computer Programming, Specific Applications
- Computer Science
- Drama and Dramatics/Theatre Arts, General
- Education, General
- Elementary Education and Teaching
- English Language and Literature, General
- Geology/Earth Science, General
- History, General
- Human Resources Management/Personnel Administration, General
- Junior High/Intermediate/Middle School Education and Teaching
- Management Information Systems, General
- Marketing/Marketing Management, General
- Mathematics, General
- Music, General
- Nursing/Registered Nurse Training
- Parks, Recreation and Leisure Facilities Management
- Physical Education Teaching and Coaching
- Physical Sciences
- Political Science and Government, General
- Pre-Dentistry Studies
- Pre-Medicine/Pre-Medical Studies
- Pre-Veterinary Studies
- Psychology, General
- Social Sciences, General
- Sociology
- Special Education and Teaching, General

GEORGIA SOUTHERN UNIVERSITY

PO Box 8055
Statesboro, GA 30460

(912) 681-5611
http://www.georgiasouthern.edu/

BIG DEAL

UNIVERSITY 101
Extended orientation program; upperclassman mentors; optional first-year residential learning communities; optional first-year Success Series workshops; first-year summer Eagle Incentive Program designed for first-year students who do not meet all admissions requirements.

BIG FISH

What do Bill Clinton, Ted Danson, and Maya Angelou have in common?

They are among the many notable celebrities, politicians, and authors who have shared their thoughts on writing with the "Wall of Fame" at Georgia Southern's Writing Center. The Writing Center is part of the school's academic Success Center, which provides support for all students. Students have access to free tutoring services (both private and online), academic workshops, and computer labs. The center also organizes weekly group-study sessions for classes that are known to be difficult. First-years are treated with a personal touch. Georgia Southern's first-year experience program provides residential learning communities, a peer mentoring program, and a series of workshops that focus on helping students overcome typical first-year problems.

GEORGIA SOUTHERN UNIVERSITY

WHAT IT IS

Georgia Southern University was founded almost 100 years ago and became the first university in the southern part of the state in 1990. The university focuses on undergraduate education and producing successful graduates through a combination of superior teaching and a challenging academic program. Students come from every state in the nation and 80 foreign countries, and the resulting diversity greatly enhances the educational experience. The university offers majors in more than 120 areas of study, and exceptionally talented students can apply to be part of an honors program. This program provides students with challenging courses, which integrate in-class lessons with hands-on learning in the surrounding community. As the largest and most comprehensive institution of higher education in the area, Georgia Southern makes a particular effort to reach out to the surrounding communities. Programs in economic development, education, health, and cultural opportunities all help to build a mutually beneficial relationship between the university and its neighbors.

WHERE IT'S AT

Georgia Southern University's 675-acre Statesboro campus is situated in an area of natural beauty, with dramatic lawns, peaceful lakes, and towering pine trees dotting the landscape. At the center of campus are redbrick and white-columned buildings, framed by arches of oak trees. Recently, the school has embarked on an ambitious expansion plan, with more than $200 million dedicated to construction of new buildings and renovation of existing facilities. Major campus attractions include the Center for Wildlife Education, a botanical garden, and the performing arts center. The latter venue is state of the art and hosts performances by both student groups and nationally known artists, such as the Alvin Ailey American Dance Theater and Vienna Boys Choir.

THE DETAILS

Campus setting:	small town
Degrees:	bachelor's, master's, doctoral
Calendar:	semesters
Public/Private:	public state
Number of full-time faculty:	630
Student-to-teacher ratio:	20:1
Admissions requirements:	

- **Options:** common application, deferred entrance, early admission, electronic application
- **Application fee:** $20
- **Required:** high school transcript, SAT or ACT
- **Application deadlines:** 8/1 (freshmen), 7/1 (transfer)
- **Early decision:** —
- **Notification:** continuous (freshmen), continuous (transfer)

Average high school GPA:	3.08
Average freshman SAT verbal/math score:	544 / 546
Average freshman ACT score:	22
Number of applicants:	8,434
Number of applicants accepted:	4,575
Percentage of students from out of state:	4%
Total freshman enrollment:	2,983
Total enrollment:	16,100
Percentage of students who live in campus housing:	23%
Total in-state tuition, fees & expenses:	$10,062
Total out-of-state tuition, fees & expenses:	$17,120
Average financial aid package:	$6,606

GEORGIA SOUTHERN UNIVERSITY

MAJORS

- Accounting
- Anthropology
- Apparel and Textiles, General
- Art/Art Studies, General
- Art Teacher Education
- Athletic Training/Trainer
- Biology/Biological Sciences, General
- Biology Teacher Education
- Business/Managerial Economics
- Business Administration and Management, General
- Business Teacher Education
- Chemistry, General
- Chemistry Teacher Education
- Civil Engineering Technology/Technician
- Clinical Laboratory Science/Medical Technology/Technologist
- Communication Studies/Speech Communication and Rhetoric
- Computer and Information Sciences, General
- Construction Engineering Technology/Technician
- Criminal Justice/Safety Studies
- Development Economics and International Development
- Drama and Dramatics/Theatre Arts, General
- Economics, General
- Education, General
- Electrical, Electronic and Communications Engineering Technology/Technician
- English/Language Arts Teacher Education
- English Language and Literature, General
- Family and Consumer Sciences/Home Economics Teacher Education
- Finance, General
- Foods, Nutrition, and Wellness Studies, General
- French Language and Literature
- French Language Teacher Education
- General Studies
- Geography
- Geology/Earth Science, General
- German Language and Literature
- German Language Teacher Education
- Graphic and Printing Equipment Operator, General Production
- Health and Physical Education, General
- History, General
- History Teacher Education
- Hotel/Motel Administration/Management
- Human Development and Family Studies, General
- Industrial Production Technologies/Technicians, Other
- Industrial Technology/Technician
- Interior Design
- International Business/Trade/Commerce
- International Relations and Affairs
- Journalism
- Junior High/Intermediate/Middle School Education and Teaching
- Kindergarten/Preschool Education and Teaching
- Kinesiology and Exercise Science
- Logistics and Materials Management
- Management Information Systems, General
- Marketing/Marketing Management, General
- Mathematics, General
- Mathematics Teacher Education
- Mechanical Engineering/Mechanical Technology/Technician
- Music, General
- Music Performance, General
- Music Teacher Education
- Music Theory and Composition
- Nursing/Registered Nurse Training
- Parks, Recreation and Leisure Studies
- Philosophy
- Physical Education Teaching and Coaching
- Physics, General
- Physics Teacher Education
- Political Science and Government, General
- Psychology, General
- Public Health Education and Promotion
- Public Relations/Image Management
- Radio and Television
- Sociology
- Spanish Language and Literature
- Spanish Language Teacher Education
- Special Education and Teaching, General
- Speech and Rhetorical Studies
- Sport and Fitness Administration/Management
- Technology Teacher Education/Industrial Arts Teacher Education

GEORGIA STATE UNIVERSITY

PO Box 3965
Atlanta, GA 30303

(404) 651-2000
http://www.gsu.edu/

BIG DEAL

UNIVERSITY 101
Extended orientation program; optional first-year residential learning communities; optional first-year transitional seminar; special academic advisors assigned to first-years.

BIG FISH

Georgia State's College of Health and Human Services wants to make its students all-around stars.

The college adopts an interdisciplinary approach for each of its five undergraduate majors, giving students a multifaceted view of their chosen disciplines. Students learn from an 80-member faculty team who are nationally recognized as being experts in their field. Undergrads also receive guidance from domestic and international community leaders who have experience with the latest equipment and teaching techniques. Almost all majors require a work-placement component, forcing students to have proven field experience before hitting the job market.

GEORGIA STATE UNIVERSITY

WHAT IT IS

Since Georgia State University's establishment more than 90 years ago, the institution has grown into the second-largest institution of higher education in the state. Virtually anyone can find his or her niche at this major research university, which has an enrollment of about 27,000 students in six separate colleges. Students enroll at Georgia State from all over the nation, as well as from more than 145 countries. This diversity matches the university's range of programs—the institution offers more than 52 degree programs, with 250 fields of study. Facilities and services are equally comprehensive; the school's libraries, for example, contain more than 3.3 million volumes. Although Georgia State was for many years primarily a commuter school, the residential population has been on the rise in past years. In 1996, the institution began to develop a housing plan. Designed for the needs of contemporary students, the plan features stylish, urban apartment complexes rather than the generic cinder-block monoliths so common at many large state universities.

WHERE IT'S AT

Georgia State University occupies a vibrant urban campus in the heart of downtown Atlanta. In recent years, the university has focused on developing its "Main Street Master Plan," with the goal of creating an inviting, livable campus setting for students, faculty, staff, and the surrounding community. Recent campus development includes the Rialto Center for the Performing Arts, the construction of modern residence halls, and new student and recreation centers. Atlanta itself is a thriving city with a population of about 475,000 (the metro area is home to about 4.7 million people). When students aren't busy studying, they often take in a Braves game at Turner Field; hit East Atlanta; or visit the trendy bars, restaurants, and shops in the Little Five Points neighborhoods.

THE DETAILS

Campus setting:	urban
Degrees:	bachelor's, master's, doctoral
Calendar:	semesters
Public/Private:	public state
Number of full-time faculty:	1,027
Student-to-teacher ratio:	19:1

Admissions requirements:
- **Options:** deferred entrance, electronic application
- **Application fee:** $50
- **Required:** high school transcript, SAT or ACT
- **Application deadlines:** 3/1 (freshmen), 6/1 (transfer)
- **Early decision:** —
- **Notification:** continuous (freshmen), continuous (transfer)

Average high school GPA:	3.31
Average freshman SAT verbal/math score:	547 / 554
Average freshman ACT score:	22
Number of applicants:	8,481
Number of applicants accepted:	4,775
Percentage of students from out of state:	3%
Total freshman enrollment:	2,209
Total enrollment:	27,267
Percentage of students who live in campus housing:	10%
Total in-state tuition, fees & expenses:	$11,832
Total out-of-state tuition, fees & expenses:	$22,746
Average financial aid package:	$7,780

GEORGIA STATE UNIVERSITY

MAJORS

- Accounting
- Actuarial Science
- African-American/Black Studies
- Anthropology
- Art/Art Studies, General
- Art Teacher Education
- Biology/Biological Sciences, General
- Business/Managerial Economics
- Business Administration and Management, General
- Chemistry, General
- Classics and Languages, Literatures and Linguistics, General
- Computer and Information Sciences, General
- Criminal Justice/Safety Studies
- Early Childhood Education and Teaching
- Economics, General
- Elementary Education and Teaching
- English Language and Literature, General
- Facilities Planning and Management
- Film/Cinema Studies
- Finance, General
- Fine/Studio Arts, General
- Foods, Nutrition, and Wellness Studies, General
- French Language and Literature
- Geography
- Geology/Earth Science, General
- German Language and Literature
- History, General
- Human Resources Development
- Insurance
- Journalism
- Marketing/Marketing Management, General
- Mathematics, General
- Multi-/Interdisciplinary Studies, Other
- Music Management and Merchandising
- Music Performance, General
- Nursing/Registered Nurse Training
- Philosophy
- Physics, General
- Political Science and Government, General
- Psychology, General
- Real Estate
- Religion/Religious Studies
- Respiratory Care Therapy/Therapist
- Social Work
- Sociology
- Spanish Language and Literature
- Speech and Rhetorical Studies
- Urban Studies/Affairs
- Women's Studies

LAGRANGE COLLEGE

601 Broad Street
LaGrange, GA 30240

(706) 880-8000
http://www.lagrange.edu/

BIG IDEA

UNIVERSITY 101
Extended orientation program; special academic advisors assigned to first-year students; required first-year transitional seminar; upperclassman mentors.

Winter is when academics heat up at LaGrange.

The January interim term gives students a break from semester-long coursework and allows them to focus their energy on one project. LaGrange always encourages students to direct their own independent projects; original research studies and creative endeavors make great January Term assignments. Soak up some culture with a winter study abroad trip to western Europe, Haiti, or the Czech Republic, or get a glimpse of life beyond college while completing an off-campus internship. On-campus courses boldly go where academia has never gone before, exploring such topics as the Science in Science Fiction, Build Your Own Computer from Scratch, and Satire as an Antidote to Human Folly. LaGrange's low average class size will ensure that you'll have plenty of chances to add your two cents.

LAGRANGE COLLEGE

WHAT IT IS

Founded in 1831, LaGrange College is the oldest private college in Georgia. A liberal arts and sciences institution affiliated with the United Methodist Church, LaGrange holds fast to its long-standing mission of challenging students' minds, inspiring their souls, and changing their lives.

LaGrange College students can start their own special interest group or join one of more than 40 clubs and organizations, including student government, honor societies, service clubs, sororities and fraternities, performance groups, religious organizations, and student publications. Students also can get involved in such service efforts as building homes through Habitat for Humanity or traveling to Costa Rica or the Czech Republic on a mission trip. One of the unique activities LaGrange students enjoy is "dive-in movies," in which popular films are beamed onto a 35-foot screen by the college's indoor pool, and students watch while drifting about in floats, inner tubes, and rafts. Other on-campus activities include intramural sports tournaments, theater performances, karaoke and open-mike competitions, art exhibitions, and Greek Week. Off-campus excursions are planned each semester, such as snow-skiing trips to North Carolina. LaGrange College's athletic facilities include an indoor competition swimming pool, an outdoor recreational swimming pool, a fully equipped fitness center, a recently completed $2 million baseball facility, two gymnasiums, two lighted softball fields, a lighted soccer field, and a training facility.

WHERE IT'S AT

The college is located in a residential section of LaGrange, Georgia, which has a population of 30,000 and was named Intelligent City of the Year by the World Teleport Association for its telecommunication infrastructure and Internet initiatives. LaGrange is home to Fortune 500 companies, unique shops and restaurants, and historic landmarks. Nearby are the world-famous Callaway Gardens, the Warm Springs Foundation, and Franklin D. Roosevelt's Little White House. The West Point Dam on the Chattahoochee River provides one of the largest lakes in the region, and waterfronts and a marina are within the city limits. The city is located 65 miles southwest of Atlanta and 55 miles southwest of Hartsfield-Jackson Atlanta International Airport.

THE DETAILS

Campus setting:	small town
Degrees:	bachelor's, master's
Calendar:	quarters
Public/Private:	private religious
Number of full-time faculty:	66
Student-to-teacher ratio:	11:1

Admissions requirements:
- **Options:** deferred entrance, early admission, electronic application
- **Application fee:** $20
- **Required:** essay or personal statement, high school transcript, letter of recommendation, SAT or ACT
- **Application deadlines:** 8/30 (freshmen), 8/15 (transfer)
- **Early decision:** —
- **Notification:** continuous (freshmen), continuous (transfer)

Average high school GPA:	3.19
Average freshman SAT verbal/math score:	520 / 521
Average freshman ACT score:	20
Number of applicants:	1,226
Number of applicants accepted:	669
Percentage of students from out of state:	12%
Total freshman enrollment:	218
Total enrollment:	1,044
Percentage of students who live in campus housing:	61%
Total tuition:	$15,206
Total cost with fees & expenses:	$22,324
Average financial aid package:	$12,596

LAGRANGE COLLEGE

MAJORS

- Accounting
- Biochemistry
- Biology/Biological Sciences, General
- Business/Commerce, General
- Business/Managerial Economics
- Business Administration and Management, General
- Chemistry, General
- Computer and Information Sciences, General
- Computer Science
- Drama and Dramatics/Theatre Arts, General
- Early Childhood Education and Teaching
- Economics, General
- Education, General
- Elementary Education and Teaching
- English Language and Literature, General
- History, General
- Human Services, General
- Junior High/Intermediate/Middle School Education and Teaching
- Mathematics, General
- Music, General
- Nursing/Registered Nurse Training
- Organizational Behavior Studies
- Political Science and Government, General
- Pre-Dentistry Studies
- Pre-Law Studies
- Pre-Medicine/Pre-Medical Studies
- Pre-Veterinary Studies
- Psychology, General
- Religion/Religious Studies
- Religious Education
- Social Work
- Spanish Language and Literature
- Visual and Performing Arts, General

MERCER UNIVERSITY

1400 Coleman Avenue
Macon, GA 31207

(478) 301-2700
http://www.mercer.edu/

BIG FISH

UNIVERSITY 101
Required first-year humanities seminars; Office of First-Year Programs to help answer questions and solve problems; special academic advisors assigned to first-years; midterm report cards for first-year students; required first-year transitional seminar or first-year humanities seminar; optional first-year transitional workshops; optional first year–only honor society.

Attention, bookworms!

Mercer University students have the option of enrolling in the Great Books program, an eight-semester series of courses that use only primary source texts as curriculum readings. Great Books students begin learning about ancient Greece and Rome and work their way up to the mid-twentieth century, all while reading Homer, Cicero, the Bible, Dante, Chaucer, Descartes, Milton, Kant, Marx, and Freud. Great Books courses are writing-intensive, discussion-based seminars limited to 20 students. Students are graded based on their contribution to the class and the portfolios they construct throughout the semester.

MERCER UNIVERSITY

WHAT IT IS

Founded in 1833, Mercer University has an enduring Baptist heritage. The university is composed of 10 colleges and schools: the College of Liberal Arts, Eugene W. Stetson School of Business and Economics, School of Engineering, Tift College of Education, Georgia Baptist College of Nursing, School of Medicine, Walter F. George School of Law, Southern School of Pharmacy, James and Carolyn McAfee School of Theology, and College of Continuing and Professional Studies. Tradition plays a key role in creating Mercer's unique identity as an institution committed to Judeo-Christian principles as well as the tenets of religious and intellectual freedom. Students benefit from Mercer's welcoming atmosphere, small classes, and superb faculty, who are distinguished for both teaching and research activities.

A variety of on-campus housing facilities—including residence halls, apartments, and Greek houses—are available to undergraduate students. The university's more than 80 on-campus organizations include a wide range of academic clubs and honor societies as well as performing arts, special interest, and religious groups. Six sororities and 10 fraternities create a vibrant social atmosphere, and members participate in numerous community service projects. Mercer also offers the U.S. Army ROTC program.

WHERE IT'S AT

Mercer University's main undergraduate campus is in Macon, Georgia, and its graduate and professional center is in Atlanta. Historic buildings and majestic magnolia trees provide the setting on Mercer's beautiful 130-acre campus in Macon—a welcoming community with small-town values and big-city amenities, just one hour from Atlanta. Mercer's convenient location in the center of the state also makes travel to Georgia's coast, Florida's beaches, and the Blue Ridge Mountains an easy drive. Macon is also home to a professional football team, the annual Cherry Blossom Festival, the Georgia Music Hall of Fame, and the Georgia Sports Hall of Fame. Easily accessible from two interstate highways, I-75 and I-16, Macon is the fifth-largest city in Georgia and the educational, medical, cultural, and commercial hub of central Georgia.

THE DETAILS

Campus setting:	suburban
Degrees:	bachelor's, master's, doctoral
Calendar:	semesters
Public/Private:	private religious
Number of full-time faculty:	343
Student-to-teacher ratio:	14:1

Admissions requirements:
- **Options:** common application, deferred entrance, early admission, early action, electronic application
- **Application fee:** $50
- **Required:** high school transcript, letter of recommendation, SAT or ACT
- **Application deadlines:** 6/1 (freshmen), continuous (transfer)
- **Early action:** 11/1
- **Notification:** continuous (freshmen), continuous (transfer), 12/15 (early action)

Average high school GPA:	3.5
Average freshman SAT verbal/math score:	593 / 593
Average freshman ACT score:	24
Number of applicants:	2,711
Number of applicants accepted:	2,298
Percentage of students from out of state:	22%
Total freshman enrollment:	635
Total enrollment:	7,180
Percentage of students who live in campus housing:	65%
Total tuition:	$22,050
Total cost with fees & expenses:	$29,910
Average financial aid package:	$22,126

MERCER UNIVERSITY

MAJORS

- African-American/Black Studies
- Art/Art Studies, General
- Biochemistry
- Biology/Biological Sciences, General
- Business/Commerce, General
- Business Administration, Management and Operations, Other
- Chemistry, General
- Christian Studies
- Classics and Languages, Literatures and Linguistics, General
- Communication, Journalism and Related Programs, Other
- Community Organization and Advocacy
- Computer Science
- Criminal Justice/Safety Studies
- Drama and Dramatics/Theatre Arts, General
- Economics, General
- Education, Other
- Elementary Education and Teaching
- Engineering, General
- English Language and Literature, General
- Environmental Science
- Environmental Studies
- French Language and Literature
- German Language and Literature
- Health/Medical Preparatory Programs, Other
- History, General
- Human Services, General
- Information Science/Studies
- International Relations and Affairs
- Journalism
- Junior High/Intermediate/Middle School Education and Teaching
- Latin Language and Literature
- Liberal Arts and Sciences/Liberal Studies
- Mass Communication/Media Studies
- Mathematics, General
- Multi-/Interdisciplinary Studies, Other
- Music, General
- Music, Other
- Music Performance, General
- Music Teacher Education
- Nursing/Registered Nurse Training
- Philosophy
- Physics, General
- Political Science and Government, General
- Pre-Dentistry Studies
- Pre-Medicine/Pre-Medical Studies
- Psychology, General
- Regional Studies (U.S., Canadian, Foreign)
- Sociology
- Spanish Language and Literature

MOREHOUSE COLLEGE

830 Westview Drive, SW
Atlanta, GA 30314

(404) 681-2800
http://www.morehouse.edu/

BIG FISH

UNIVERSITY 101
Extended orientation program; required first-year theme housing; required first-year transitional seminar; required first-year cultural events.

The largest private, liberal arts college for African American men in the nation, Morehouse has been producing leaders since 1867.

At Morehouse College, students are presented with myriad learning opportunities and choose what best fits their academic and career goals. Cooperative education programs, study abroad trips, dual- and combined-degree options, paid and unpaid undergraduate research opportunities, community service projects, an honors program, three kinds of ROTC training, and a self-designed major option allows Morehouse students to custom-tailor their collegiate experience. Now isn't too early to think about applying. The school's annual Summer Scholars program provides residential college preparatory courses for high school juniors and seniors.

MOREHOUSE COLLEGE

WHAT IT IS

Morehouse College is one of just a few all-male colleges in the United States and the country's only institution of higher education that is primarily dedicated to the education of black men. This private liberal arts college grants more bachelor's degrees to black men than any other institution in the world. Founded in 1867 in the basement of the Springfield Baptist Church (the oldest independent black church in the United States), Morehouse began to develop its comprehensive programs in the liberal arts in the early twentieth century. Today, Morehouse places a special emphasis on teaching its students about the history and culture of black people, while offering rigorous courses in many other academic areas. The college offers a variety of programs to complement the traditional curriculum, including programs offered at the Andrew Young Center for International Affairs and the Morehouse Research Institute. The success of Morehouse graduates is evidence of the college's quality education: Several students have been named Rhodes scholars, and famous alums include leaders in the political and arts worlds.

WHERE IT'S AT

Morehouse College occupies a 66-acre campus near the historic West End neighborhood in Atlanta, Georgia. The college is just three miles from this southern community's thriving downtown area. Atlanta is one of the fastest-growing cities in the country, and students can take advantage of internship opportunities and entertainment there. Several prominent companies and other institutions are based in Atlanta, including Coca-Cola, CNN, and the National Centers for Disease Control and Prevention. Morehouse College is also a member of the Atlanta University Center, a consortium of area schools, which includes Spelman College and Clark Atlanta University. The members of the consortium work together to provide the best possible education and services to the area's black students.

THE DETAILS

Campus setting:	urban
Degrees:	bachelor's
Calendar:	semesters
Public/Private:	private nonprofit
Number of full-time faculty:	159
Student-to-teacher ratio:	15:1

- **Admissions requirements:**
  - **Options:** common application, deferred entrance, early admission, early decision, electronic application
  - **Application fee:** $45
  - **Required:** essay or personal statement, high school transcript, letter of recommendation, SAT or ACT
  - **Application deadlines:** 2/15 (freshmen), 2/15 (transfer)
  - **Early decision:** 10/15
  - **Notification:** 4/1 (freshmen), 4/1 (transfer), 12/15 (early decision)

Average high school GPA:	3.24
Average freshman SAT verbal/math score:	533 / 535
Average freshman ACT score:	21
Number of applicants:	2,277
Number of applicants accepted:	1,536
Percentage of students from out of state:	70%
Total freshman enrollment:	700
Total enrollment:	2,891
Percentage of students who live in campus housing:	40%
Total tuition:	$14,318
Total cost with fees & expenses:	$25,338
Average financial aid package:	$11,079

MOREHOUSE COLLEGE

MAJORS

- Accounting
- Adult and Continuing Education and Teaching
- African-American/Black Studies
- Art/Art Studies, General
- Biology/Biological Sciences, General
- Business Administration and Management, General
- Chemistry, General
- Computer and Information Sciences, General
- Drama and Dramatics/Theatre Arts, General
- Economics, General
- Elementary Education and Teaching
- Engineering, General
- English Language and Literature, General
- Finance, General
- French Language and Literature
- German Language and Literature
- History, General
- Interdisciplinary Studies
- International Relations and Affairs
- Junior High/Intermediate/Middle School Education and Teaching
- Marketing/Marketing Management, General
- Mathematics, General
- Music, General
- Philosophy
- Physical Education Teaching and Coaching
- Physics, General
- Political Science and Government, General
- Psychology, General
- Religion/Religious Studies
- Secondary Education and Teaching
- Sociology
- Spanish Language and Literature
- Urban Studies/Affairs

NORTH GEORGIA COLLEGE AND STATE UNIVERSITY

82 College Circle (706) 864-1400
Dahlonega, GA 30597 http://www.ngcsu.edu/

BIG DEAL

UNIVERSITY 101
Extended orientation program; optional first-year transitional seminar; faculty mentors (for seminar students only); optional first-year residential learning community.

BIG IDEA

Atten-tion! North Georgia is the only military, co-ed, public liberal arts school in the world.

North Georgia has produced 36 generals and admirals. In partnership with the Defense Language Institute in Monterey, California, the U.S. Army pays ROTC cadets to attend North Georgia for one semester, then transfer to the West Coast to learn a foreign language and receive training in interrogation, interpreting, or cryptology. To complete this program, the institution expects students to learn a "critical need" language like Arabic and requires them to have top security clearance. When the program is complete, cadets will be commissioned as officers in the U.S. Army.

NORTH GEORGIA COLLEGE AND STATE UNIVERSITY

WHAT IT IS

North Georgia College and State University is the second-oldest institution of higher education in Georgia and was the first public college in Georgia to offer co-education.

The university emphasizes liberal arts and professional programs and is also a military college. North Georgia is one of only six military colleges in the United States, and 15 percent of students enroll as cadets. Cadets and traditional students alike choose from more than 50 majors, which prepare students for a variety of careers. The university is large enough to provide myriad academic options but small enough to foster a true sense of community. A residency requirement also contributes to a close-knit campus environment; students who have completed fewer than 90 semester hours must live on campus.

WHERE IT'S AT

Tucked in the scenic Blue Ridge Mountains of north Georgia, the quiet town of Dahlonega is home to North Georgia College and State University. Dahlonega has a population of fewer than 4,000 and is located 90 minutes from Atlanta. Fishing, hunting, canoeing, and camping are popular area activities, and restaurants, shops, and other amenities are all within walking distance of campus.

North Georgia's campus occupies 112 acres and includes more than 50 buildings. Price Memorial Hall is a campus landmark; the building was once a U.S. Mint, and its steeple is covered in gold. The school also owns 610 additional acres in neighboring parks and forests.

THE DETAILS

Campus setting:	small town
Degrees:	bachelor's, master's
Calendar:	semesters
Public/Private:	public state
Number of full-time faculty:	185
Student-to-teacher ratio:	15:1

Admissions requirements:
- **Options:** early admission, electronic application
- **Application fee:** $25
- **Required:** high school transcript, SAT or ACT
- **Application deadlines:** 7/1 (freshmen), continuous (transfer)
- **Early decision:** —
- **Notification:** continuous (freshmen), continuous (transfer)

Average high school GPA:	3.26
Average freshman SAT verbal/math score:	545 / 555
Average freshman ACT score:	21
Number of applicants:	2,103
Number of applicants accepted:	1,257
Percentage of students from out of state:	5%
Total freshman enrollment:	728
Total enrollment:	4,552
Percentage of students who live in campus housing:	37%
Total in-state tuition, fees & expenses:	$8,102
Total out-of-state tuition, fees & expenses:	$15,070
Average financial aid package:	$5,973

NORTH GEORGIA COLLEGE AND STATE UNIVERSITY

MAJORS

- Accounting
- Art/Art Studies, General
- Art Teacher Education
- Biology/Biological Sciences, General
- Business/Managerial Economics
- Business Administration and Management, General
- Chemistry, General
- Computer and Information Sciences, General
- Computer Science
- Crafts/Craft Design, Folk Art and Artisanry
- Criminal Justice/Law Enforcement Administration
- Criminal Justice/Safety Studies
- Drawing
- Education, General
- Educational Leadership and Administration, General
- Elementary Education and Teaching
- English/Language Arts Teacher Education
- English Language and Literature, General
- Family Practice Nurse/Nurse Practitioner
- Finance, General
- French Language and Literature
- History, General
- Information Science/Studies
- Junior High/Intermediate/Middle School Education and Teaching
- Kindergarten/Preschool Education and Teaching
- Marketing/Marketing Management, General
- Mathematics, General
- Mathematics Teacher Education
- Music, General
- Music Teacher Education
- Nursing/Registered Nurse Training
- Physical Education Teaching and Coaching
- Physics, General
- Political Science and Government, General
- Pre-Dentistry Studies
- Pre-Medicine/Pre-Medical Studies
- Pre-Veterinary Studies
- Psychology, General
- Public Administration
- Purchasing, Procurement/Acquisitions and Contracts Management
- Reading Teacher Education
- Science Teacher Education/General Science Teacher Education
- Secondary Education and Teaching
- Social Sciences, General
- Social Science Teacher Education
- Sociology
- Spanish Language and Literature
- Special Education and Teaching, General

OGLETHORPE UNIVERSITY

4484 Peachtree Road, NE
Atlanta, GA 30319

(404) 261-1441
http://www.oglethorpe.edu/

BIG FISH

UNIVERSITY 101
Required first-year core courses; upperclassman mentors; extended orientation program; special academic advisors assigned to first-year students; required first-year transitional seminar; first-year tutors for general education courses.

Who are we? Why are we here?

Core classes at Oglethorpe dig deep and beg us to question our conceptions of self and the universe. The Oglethorpe core curriculum was revolutionary for its time and remains one of the best liberal arts programs in the South. Funded in part by the National Endowment for the Humanities, Oglethorpe students take seven integrated, interdisciplinary humanities seminars spread out over four years. These classes cover how we understand ourselves, how we understand one another, how history influences our sense of self, and how science influences our understanding of the world. Core courses have a small average class size, are 100 percent faculty taught (like all other Oglethorpe classes), and are writing intensive.

OGLETHORPE UNIVERSITY

WHAT IT IS

Standing as a landmark in north Atlanta since the beginning of the twentieth century, Oglethorpe University is located on 126 acres of unquestionable beauty. Only 10 miles from the heart of downtown Atlanta, the campus, with its classic neo-Gothic architecture, maintains an Old World charm. Oglethorpe students learn to make a life, make a living, and make a difference. Its graduates become community leaders who are distinctive in their ability to think, communicate, and contribute.

Numerous activities are offered on campus, such as concerts, exhibits, and social affairs. The university has a student center, six tennis courts, a Resilite track, a swimming pool, an intramural field, a recreational sports facility, and a basketball arena with seating for 2,000. There are many avenues for developing leadership potential, including the Rich Foundation Urban Leadership Certificate Program. Omicron Delta Kappa, a national leadership organization, recognizes outstanding leadership on campus. Alpha Phi Omega, a national service fraternity that is open to both men and women, is one of Oglethorpe's largest organizations; its purpose is to serve the school, the community, and the nation. More than 60 clubs and organizations are open to students, including fraternities and sororities, honor societies, academic societies, and special interest groups. A distinctive feature of Oglethorpe is the interest and support that the university gives to such activities. This is in keeping with the goals of the institution, which are to build a community of leaders and to stimulate personal and intellectual growth and development.

WHERE IT'S AT

Students enjoy the many benefits of being on a small suburban campus near a large metropolitan cultural center. Metropolitan Atlanta's population is more than 4 million, and the community offers all the entertainment advantages of a large city, including professional athletics, world-renowned museums, concerts by well-known artists, theaters, and restaurants. Cultural centers and recreational facilities are easily accessible. Home to one of the busiest airports in the world, Hartsfield-Jackson Atlanta International Airport, the city is a major international transportation hub.

THE DETAILS

Campus setting:	suburban
Degrees:	bachelor's, master's
Calendar:	semesters
Public/Private:	private nonprofit
Number of full-time faculty:	57
Student-to-teacher ratio:	11:1

Admissions requirements:
- **Options:** common application, deferred entrance, early action, electronic application
- **Application fee:** $35
- **Required:** essay or personal statement, high school transcript, letter of recommendation, SAT and SAT Subject Tests, or ACT
- **Application deadlines:** continuous (freshmen), continuous (transfer)
- **Early action:** 12/1
- **Notification:** continuous (freshmen), continuous (transfer), 1/1 (early action)

Average high school GPA:	3.6
Average freshman SAT verbal/math score:	583 / 559
Average freshman ACT score:	23
Number of applicants:	1,261
Number of applicants accepted:	812
Percentage of students from out of state:	37%
Total freshman enrollment:	223
Total enrollment:	1,053
Percentage of students who live in campus housing:	58%
Total tuition:	$22,200
Total cost with fees & expenses:	$30,900
Average financial aid package:	$20,779

OGLETHORPE UNIVERSITY

MAJORS

- Accounting
- American/United States Studies/Civilization
- Art/Art Studies, General
- Biology/Biological Sciences, General
- Business/Managerial Economics
- Business Administration and Management, General
- Chemistry, General
- Computer Science
- Economics, General
- Education, General
- Elementary Education and Teaching
- English Language and Literature, General
- History, General
- Interdisciplinary Studies
- International Relations and Affairs
- Junior High/Intermediate/Middle School Education and Teaching
- Kindergarten/Preschool Education and Teaching
- Mass Communication/Media Studies
- Mathematics, General
- Philosophy
- Physics, General
- Political Science and Government, General
- Pre-Dentistry Studies
- Pre-Law Studies
- Pre-Medicine/Pre-Medical Studies
- Pre-Veterinary Studies
- Psychology, General
- Secondary Education and Teaching
- Social Work
- Sociology
- Urban Studies/Affairs

PIEDMONT COLLEGE

PO Box 10, 165 Central Avenue
Demorest, GA 30535

(706) 778-3000
http://www.piedmont.edu/

BIG FISH

UNIVERSITY 101
Required first-year transitional seminar; extended orientation program.

Want to make sure your voice is heard?

Piedmont's Writing and Speaking Across the Curriculum program requires students to enroll in courses that emphasize composition and communication skills. Students who want to take their foundational communications skills one step further have a wide range of degree programs and off-campus options available through the college's mass communications department. Mass communications students create their own interdisciplinary majors based on their particular interests and are free to take part in internships, study abroad trips, and service-learning projects related to their programs. For students who want to spread the word on campus, the department also operates the school newspaper, radio station, television station, yearbook, debate team, magazine, film festival, and leadership council.

PIEDMONT COLLEGE

WHAT IT IS

Inspired by the liberal arts tradition and a historical association with the Congregational Christian Churches, Piedmont College cultivates a diverse, challenging, and caring intellectual environment to encourage academic success and spiritual development. The college is also committed to its Writing and Speaking Across the Curriculum program as a component of its general education requirements and assessment. At each academic level, students are required to enroll in courses that emphasize and assess writing and speaking.

The college offers both day and evening classes, with limited weekend offerings. During the fall and spring semesters, evening and weekend classes are offered in two 8-week sessions, as are all classes at the Athens Center. Campus-life programs offer numerous opportunities for resident and commuter students to participate in a wide variety of planned and spontaneous activities. The Campus Activity Board is responsible for planning events for orientation, homecoming, and special dinners. CAB also schedules various entertainers, lip-synching and talent-show competitions, and other ventures, such as movie nights, shopping trips, roller-skating, tubing, and various Atlanta-based sporting and theatrical events.

WHERE IT'S AT

Located in the heart of the northeast Georgia mountains, Piedmont College's 100-acre main campus provides ample opportunity for outdoor activities that include hiking, white-water rafting, fishing, and rappelling. For students interested in city life, Piedmont College is about an hour's drive from Atlanta or Greenville, South Carolina. These cities offer an abundance of museums, botanical gardens, concert venues, and sporting events, as well as outstanding shopping and dining experiences.

THE DETAILS

Campus setting:	rural
Degrees:	bachelor's, master's
Calendar:	semesters
Public/Private:	private religious
Number of full-time faculty:	96
Student-to-teacher ratio:	14:1

Admissions requirements:
- **Options:** common application, deferred entrance, early admission, electronic application
- **Application fee:** —
- **Required:** high school transcript, SAT or ACT
- **Application deadlines:** 7/1 (freshmen), 7/1 (transfer)
- **Early decision:** —
- **Notification:** —

Average high school GPA:	3.40
Average freshman SAT verbal/math score:	508 / 516
Average freshman ACT score:	21
Number of applicants:	862
Number of applicants accepted:	532
Percentage of students from out of state:	4%
Total freshman enrollment:	167
Total enrollment:	2,222
Percentage of students who live in campus housing:	16%
Total tuition:	$13,500
Total cost with fees & expenses:	$19,400
Average financial aid package:	$11,682

PIEDMONT COLLEGE

MAJORS

- Biology/Biological Sciences, General
- Business Administration and Management, General
- Chemistry, General
- Computer Science
- Criminal Justice/Law Enforcement Administration
- Drama and Dramatics/Theatre Arts, General
- Elementary and Middle School Administration/Principalship
- English Language and Literature, General
- Environmental Science
- Environmental Studies
- Fine/Studio Arts, General
- History, General
- Interdisciplinary Studies
- Junior High/Intermediate/Middle School Education and Teaching
- Kindergarten/Preschool Education and Teaching
- Mass Communication/Media Studies
- Mathematics, General
- Mathematics and Computer Science
- Music, General
- Music Performance, General
- Nursing/Registered Nurse Training
- Philosophy
- Political Science and Government, General
- Psychology, General
- Religion/Religious Studies
- Social Sciences, General
- Sociology
- Spanish Language and Literature
- Special Education and Teaching, General

REINHARDT COLLEGE

7300 Reinhardt College Circle
Waleska, GA 30183

(770) 720-5600
http://www.reinhardt.edu/

BIG FISH

UNIVERSITY 101
Extended orientation program; required first-year transitional seminar; special academic advisors assigned to first-year students.

A tiny power pack, Reinhardt College has programs unlike any other school in the state.

Reinhardt students apply their financial aid packages (including HOPE scholarships) to study, intern, or work abroad programs anywhere from Greece to Ghana. An international education consortium allows students to study in 57 institutions around the world. Also, if you'd prefer a more service-oriented trip, Campus Ministries offers domestic and international mission trips every year. On campus, the Funk Heritage Center has an extensive collection of Native American art, a 5-ton petroglyph (a carved boulder), and a restored 1835 cabin.

REINHARDT COLLEGE

WHAT IT IS

Reinhardt College was founded in 1883 and offers students 40 baccalaureate degrees in 33 fields of study. Since it began offering four-year degrees in 1992, the college has grown quickly, adding such programs as psychology, sociology, communications, art, and religion. Student activities have also expanded, with new programs in volleyball and baseball, for example. A low student-faculty ratio means that students receive individual attention in the classroom. Study abroad programs, internships, and service projects supplement traditional learning experiences. The college also provides students with more than 30 clubs and organizations, and student activities include intramural sports, musical groups, a literary magazine, and student-run television and radio stations.

WHERE IT'S AT

Reinhardt College's 540-acre main campus is located in Waleska, Georgia. This tiny community of fewer than 700 residents is about 45 minutes from Atlanta. The school also operates a second, satellite campus in Alpharetta, Georgia. Students study within a naturally beautiful setting, close to the scenic mountains of north Georgia. Reinhardt is transitioning to a more residential campus. Two apartment-style residences with accommodations for about 200 students opened in 2004, and about 50 percent of students on the main campus live in college housing. The Funk Heritage Center is a major campus landmark, and its exhibits focus on the history and art of the area's Native American tribes and the later European settlers.

THE DETAILS

Campus setting:	rural
Degrees:	bachelor's
Calendar:	semesters
Public/Private:	private religious
Number of full-time faculty:	52
Student-to-teacher ratio:	10:1

Admissions requirements:
- **Options:** common application, deferred entrance, early admission, electronic application
- **Application fee:** $25
- **Required:** high school transcript, SAT or ACT
- **Application deadlines:** continuous (freshmen), continuous (transfer)
- **Early decision:** —
- **Notification:** continuous (freshmen), continuous (transfer)

Average high school GPA:	2.68
Average freshman SAT verbal/math score:	481 / 481
Average freshman ACT score:	19
Number of applicants:	958
Number of applicants accepted:	494
Percentage of students from out of state:	4%
Total freshman enrollment:	308
Total enrollment:	1,096
Percentage of students who live in campus housing:	39%
Total tuition:	$12,000
Total cost with fees & expenses:	$18,462
Average financial aid package:	$6,570

REINHARDT COLLEGE

MAJORS

- Accounting
- Art/Art Studies, General
- Bible/Biblical Studies
- Biology/Biological Sciences, General
- Business/Commerce, General
- Business Administration and Management, General
- English Language and Literature, General
- Entrepreneurship/Entrepreneurial Studies
- Health and Physical Education/Fitness, Other
- History, General
- Information Science/Studies
- Junior High/Intermediate/Middle School Education and Teaching
- Kindergarten/Preschool Education and Teaching
- Liberal Arts and Sciences/Liberal Studies
- Mass Communication/Media Studies
- Music, General
- Physical Education Teaching and Coaching
- Psychology, General
- Sociology
- Sport and Fitness Administration/Management

SAVANNAH COLLEGE OF ART AND DESIGN

342 Bull Street, PO Box 3146
Savannah, GA 31402

(912) 525-5000
http://www.scad.edu/

BIG IDEA

UNIVERSITY 101
Extended orientation program; required first-year foundational art courses.

BIG FISH

According to the dictionary, the word *scads* means "oodles."

At SCAD, it means a multitude of exciting programs for the students of visual, performing, and written arts. Programs ranging from metals and jewelry to interactive design and game development give students the chance to explore mediums, materials, techniques, and styles. The SCAD curriculum promotes learning by doing; every student must produce a full body of work. Students are encouraged—in some cases required—to take on internships and apprenticeships, study abroad, display their work at local venues, or become a part of the blossoming Savannah arts scene. SCAD attracts working visionaries from around the world, including musicians like Wilco, actress Jane Fonda, and author Amy Tan.

SAVANNAH COLLEGE OF ART AND DESIGN

WHAT IT IS

The Savannah College of Art and Design prepares students for careers in the visual and performing arts, design, the building arts, and the history of art and architecture. Founded in 1978, the college, which is the largest art school in the United States, offers a solid, innovative curriculum that attracts students from every state and more than 80 countries. SCAD has locations in Savannah, Atlanta, and Lacoste, France. Online programs are offered via SCAD e-Learning. A graduate certificate program is offered to provide special preparation in an area complementary to the student's major or profession.

The college has been recognized by the National Trust for Historic Preservation, American Institute of Architects, and International Downtown Association, among others, for adaptive re-use of historic buildings. The college encourages collaboration inside and outside of the classroom, with several active student clubs linked to professional organizations and others formed purely according to interests. The college provides residence halls, dining halls, book and supply stores, and galleries, as well as a full calendar of lectures, performances, festivals, and other cultural events.

WHERE IT'S AT

SCAD is located in the charming southern city of Savannah, Georgia, minutes from the Atlantic Ocean. Savannah's renowned National Historic Landmark district provides a culturally diverse, active, and inspiring urban environment for students. The college has grown to occupy more than 1 million square feet in more than 50 buildings in Savannah's historic districts. Many buildings are located on the famous 24 squares of the old town, which are laden with monuments, live oaks, horse-and-buggy tours, and an undeniable Southern Gothic feel that is sought by the many movies filmed there. Two nearby attractions are the Riverfront Plaza and Factors' Walk (a group of nineteenth-century warehouses and passageways that have been remodeled to include shops, bars, and restaurants) and the City Market (a renovated shopping area that features antique and souvenir shops, as well as unique eateries).

THE DETAILS

Campus setting:	urban
Degrees:	bachelor's, master's
Calendar:	quarters
Public/Private:	private nonprofit
Number of full-time faculty:	319
Student-to-teacher ratio:	18:1

Admissions requirements:
- **Options:** early admission, electronic application
- **Application fee:** $50
- **Required:** high school transcript, 3 letters of recommendation, SAT or ACT
- **Application deadlines:** continuous (freshmen), continuous (transfer)
- **Early decision:** —
- **Notification:** continuous (freshmen), continuous (transfer)

Average high school GPA:	—
Average freshman SAT verbal/math score:	552 / 538
Average freshman ACT score:	23
Number of applicants:	4,100
Number of applicants accepted:	2,960
Percentage of students from out of state:	85%
Total freshman enrollment:	1,285
Total enrollment:	6,776
Percentage of students who live in campus housing:	33%
Total tuition:	$21,600
Total cost with fees & expenses:	$32,300
Average financial aid package:	$8,100

SAVANNAH COLLEGE OF ART AND DESIGN

MAJORS

- Animation, Interactive Technology, Video Graphics and Special Effects
- Applied Art
- Architectural History and Criticism, General
- Architecture
- Art History, Criticism and Conservation
- Cinematography and Film/Video Production
- Computer Graphics
- Design and Applied Arts, Other
- Design and Visual Communications, General
- Digital Communication and Media/Multimedia
- Drama and Dramatics/Theatre Arts, General
- Fashion/Apparel Design
- Fiber, Textile and Weaving Arts
- Graphic Design
- Historic Preservation and Conservation
- Illustration
- Industrial Design
- Interior Design
- Metal and Jewelry Arts
- Painting
- Photography
- Recording Arts Technology/Technician

SAVANNAH STATE UNIVERSITY

3219 College Avenue
Savannah, GA 31404

(912) 356-2186
http://www.savstate.edu/

BIG DEAL

BIG FISH

UNIVERSITY 101
Freshman Year Experience Office to help answer questions and solve problems; required first-year transitional seminar; special academic advisors assigned to first-years; upperclassman mentors; optional first-year residential learning communities; optional first-year leadership program; extended orientation program.

Historic charm and lively culture might draw you to Savannah State, but its environmental programs will keep you there.

In a state known for schools with strong engineering and technology programs, Savannah State offers unique environmental and marine science degree options. Just 10 minutes from the Atlantic Ocean, the school's location provides the perfect natural laboratory for hands-on work. Students learn about the ecology, biology, and preservation of our earth by exploring Georgia's waterways on university-owned boats. Courses may take place in on-campus laboratories or directly in the middle of salt marshes, beaches, or the ocean.

SAVANNAH STATE UNIVERSITY

WHAT IT IS

As the oldest public, historically black institution in Georgia, Savannah State University has transformed the lives of generations of students in a nurturing learning environment since its founding in 1890. As a senior unit of the University System of Georgia, Savannah State continues that tradition in classrooms in which cutting-edge instruction is complemented by one of the lowest student-faculty ratios in the region. Its programs are designed to provide opportunities for students to improve themselves, attain career objectives, and compete effectively in the job market. Savannah State offers degrees through its Colleges of Business Administration, Liberal Arts and Social Sciences, and Sciences and Technology.

Most undergraduate students enrolled at Savannah State University are Georgia residents, although 18 states and 17 other countries are represented. Students can participate in numerous social and academic organizations, as well as intercollegiate and intramural sports. Campus housing options include traditional residence halls and an apartment-style complex that features fully furnished one-, two-, and four-bedroom apartments. A Freshman Living Learning Center opened August 2003 to house new students in a state-of-the-art environment.

WHERE IT'S AT

The university is located in beautiful, historic Savannah, Georgia. The campus is a 10-minute drive from the Atlantic Ocean and the sandy beaches of Tybee Island. Students at Savannah State enjoy the best of two worlds—the cultural advantages of a metropolitan city and the sun and surf of the ocean and boating, fishing, and waterskiing on the many area rivers. The city also offers excellent golfing and tennis facilities. Culturally, the city offers the Savannah Symphony Orchestra, ballet and theater groups, the Telfair Museum of Arts and Sciences, the King-Tisdell Black Heritage Museum, and special celebrations and festivals such as Night in Old Savannah. Savannah State University partners with the city to produce the annual Black Heritage Festival, a monthlong heritage celebration that includes lectures, dance performances, concerts, and more. Savannah is also famous for its Low Country cuisine, scenic boat tours, specialty shops, and riverfront activities.

THE DETAILS

Campus setting:	suburban
Degrees:	bachelor's, master's
Calendar:	semesters
Public/Private:	public state
Number of full-time faculty:	123
Student-to-teacher ratio:	18:1

Admissions requirements:
- **Options:** common application, deferred entrance, early admission, electronic application
- **Application fee:** $20
- **Required:** high school transcript, SAT or ACT, SAT (recommended)
- **Application deadlines:** 6/1 (freshmen), 6/1 (transfer)
- **Early decision:** —
- **Notification:** continuous (freshmen), continuous (transfer)

Average high school GPA:	2.82
Average freshman SAT verbal/math score:	459 / 455
Average freshman ACT score:	17
Number of applicants:	3,926
Number of applicants accepted:	1,254
Percentage of students from out of state:	17%
Total freshman enrollment:	568
Total enrollment:	2,800
Percentage of students who live in campus housing:	45%
Total in-state tuition, fees & expenses:	$8,038
Total out-of-state tuition, fees & expenses:	$15,006
Average financial aid package:	$3,200

SAVANNAH STATE UNIVERSITY

MAJORS

- Accounting
- African-American/Black Studies
- Biology/Biological Sciences, General
- Business Administration and Management, General
- Chemical Engineering
- Chemistry, General
- Civil Engineering, General
- Civil Engineering Technology/Technician
- Computer Engineering, General
- Computer Engineering Technology/Technician
- Criminal Justice/Law Enforcement Administration
- Electrical, Electronic and Communications Engineering Technology/Technician
- English Language and Literature, General
- Environmental Studies
- History, General
- International Business/Trade/Commerce
- Management Information Systems, General
- Marine Biology and Biological Oceanography
- Marketing/Marketing Management, General
- Mass Communication/Media Studies
- Mathematics, General
- Mechanical Engineering/Mechanical Technology/Technician
- Music, General
- Parks, Recreation and Leisure Facilities Management
- Political Science and Government, General
- Social Work
- Sociology
- Visual and Performing Arts, General

SOUTHERN POLYTECHNIC STATE UNIVERSITY

1100 South Marietta Parkway
Marietta, GA 30060

(678) 915-7778
http://www.spsu.edu/

BIG DEAL

UNIVERSITY 101
Extended orientation program; first-year extracurricular and social activities; required first-year residential learning communities; mandatory first-year residential tutoring for general-education courses; special academic advisors assigned to first-years.

BIG IDEA

Calling all geeks! Southern Polytechnic wants *you*.

Science- and technology-related majors are the only academic programs offered on this campus. Bonus: Students graduate with more than just a degree. The school's Cooperative Education program provides work experience and a sizable paycheck (by college student standards). Co-ops are open to all majors and pay an average of $2,152 per month for students starting out and $2,468 for veteran co-opers. Students may either take a semester (or two) off to work with their co-op employer full-time or choose to work part-time while still taking classes. If you're thinking about taking advantage of this program, you'd better plan ahead. Co-ops last a minimum of three semesters.

SOUTHERN POLYTECHNIC STATE UNIVERSITY

WHAT IT IS

Since Southern Polytechnic State University was founded in 1948 as a two-year technical institute, the university has developed an excellent academic reputation and is home to a diverse population of approximately 4,000 students. The university focuses on the sciences and technology and aims to produce graduates who will be successful in their chosen fields. Professors have extensive research and work experience in their fields, and active, experiential learning is their educational approach. Southern Polytechnic State also offers innovative programs to give students a background in the latest technology. For example, the institution was one of the first in the country to offer an undergraduate degree in engineering technology. Further, the university offers several evening and weekend courses to meet the various needs and schedules of its students. Many students take advantage of internship opportunities with companies in nearby Atlanta, and it's not unusual for the same corporations to recruit Southern Polytechnic alums after graduation.

WHERE IT'S AT

Students at Southern Polytechnic State University live and work on the school's 193-acre campus in Marietta, Georgia. The institution's 35 buildings are spread out across a peaceful, wooded landscape that provides the perfect environment for studying. Historic downtown Marietta is the center of this vibrant community and features numerous unique shops, restaurants, and businesses. Students are just a 20-minute drive from downtown Atlanta, where they might take in an Atlanta Braves baseball game or a play at one of the city's theaters. Between the campus, the town, and the city, students have the best of all worlds.

THE DETAILS

Campus setting:	suburban
Degrees:	bachelor's, master's
Calendar:	semesters
Public/Private:	public state
Number of full-time faculty:	137
Student-to-teacher ratio:	17:1

Admissions requirements:
- **Options:** early admission
- **Application fee:** $20
- **Required:** high school transcript, SAT or ACT
- **Application deadlines:** 8/1 (freshmen), 8/1 (transfer)
- **Early decision:** —
- **Notification:** continuous (freshmen), continuous (transfer)

Average high school GPA:	3.17
Average freshman SAT verbal/math score:	553 / 576
Average freshman ACT score:	22
Number of applicants:	1,069
Number of applicants accepted:	668
Percentage of students from out of state:	5%
Total freshman enrollment:	439
Total enrollment:	3,801
Percentage of students who live in campus housing:	12%
Total in-state tuition, fees & expenses:	$8,838
Total out-of-state tuition, fees & expenses:	$16,120
Average financial aid package:	$2,406

SOUTHERN POLYTECHNIC STATE UNIVERSITY

MAJORS

- Architectural Engineering Technology/Technician
- Architecture
- Biology/Biological Sciences, General
- Civil Engineering Technology/Technician
- Computer and Information Sciences, General
- Computer and Information Sciences and Support Services, Other
- Computer Engineering Technology/Technician
- Construction Engineering Technology/Technician
- Electrical, Electronic and Communications Engineering Technology/Technician
- Electrical and Electronic Engineering Technologies/Technicians, Other
- Entrepreneurship/Entrepreneurial Studies
- Industrial Production Technologies/Technicians, Other
- Industrial Technology/Technician
- Information Science/Studies
- International Relations and Affairs
- Mathematics, General
- Mechanical Engineering/Mechanical Technology/Technician
- Organizational Behavior Studies
- Physics, General
- Survey Technology/Surveying
- Technical and Business Writing
- Telecommunications

SPELMAN COLLEGE

350 Spelman Lane, SW
Atlanta, GA 30314

(404) 681-3643
http://www.spelman.edu/

BIG FISH

UNIVERSITY 101
Extended orientation program; required first-year transitional seminar; special academic advisors assigned to first-years; first year–only extracurricular and social events; special academic advising, peer tutoring, and study rooms available for first-year science, engineering, and mathematics students.

Spelman expects a lot from the women accepted into its programs.

In return, students get a first-rate education on a gorgeous campus just minutes from downtown Atlanta. Through the Spelman ALIVE initiative, the school has vowed to maintain its high standards through a combined program of academic excellence, leadership development, improved environment, visible achievements, and exemplary customer service. Students are put through the ringer in tough classes taught by tenured and accomplished faculty (84 percent have their PhDs). A low student-teacher ratio means that you'll have teachers around to mentor you and answer your questions for all four years. The college is a member of the largest consortium of historically black institutions in the world.

SPELMAN COLLEGE

WHAT IT IS

An historically black, liberal arts college for women, Spelman College was founded in 1881. The campus has grown from only nine acres of drill ground and five frame barracks used for federal troops after the Civil War to 32 acres and 26 buildings. As an integral part of the Atlanta University Center, Spelman benefits from proximity to and cooperation with the other member institutions, but it maintains its own identity nonetheless, thus offering outstanding opportunities for the education of women for leadership roles.

A focal point of campus activity is the Manley College Center, which houses the dining hall, a food court, faculty and student lounges, and student government and administrative offices. There is a varied program of student and professional cultural activities on the campus. Many of the extracurricular activities are planned and sponsored by the Student Government Association. Others are presented by departmental honor societies and clubs, excellent dance groups, and both jazz and classical instrumental ensembles. The strong tradition in fine arts at Spelman gives students maximum cultural exposure through the renowned Spelman Glee Club, the Spelman-Morehouse Chorus, and the Spelman-Morehouse Players. Health and physical education facilities include a gymnasium, tennis courts, a swimming pool, bowling lanes, dance studios, and a weight room. Student thought is expressed through several publications: *Reflections*, the yearbook; *Spotlight*, the newspaper; and *Focus*, the literary magazine. Religious life and services form an important part of campus life. Opportunities to experience fellowship meaningfully, special convocations, and counseling are provided.

WHERE IT'S AT

Spelman College is located in Atlanta, known as "The Gateway to the South," a city that is rapidly becoming one of the most dynamic and vital urban areas in the country. Proximity to other colleges and universities in the area provides additional educational, social, and cultural opportunities. The city is one of the most exciting learning laboratories imaginable. Here, women can observe politics at work and can meet some of the world's leaders. As an urban center with crucial social problems, Atlanta challenges students to become involved in community programs. An extensive community services program coordinates the placement of students in community agencies.

THE DETAILS

Campus setting:	urban
Degrees:	bachelor's
Calendar:	semesters
Public/Private:	private nonprofit
Number of full-time faculty:	164
Student-to-teacher ratio:	12:1

Admissions requirements:
- **Options:** common application, deferred entrance, early admission, early action, electronic application
- **Application fee:** $35
- **Required:** essay or personal statement, high school transcript, 2 letters of recommendation, SAT or ACT
- **Application deadlines:** 2/1 (freshmen), 2/1 (transfer)
- **Early action:** —
- **Notification:** 4/1 (freshmen), 4/1 (transfer), — (early action)

Average high school GPA:	3.49
Average freshman SAT verbal/math score:	545 / 530
Average freshman ACT score:	22
Number of applicants:	3,978
Number of applicants accepted:	1,887
Percentage of students from out of state:	70%
Total freshman enrollment:	590
Total enrollment:	2,186
Percentage of students who live in campus housing:	53%
Total tuition:	$13,525
Total cost with fees & expenses:	$24,400
Average financial aid package:	$4,473

SPELMAN COLLEGE

MAJORS

- Anthropology
- Art/Art Studies, General
- Biochemistry
- Biology/Biological Sciences, General
- Chemistry, General
- Computer Science
- Developmental and Child Psychology
- Drama and Dramatics/Theatre Arts, General
- Economics, General
- Engineering, General
- English Language and Literature, General
- Environmental Studies
- French Language and Literature
- History, General
- Mathematics, General
- Music, General
- Natural Sciences
- Philosophy
- Physics, General
- Political Science and Government, General
- Psychology, General
- Religion/Religious Studies
- Sociology
- Spanish Language and Literature
- Women's Studies

THOMAS UNIVERSITY

1501 Millpond Road
Thomasville, GA 31792

(229) 226-1621
http://www.thomasu.edu/

BIG FISH

UNIVERSITY 101
Required first-year transitional seminar; extended orientation program.

Want a school where everyone knows your name?

Everyone knows everyone on this 600-plus-student Thomasville campus, and the school maintains a low student-teacher ratio. Thomas faculty members are known for having a vested interest in their school. You'll see your professors in class, of course, but there's a good chance that you'll also see them supporting student productions, hosting exam review sessions, giving students extra help after class, or helping students with their independent projects. Acting as mentors, teachers, and advisors, Thomas faculty give education a personal touch.

THOMAS UNIVERSITY

WHAT IT IS

Since Thomas University's first classes (with only nine students) were held in 1954, the institution has been committed to providing a high-quality education to both traditional and nontraditional students. The school began offering four-year degrees in 1988 and focuses on developing programs that prepare graduates for careers. At the same time, the university ensures that students graduate with a solid foundation in the liberal arts. Popular programs include education, nursing, and criminal justice.

The university has an enrollment of fewer than 700 and an average class size of fewer than 10. Students receive individual attention from their professors, who often lead them on trips abroad and to professional meetings or coordinate service projects in the local community. Thomas University has a history of placing nearly all of its graduates in major-related jobs after graduation.

WHERE IT'S AT

Thomas University is located in Thomasville, Georgia, a town with a population of about 18,000. This community in the rural southwestern part of the state is 55 miles south of Albany, 45 miles west of Valdosta, and 35 miles north of Tallahassee, Florida. The university's campus was once the grounds of Birdwood Plantation, the former home of the U.S. ambassador to Japan. Thomasville and the surrounding area are home to many stately antebellum mansions, and the landscape is dotted with azaleas, moss-covered oak trees, and rose gardens. The city's annual spring rose festival is a popular attraction, as are the shops and restaurants in the Victorian-era downtown. The local farmers' market is one of the largest in the state.

THE DETAILS

Campus setting:	small town
Degrees:	bachelor's, master's
Calendar:	semesters
Public/Private:	private nonprofit
Number of full-time faculty:	46
Student-to-teacher ratio:	10:1

Admissions requirements:
- **Options:** deferred entrance, early admission, electronic application
- **Application fee:** $25
- **Required:** high school transcript
- **Application deadlines:** continuous (freshmen), continuous (transfer)
- **Early decision:** —
- **Notification:** continuous (freshmen), continuous (transfer)

Average high school GPA:	—
Average freshman SAT verbal/math score:	—/—
Average freshman ACT score:	—
Number of applicants:	—
Number of applicants accepted:	—
Percentage of students from out of state:	4%
Total freshman enrollment:	74
Total enrollment:	783
Percentage of students who live in campus housing:	9%
Total tuition:	$10,200
Total cost with fees & expenses:	$11,620
Average financial aid package:	$5,119

THOMAS UNIVERSITY

MAJORS

- Accounting
- Biology/Biological Sciences, General
- Business Administration and Management, General
- Communication Studies/Speech Communication and Rhetoric
- Criminal Justice/Law Enforcement Administration
- Criminology
- Early Childhood Education and Teaching
- English Language and Literature, General
- Humanities/Humanistic Studies
- Junior High/Intermediate/Middle School Education and Teaching
- Kindergarten/Preschool Education and Teaching
- Liberal Arts and Sciences/Liberal Studies
- Nursing/Registered Nurse Training
- Parks, Recreation and Leisure Facilities Management
- Political Science and Government, General
- Psychology, General
- Rehabilitation Therapy
- Secondary Education and Teaching
- Social Sciences, General
- Social Work
- Sociology

UNIVERSITY OF GEORGIA

Terrell Hall
Athens, GA 30602

(706) 542-3000
http://www.uga.edu/

BIG DEAL

BIG REP

UNIVERSITY 101
Extended orientation program; optional first-year transitional seminar; optional first-year leadership trips; optional first-year service-learning projects; optional first-year wilderness trips; optional first-year summer intensive courses taking place on campus three weeks before classes start.

Welcome to Smartypants U.

At the University of Georgia, you can take classes with Pulitzer Prize winners, Fulbright scholars, and members of the National Academy of Sciences, American Academy of Arts and Science, and National Society of Engineers. You can also find yourself receiving a grade from a certified genius. In 2003, Eve Troutt Powell, an associate professor of history, landed a $500,000 grant from the MacArthur Foundation, nicknamed "the Genius Award." Get the picture? Also in 2003, the school spent more than $299 million on faculty and student research, more than any other institution without a medical or engineering school. Georgia students are just as driven as their teachers. In the 2003–2004 academic year, the Georgia student body scored three Goldwater Scholarships, two Truman Scholarships, two Mellon Fellowships, and one Marshall Scholarship. Since being founded in 1784, the university has also produced 19 Rhodes scholars.

UNIVERSITY OF GEORGIA

WHAT IT IS

Chartered in 1785, the University of Georgia is the oldest state-chartered public university in the United States. UGA is the state's flagship institution of higher education. It is also the state's most comprehensive and most diversified institution of higher education. Its motto, "To teach, to serve, and to inquire into the nature of things," reflects the university's integral and unique role in conserving and enhancing our intellectual, cultural, and environmental heritage. As a public research institution, UGA offers numerous opportunities for academic research, study abroad, and interdisciplinary study.

Approximately 25,000 of the university's total enrollment are students attending the university as undergraduates. The university attracts students from all 50 states and the District of Columbia, as well as more than 130 countries. Its proximity to the large metropolitan area of Atlanta provides students opportunities for internships and externships, research opportunities, and careers after graduation.

WHERE IT'S AT

The university's main campus, in Athens, Georgia, covers 706 acres and includes 367 buildings. To its north, the campus adjoins historic downtown Athens, which features many boutiques, restaurants, entertainment options, and service businesses. The university covers 4,308 acres in Clarke County and owns a total of 42,064 acres throughout the state. Considered one of the nation's best college towns, Athens is home to a vibrant and popular music scene, earning recognition by *Rolling Stone* magazine in 2003 as the number-one music city in the United States. In proximity to the foothills of the Blue Ridge Mountains, Athens is approximately 70 miles northeast of Atlanta, making it easily accessible.

THE DETAILS

Campus setting:	suburban
Degrees:	bachelor's, master's, doctoral
Calendar:	semesters
Public/Private:	public state
Number of full-time faculty:	1,661
Student-to-teacher ratio:	15:1

Admissions requirements:
- **Options:** deferred entrance, early admission, early action, electronic application
- **Application fee:** $50
- **Required:** high school transcript, SAT or ACT
- **Application deadlines:** 2/1 (freshmen), 4/1 (transfer)
- **Early action:** 11/1
- **Notification:** 4/1 (freshmen), continuous (transfer), 12/15 (early action)

Average high school GPA:	3.65
Average freshman SAT verbal/math score:	616 / 620
Average freshman ACT score:	25
Number of applicants:	13,267
Number of applicants accepted:	8,197
Percentage of students from out of state:	15%
Total freshman enrollment:	4,500
Total enrollment:	33,405
Percentage of students who live in campus housing:	27%
Total in-state tuition, fees & expenses:	$11,028
Total out-of-state tuition, fees & expenses:	$22,344
Average financial aid package:	$7,058

MAJORS

- Accounting
- Advertising
- African-American/Black Studies
- Agricultural/Biological
- Engineering and Bioengineering
- Agricultural Business and Management, General
- Agricultural Economics
- Agricultural Teacher Education
- Agronomy and Crop Science
- Ancient/Classical Greek Language and Literature
- Animal Genetics
- Animal Sciences, General
- Anthropology
- Apparel and Textiles, General

UNIVERSITY OF GEORGIA

- Applied Horticulture/Horticultural Operations, General
- Art/Art Studies, General
- Art History, Criticism and Conservation
- Art Teacher Education
- Astronomy
- Biochemistry
- Biological and Physical Sciences
- Biology/Biological Sciences, General
- Biotechnology
- Botany/Plant Biology
- Broadcast Journalism
- Business/Commerce, General
- Business/Managerial Economics
- Business Administration and Management, General
- Business Teacher Education
- Cell/Cellular Biology and Histology
- Chemistry, General
- Classics and Languages, Literatures and Linguistics, General
- Cognitive Psychology and Psycholinguistics
- Communication Disorders, General
- Comparative Literature
- Computer and Information Sciences, General
- Consumer Economics
- Criminal Justice/Safety Studies
- Dairy Science
- Dietetics/Dietitians
- Drama and Dance Teacher Education
- Drama and Dramatics/Theatre Arts, General
- Ecology
- Economics, General
- Educational Psychology
- English/Language Arts Teacher Education
- English Language and Literature, General
- Entomology
- Environmental Health
- Family and Consumer Sciences/Home Economics Teacher Education
- Fashion Merchandising
- Film/Cinema Studies
- Finance, General
- Fine/Studio Arts, General
- Fishing and Fisheries Sciences and Management
- Foods, Nutrition, and Wellness Studies, General
- Food Science
- Foreign Languages and Literatures, General
- Foreign Language Teacher Education
- Forestry, General
- Forest Sciences and Biology
- French Language and Literature
- Geography
- Geology/Earth Science, General
- German Language and Literature
- Health Teacher Education
- History, General
- Housing and Human Environments, General
- Human Development and Family Studies, General
- Insurance
- International Business/Trade/Commerce
- Italian Language and Literature
- Japanese Language and Literature
- Journalism
- Junior High/Intermediate/Middle School Education and Teaching
- Kindergarten/Preschool Education and Teaching
- Landscape Architecture
- Landscaping and Groundskeeping
- Latin Language and Literature
- Liberal Arts and Sciences/Liberal Studies
- Linguistics
- Management Information Systems, General
- Marketing/Marketing Management, General
- Mass Communication/Media Studies
- Mathematics, General
- Mathematics Teacher Education
- Medical Microbiology and Bacteriology
- Music, General
- Music Performance, General
- Music Teacher Education
- Music Theory and Composition
- Music Therapy/Therapist
- Pharmacy
- Philosophy
- Physical Education Teaching and Coaching
- Plant Protection and Integrated Pest Management
- Political Science and Government, General
- Poultry Science
- Psychology, General
- Public Relations/Image Management
- Radio and Television Broadcasting Technology/Technician
- Reading Teacher Education
- Real Estate
- Religion/Religious Studies
- Russian Language and Literature
- Sales and Marketing Operations/Marketing and Distribution Teacher Education
- Science Teacher Education/General Science Teacher Education
- Slavic Languages, Literatures, and Linguistics, General
- Social Science Teacher Education
- Social Work
- Sociology
- Spanish Language and Literature
- Special Education and Teaching, General
- Speech and Rhetorical Studies
- Sport and Fitness Administration/Management
- Statistics, General
- Technology Teacher Education/Industrial Arts Teacher Education
- Turf and Turfgrass Management
- Wildlife and Wildlands Science and Management
- Women's Studies

UNIVERSITY OF WEST GEORGIA

1601 Maple Street
Carrollton, GA 30118

(678) 839-5000
http://www.westga.edu/

BIG DEAL

UNIVERSITY 101
Upperclassman mentors; optional first-year residential learning communities; faculty mentors for learning community students; optional first-year leadership training for learning community students; optional first-year transitional seminar (required for learning community students); extended orientation program.

BIG FISH

How would you like to skip high school and go straight to college?

If you find high school a breeze, the University of West Georgia's Advanced Academy of Georgia can strip you from the throes of high school boredom and send you on a whirlwind educational trip. Students can apply during sophomore or junior year (exceptions have been made for younger, highly talented students). One of the only programs of its kind in the country, the academy allows students to earn high school and college credit at the same time. But this isn't an extended recess—students take normal college-level courses. If you apply as a regular first-year, you should know that UWG offers one of the most comprehensive first-year orientation and support programs around.

UNIVERSITY OF WEST GEORGIA

WHAT IT IS

The University of West Georgia is a charter member of the University System of Georgia. From its beginnings in 1906 as the Fourth District Agricultural and Mechanical School, West Georgia has grown into a leading comprehensive university that offers programs of study through three colleges—the College of Arts and Sciences, the Richards College of Business, and the College of Education. In addition, the Honors College, the only college of its kind in Georgia, offers an honors curriculum, and the university's Advanced Academy of Georgia is one of fewer than 12 programs in the nation that allows gifted high school juniors and seniors to live and study full-time at a university while completing high school graduation requirements in absentia.

UWG takes its motto of "Educational excellence in a personal environment" seriously. First-years live on campus in one of 13 residence halls and can join a learning community of students who live in the same hall and share classes. Those who participate often earn higher grades as a result. Extracurricular activities are sponsored through approximately 100 student organizations, which cover academics, professional and honor groups, politics, religion, service, recreation and sports, social fraternities and sororities, and a national champion debate team. West Georgia also has a nationally competitive cheerleading program, featuring the national champion co-ed team for four consecutive years (2002–2005), the 2004 national champion all-female squad, and a partner stunt team that ranked second in the United States in 2004 and 2005.

WHERE IT'S AT

Fifty miles west of Atlanta, the campus extends over more than 600 wooded acres in Carrollton—the cultural, educational, health-care, and commercial center for the west Georgia region. A progressive city of about 20,000, with a diverse economic base, Carrollton offers a wide range of opportunities for professional and cultural experiences. Shops, galleries, and restaurants line the downtown square, and the city offers movies, dancing, theatrical productions, and dining that ranges from Southern to gourmet and international cuisine. A new $6 million Cultural Arts Center showcases the arts, and recreational activities abound through the county's 33,421 acres of state, public, and private recreational parks and facilities.

THE DETAILS

Campus setting:	small town
Degrees:	bachelor's, master's, doctoral
Calendar:	semesters
Public/Private:	public state
Number of full-time faculty:	384
Student-to-teacher ratio:	19:1

Admissions requirements:
- **Options:** early admission, electronic application
- **Application fee:** $20
- **Required:** high school transcript, letter of recommendation, SAT or ACT
- **Application deadlines:** 7/1 (freshmen), 6/1 (transfer)
- **Early decision:** —
- **Notification:** 8/1 (freshmen), continuous (transfer)

Average high school GPA:	2.97
Average freshman SAT verbal/math score:	511 / 505
Average freshman ACT score:	21
Number of applicants:	4,953
Number of applicants accepted:	3,031
Percentage of students from out of state:	3%
Total freshman enrollment:	1,860
Total enrollment:	10,216
Percentage of students who live in campus housing:	30%
Total in-state tuition, fees & expenses:	$8,056
Total out-of-state tuition, fees & expenses:	$15,024
Average financial aid package:	$6,771

UNIVERSITY OF WEST GEORGIA

MAJORS

- Accounting
- Anthropology
- Art/Art Studies, General
- Biology/Biological Sciences, General
- Biology Teacher Education
- Business/Managerial Economics
- Business Administration and Management, General
- Business Teacher Education
- Chemistry, General
- Chemistry Teacher Education
- Computer and Information Sciences, General
- Criminal Justice/Safety Studies
- Drama and Dramatics/Theatre Arts, General
- Economics, General
- Economics, Other
- Education/Teaching of Individuals with Mental Retardation
- Elementary Education and Teaching
- English Language and Literature, General
- Environmental Studies
- Finance, General
- French Language and Literature
- Geography
- Geological and Earth Sciences/Geosciences, Other
- Geology/Earth Science, General
- German Language and Literature
- History, General
- International Economics
- International Relations and Affairs
- Journalism
- Junior High/Intermediate/Middle School Education and Teaching
- Management Information Systems, General
- Marketing/Marketing Management, General
- Mathematics, General
- Microbiological Sciences and Immunology, Other
- Music Performance, General
- Music Teacher Education
- Music Theory and Composition
- Nursing/Registered Nurse Training
- Office Management and Supervision
- Parks, Recreation and Leisure Facilities Management
- Philosophy
- Physical Education Teaching and Coaching
- Physics, General
- Physics Teacher Education
- Political Science and Government, General
- Pre-Law Studies
- Pre-Medicine/Pre-Medical Studies
- Pre-Veterinary Studies
- Psychology, General
- Real Estate
- Secondary Education and Teaching
- Sociology
- Spanish Language and Literature
- Speech-Language Pathology/Pathologist

VALDOSTA STATE UNIVERSITY

1500 North Patterson Street
Valdosta, GA 31698

(229) 333-5800
http://www.valdosta.edu/

BIG DEAL

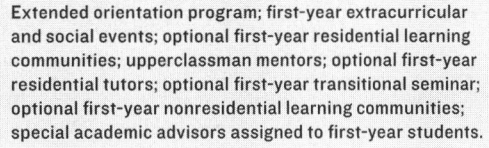

BIG FISH

UNIVERSITY 101
Extended orientation program; first-year extracurricular and social events; optional first-year residential learning communities; upperclassman mentors; optional first-year residential tutors; optional first-year transitional seminar; optional first-year nonresidential learning communities; special academic advisors assigned to first-year students.

Brick-and-mortar classrooms? Yup. Online? Uh-huh. Distince-learning? You bet.

Valdosta's got you covered, no matter how you want to get an education. Valdosta's online and distance-learning programs are just as strong as their in-class counterparts. Valdosta students have the freedom to choose how and where they want to complete their degrees. Traditional day classes are always an option, but students may also choose to fulfill their degree requirements completely or partially online, during a semester or year abroad, or in a work-placement setting. The university also operates 11 satellite campuses and two campuses on military bases to provide learning opportunities to all students throughout Georgia.

VALDOSTA STATE UNIVERSITY

WHAT IT IS

Established in 1906, Valdosta State University offers students from nearly every state and 63 countries an education in such areas as health care and teaching. The school currently awards baccalaureate degrees in 53 subject areas, and the most popular majors include accounting, biology, criminal justice, nursing, early childhood education, and communications.

Students receive individualized attention from full professors (not graduate assistants), and enormous lectures are hard to come by with its low average undergraduate class size. The school has also invested heavily in new technology, with 73 student computer labs and a state-of-the-art fiber optic data network.

A recent library expansion project added an Internet café and workstations, which provide students with access to an array of materials that are not included in the university's collection of 1.7 million volumes.

WHERE IT'S AT

Valdosta, Georgia, is located in the southern part of the state, midway between Atlanta and Orlando, Florida. It is the tenth-largest city in Georgia—the population of the city and surrounding area is about 123,000—and located just 15 miles from the Florida border. The school's two campuses, landscaped with palm trees and azaleas, occupy more than 170 acres; its buildings are beautiful examples of Spanish Mission– and modified Georgian–style architecture. Recently, the university embarked on a major building project, beginning construction on new student housing and renovating existing residences. The Atlantic coast is about three hours from campus, making a day or weekend trip to the beach easy for students who need a break from their studies.

THE DETAILS

Campus setting:	small town
Degrees:	bachelor's, master's, doctoral
Calendar:	semesters
Public/Private:	public state
Number of full-time faculty:	420
Student-to-teacher ratio:	21:1

Admissions requirements:
- **Options:** early admission, electronic application
- **Application fee:** $20
- **Required:** high school transcript, SAT or ACT
- **Application deadlines:** 7/1 (freshmen), 8/1 (transfer)
- **Early decision:** —
- **Notification:** continuous (freshmen), continuous (transfer)

Average high school GPA:	3.03
Average freshman SAT verbal/math score:	517 / 517
Average freshman ACT score:	22
Number of applicants:	5,224
Number of applicants accepted:	3,440
Percentage of students from out of state:	6%
Total freshman enrollment:	1,690
Total enrollment:	10,400
Percentage of students who live in campus housing:	17%
Total in-state tuition, fees & expenses:	$8,950
Total out-of-state tuition, fees & expenses:	$15,918
Average financial aid package:	$8,045

VALDOSTA STATE UNIVERSITY

MAJORS

- Accounting
- Administrative Assistant and Secretarial Science, General
- Applied Mathematics
- Art/Art Studies, General
- Art Teacher Education
- Astronomy
- Biology/Biological Sciences, General
- Business/Commerce, General
- Business/Managerial Economics
- Business Administration and Management, General
- Business Teacher Education
- Chemistry, General
- Chemistry Teacher Education
- Communication Studies/Speech Communication and Rhetoric
- Computer and Information Sciences, General
- Computer Systems Analysis/Analyst
- Criminal Justice/Safety Studies
- Early Childhood Education and Teaching
- Economics, General
- Elementary Education and Teaching
- Engineering Technology, General
- English/Language Arts Teacher Education
- English Language and Literature, General
- Finance, General
- Foreign Language Teacher Education
- French Language and Literature
- General Studies
- Health and Physical Education, General
- History, General
- Information Science/Studies
- Interior Design
- Junior High/Intermediate/Middle School Education and Teaching
- Kinesiology and Exercise Science
- Legal Assistant/Paralegal
- Marketing/Marketing Management, General
- Mathematics, General
- Mathematics Teacher Education
- Music, General
- Music Performance, General
- Music Teacher Education
- Natural Resources/Conservation, General
- Nursing/Registered Nurse Training
- Philosophy
- Physical Education Teaching and Coaching
- Physics, General
- Political Science and Government, General
- Psychology, General
- School Psychology
- Science Teacher Education/General Science Teacher Education
- Secondary Education and Teaching
- Social Studies Teacher Education
- Sociology
- Spanish Language and Literature
- Special Education and Teaching, General
- Speech-Language Pathology/Pathologist
- Trade and Industrial Teacher Education
- Visual and Performing Arts, General

WESLEYAN COLLEGE

4760 Forsyth Road
Macon, GA 31210

(478) 477-1110
http://www.wesleyancollege.edu/

BIG IDEA

UNIVERSITY 101
Extended orientation program; first-year residential computer assistants; special academic advisors assigned to first-year students.

Wesleyan is a college of "firsts."

The world's oldest college for women, Wesleyan trained the first female medical doctor and the first woman to argue a case before the Georgia Supreme Court. Accomplished and available, professors encourage their students to continue their studies outside of the classroom through off-campus work-placement programs and study abroad trips. Through partnerships with the National Student Exchange and the Institute for the International Education of Students, Wesleyan students can study abroad just about anywhere in the world. More than 175 domestic sites and 15 countries around the globe host Wesleyan students each semester during long- and short-term excursions.

WHAT IT IS

Wesleyan College, chartered in 1836, has the distinction of being the world's first college chartered to grant degrees to women. Today, Wesleyan is regarded as one of the nation's finest colleges and remains dedicated to the education of women. Wesleyan is a Methodist-related liberal arts college, and enrollment is limited to fewer than 1,000 students. This is done primarily to support a learner-based curriculum that limits classes to no more than 20 students and to provide opportunities for meaningful participation in the life of the college community.

The Georgian-style brick buildings on campus include two student apartment buildings. All residential halls have been recently renovated and offer single rooms and suites. A multipurpose athletic facility includes a fitness center, an equestrian center, tennis courts, and soccer and softball fields. Among other recreational facilities are a gymnasium with a heated pool and a lake with a jogging trail. The Campus Activities Board plans concert-dance weekends, events with nearby colleges, international fashion shows, holiday trips, and special dinners. The Council on Religious Concerns encourages religious life on campus and sponsors activities that involve students with community life. Students volunteer at local institutions, such as the Georgia Academy for the Blind, the Methodist Children's Home, and neighborhood schools and churches. They also participate in special interest clubs, student publications, performing arts groups, honor societies, and professional fraternities. A number of college traditions are perpetuated by spirited but friendly competition among the four classes.

WHERE IT'S AT

The college is located on a 200-acre wooded campus in a suburb of the beautiful, historic city of Macon, Georgia, the third-largest city in the state. Macon is the cultural, educational, medical, and economic leader of middle Georgia and located about an hour's drive south of Atlanta. The city of Macon offers varied entertainment and many cultural opportunities, including both the Georgia Music and Sports Halls of Fame. Visits by nationally and internationally acclaimed speakers and a series of popular and classical concerts are held on the Wesleyan campus each year, as are special events associated with Macon's renowned Cherry Blossom Festival.

THE DETAILS

Campus setting:	suburban
Degrees:	bachelor's, master's
Calendar:	semesters
Public/Private:	private religious
Number of full-time faculty:	50
Student-to-teacher ratio:	10:1

Admissions requirements:
- **Options:** common application, deferred entrance, early admission, early decision, early action
- **Application fee:** $30
- **Required:** essay or personal statement, high school transcript, letter of recommendation, SAT or ACT
- **Application deadlines:** 3/1 (freshmen), continuous (transfer), 2/1 (early action)
- **Early decision:** 11/15
- **Notification:** 8/1 (freshmen), 8/1 (transfer), 12/15 (early decision), 3/1 (early action)

Average high school GPA:	3.50
Average freshman SAT verbal/math score:	568/548
Average freshman ACT score:	23
Number of applicants:	400
Number of applicants accepted:	220
Percentage of students from out of state:	21%
Total freshman enrollment:	75
Total enrollment:	639
Percentage of students who live in campus housing:	63%
Total tuition:	$10,050
Total cost with fees & expenses:	$19,150
Average financial aid package:	$10,811

WESLEYAN COLLEGE

MAJORS

- Advertising
- American/United States Studies/Civilization
- Art History, Criticism and Conservation
- Biology/Biological Sciences, General
- Business Administration and Management, General
- Chemistry, General
- Communication Studies/Speech Communication and Rhetoric
- Computer and Information Sciences, General
- Early Childhood Education and Teaching
- Economics, General
- Education, General
- English Language and Literature, General
- Fine/Studio Arts, General
- French Language and Literature
- History, General
- Humanities/Humanistic Studies
- Interdisciplinary Studies
- International Business/Trade/Commerce
- International Relations and Affairs
- Junior High/Intermediate/Middle School Education and Teaching
- Mathematics, General
- Music, General
- Philosophy
- Physical Sciences
- Physics, General
- Political Science and Government, General
- Psychology, General
- Religion/Religious Studies
- Social Sciences, General
- Spanish Language and Literature

AIR TIME

We here at SparkCollege frequently re-create scenes from *Top Gun* in our downtime. So we're deeply jealous of anyone who ends up going to any of the schools listed below. Students can zip around the skies at 20,000 feet—for credit! These universities offer ground instruction and flight training. Start dreaming up your call sign now, Maverick.

Auburn University
Take classes with the Department of Aviation Management and Logistics and help manage Auburn's very own airport. You'll be off the ground in no time.

Embry-Riddle Aeronautical University
This is the oldest, biggest, and best school in the world devoted to aviation. They've got the right stuff—and then some—here.

Florida Institute of Technology
Study all things aeronautical at FIT, from aviation meteorology to aviation computer science. You can even take a course called Air Taxi. No, seriously.

Lynn University
Lucky aviation students jet to Hawaii for a "study" tour. Sure, you'll study, but you'll also get to tour Volcano National Park, hang out on Waikiki Beach, and surf the waves of the North Shore.

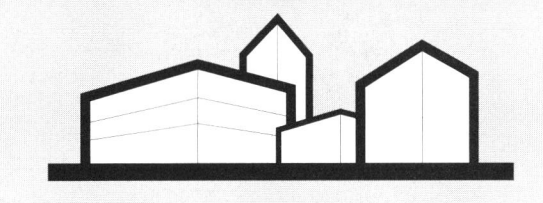

ALABAMA

ALABAMA A&M UNIVERSITY

PO Box 908
Normal, AL 35762

(256) 372-5000
http://www.aamu.edu/

BIG DEAL

UNIVERSITY 101
Extended orientation program; required first-year transitional seminar; special academic counseling, peer tutoring, and Learning Strategies workshops available for first-years who have not yet met all admission requirements.

BIG IDEA

Get ready to get dirty.

Alabama A&M's School of Agriculture and Environmental Sciences offers degree programs that will put you smack dab in the middle of the great outdoors. Students have the option of choosing a field-based major, such as forestry or food and animal sciences, or splitting their time between the classroom and lab with majors like agribusiness management or family and consumer science education. Faculty-mentored research opportunities are available to all SAES students and serve as hands-on additions to classroom education. For nontraditional students over the age of 23, Alabama A&M's distance-learning programs make all SAES degree programs available via the Internet.

ALABAMA A&M UNIVERSITY

WHAT IT IS

In 1875, Dr. William Hooper Councill, an ex-slave, educator, lawyer, publisher, and statesman, founded Alabama Agricultural & Mechanical University. Since then, the school has grown into a respected university with a focus on teaching, research, and public service. The university faculty—the most culturally diverse teaching staff of any public, four-year institution of higher education in Alabama—is engaged in cutting-edge research in areas ranging from artificial intelligence to human nutrition and rural development. Facilities include five research greenhouses and a Pelletron particle accelerator, one of just 20 in the country. Students take classes from accessible, approachable professors in a variety of disciplines. The most popular majors include telecommunications, drama, biological sciences, and computer science (AAMU was the first school in the state to offer a baccalaureate degree in computer science). Alabama A&M students are also lucky to be in the midst of Huntsville's thriving science and technology industries, where internships and jobs are available at such companies as Motorola, NASA, and Boeing and with the U.S. Army. Life outside the classroom is lively too—more than 80 percent of AAMU students participate in extracurricular activities.

WHERE IT'S AT

Situated in the foothills of the Appalachian Mountains, the 2,000-acre AAMU campus, known as "the Hill," includes significant land devoted to the agricultural sciences, but there's more here than green pastures. Huntsville, the home of Alabama A&M University, is a fast-growing city of 172,000 in northern Alabama and a major hub of the aerospace and defense industries. Museums—including the world's largest space and rocket museum—shopping, and restaurants entertain both longtime residents and AAMU students, as well as students from the University of Alabama in Huntsville. Beyond Huntsville, major southern cities such as Birmingham; Atlanta, Georgia; and Nashville, Tennessee, are within a few hours' drive.

THE DETAILS

Campus setting:	suburban
Degrees:	bachelor's, master's, doctoral
Calendar:	semesters
Public/Private:	public state
Number of full-time faculty:	299
Student-to-teacher ratio:	16:1

Admissions requirements:
- **Options:** common application, deferred entrance, electronic application
- **Application fee:** $10
- **Required:** high school transcript, letter of recommendation, ACT (recommended)
- **Application deadlines:** 7/15 (freshmen), continuous (transfer)
- **Early decision:** —
- **Notification:** continuous (freshmen), continuous (transfer)

Average high school GPA:	2.8
Average freshman SAT verbal/math score:	—/—
Average freshman ACT score:	17
Number of applicants:	8,295
Number of applicants accepted:	3,697
Percentage of students from out of state:	65%
Total freshman enrollment:	1,198
Total enrollment:	6,323
Percentage of students who live in campus housing:	45%
Total in-state tuition, fees & expenses:	$8,818
Total out-of-state tuition, fees & expenses:	$12,718
Average financial aid package:	$7,862

ALABAMA A&M UNIVERSITY

MAJORS

- Accounting
- Agricultural Economics
- Animal Sciences, General
- Biology/Biological Sciences, General
- Business/Commerce, General
- Business/Managerial Economics
- Business Administration and Management, General
- Business Statistics
- Chemistry, General
- City/Urban, Community and Regional Planning
- Civil Engineering, General
- Civil Engineering Technology/Technician
- Computer and Information Sciences, General
- Economics, General
- Education/Teaching of Individuals with Speech or Language Impairments
- Electrical, Electronics and Communications Engineering
- Elementary Education and Teaching
- English Language and Literature, General
- Family and Consumer Economics and Related Services, Other
- Finance, General
- Food Science
- Kindergarten/Preschool Education and Teaching
- Marketing/Marketing Management, General
- Mathematics, General
- Mechanical Engineering
- Mechanical Engineering/Mechanical Technology/Technician
- Music Teacher Education
- Physical Education Teaching and Coaching
- Physics, General
- Political Science and Government, General
- Psychology, General
- Radio and Television Broadcasting Technology/Technician
- Secondary Education and Teaching
- Social Work
- Sociology
- Special Education and Teaching, General

ALABAMA STATE UNIVERSITY

915 South Jackson Street
Montgomery, AL 36101

(334) 229-4100
http://www.alasu.edu/

BIG DEAL

UNIVERSITY 101
Extended orientation program; special academic advisors assigned to first-years; upperclassman mentors; optional first-year transitional seminar.

BIG FISH

Marie Curie and Jonas Salk are your heroes.

You've studied the effects of soda on baby teeth, you've charted beanstalk growth, and you're ready for more. ASU gives future scientists the tools they need to make real medical breakthroughs. Students in ASU's undergraduate biomedical research programs take courses in multiple disciplines, conduct research, and participate in preprofessional organizations. ASU's two-year START program, reserved for first-years and sophomores majoring in biology or chemistry, assigns students peer mentors to help support them through academic challenges. START students take small, rigorous courses, complete research projects, and present their findings at an annual research symposium. After completing the program, upperclassmen may be offered up to $9,700 per year to continue their honors education.

ALABAMA STATE UNIVERSITY

WHAT IT IS
Founded in 1867 to make the dream of a college education a reality for thousands of Alabamians, Alabama State University is America's oldest publicly assisted liberal arts institution for African Americans. Almost one-third of the students are non-Alabamians.

ASU is separated into six major divisions: the College of Health Sciences, the College of Arts and Sciences, the College of Business Administration, the College of Education, the School of Music, and University College. Theatre Arts is directed by the nationally acclaimed actress Dr. Tommie "Tonea" Stewart, the biomedical research program serves future leaders in the health professions, and Department of Mathematics faculty members captured national recognition for having solved a 23-year-old math mystery. College of Business Administration graduates are climbing corporate ladders in Fortune 500 companies and becoming thriving entrepreneurs. The College of Education is one of the nation's leading producers of African American teachers. The School of Music's education students are in great demand for band- and choral-directing positions upon graduation. Interested students may become involved in one of many band and choral ensembles, including the Marching Hornets, University Choir, Wind Ensemble, Chamber Singers, and Jazz Band.

WHERE IT'S AT
Montgomery, the state's capital, has a metropolitan population of more than 320,000. Centrally located in the state and on the Alabama River, Montgomery is less than two hours from Birmingham; less than three hours from the beaches of Alabama and northwest Florida's Gulf Coast, as well as Atlanta, Georgia; and four hours from the scenic mountains of Tennessee and the Carolinas. The climate is moderate year-round.

Among Montgomery's historic sites are the Civil Rights Memorial, Dexter Avenue King Memorial Baptist Church (the first pulpit of Dr. Martin Luther King Jr.), and the First White House of the Confederacy. The city offers diverse entertainment, shopping, dining, housing, and social venues. Area highlights include the Alabama Shakespeare Festival, the Montgomery Museum of Fine Arts, and Jasmine Hill Gardens.

THE DETAILS

Campus setting:	urban
Degrees:	bachelor's, master's, doctoral
Calendar:	semesters
Public/Private:	public state
Number of full-time faculty:	231
Student-to-teacher ratio:	15:1

Admissions requirements:
- **Options:** common application, deferred entrance, early admission
- **Application fee:** —
- **Required:** high school transcript, SAT or ACT (recommended)
- **Application deadlines:** 7/30 (freshmen), 7/30 (transfer)
- **Early decision:** —
- **Notification:** continuous (freshmen), continuous (transfer)

Average high school GPA:	2.79
Average freshman SAT verbal/math score:	384 / 388
Average freshman ACT score:	16
Number of applicants:	8,827
Number of applicants accepted:	4,476
Percentage of students from out of state:	35%
Total freshman enrollment:	1,139
Total enrollment:	5,653
Percentage of students who live in campus housing:	43%
Total in-state tuition, fees & expenses:	$8,708
Total out-of-state tuition, fees & expenses:	$12,716
Average financial aid package:	$7,011

ALABAMA STATE UNIVERSITY

MAJORS

- Accounting
- Administrative Assistant and Secretarial Science, General
- Art/Art Studies, General
- Art Teacher Education
- Biology/Biological Sciences, General
- Business Administration and Management, General
- Business Teacher Education
- Chemistry, General
- Clinical/Medical Laboratory Technician
- Computer Science
- Criminal Justice/Law Enforcement Administration
- Drama and Dramatics/Theatre Arts, General
- Economics, General
- Education, General
- Elementary Education and Teaching
- English Language and Literature, General
- Finance, General
- French Language and Literature
- Health Information/Medical Records Administration/Administrator
- History, General
- Information Science/Studies
- Journalism
- Kindergarten/Preschool Education and Teaching
- Liberal Arts and Sciences/Liberal Studies
- Marine Biology and Biological Oceanography
- Marketing/Marketing Management, General
- Mass Communication/Media Studies
- Mathematics, General
- Music, General
- Music Teacher Education
- Occupational Therapy/Therapist
- Parks, Recreation and Leisure Studies
- Physical Education Teaching and Coaching
- Political Science and Government, General
- Pre-Medicine/Pre-Medical Studies
- Psychology, General
- Public Relations/Image Management
- Radio and Television
- Science Teacher Education/General Science Teacher Education
- Secondary Education and Teaching
- Social Sciences, General
- Social Work
- Sociology
- Spanish Language and Literature
- Special Education and Teaching, General
- Speech and Rhetorical Studies

AUBURN UNIVERSITY

The Quad Center
Auburn University, AL 36849

(334) 844-4000
http://www.auburn.edu/

BIG DEAL

UNIVERSITY 101
Optional first-year transitional seminar; special academic advisors assigned to first-year students; upperclassman mentors; first-year residential learning communities.

BIG REP

Auburn University isn't just a good deal; it's practically a steal.

Auburn's engineering programs are among the best in the country but cost half as much as those offered by schools of equal caliber. The university has the largest engineering program in the state and produces half of Alabama's engineering grads. The College of Engineering brings in $35 million in research grants every year and has been recognized by the National Security Agency and the American Society for Engineering Education. Undergrad engineers have 15 degree options and may choose to incorporate co-op positions and study abroad trips into their program of study. Auburn alums fare well in the job market too. The Auburn Alumni Engineering Council, composed of more than 100 engineering grads, helps students find their first post-college paycheck.

ALABAMA

AUBURN UNIVERSITY

WHAT IT IS

Auburn University was chartered in 1856 as East Alabama Male College. The university has since evolved into a major comprehensive university.

A wide variety of off-campus housing is available in the form of apartments, condominiums, and trailer parks. The campus offers 19 sororities, 28 fraternities, and more than 300 other organizations. Auburn also offers an extremely active intramural sports and recreational services program in both team and individual activities. For students interested in musical organizations, there are the University Concert Choir, the University Singers, Gospel Choir, Men's Chorus, Women's Chorus, various ensembles, the University Orchestra, an opera workshop, and marching and concert bands. In addition, eight or nine theatrical productions are presented each year by the Auburn University Theatre. Auburn Studio of the Alabama Public Television Network regularly produces programs for the Alabama Educational Television network, and Auburn students operate a campus radio station, WEGL-FM. Nationally recognized ROTC programs are available in three branches of service: Air Force, Army, and Navy/Marine Corps. Each unit is ranked among the top 10 in the nation. Auburn is one of only seven schools in the Nuclear Enlisted Commissioning Program. It owns and operates the 334-acre Robert E. Pitts Auburn-Opelika Airport, providing flight education and fuel, maintenance, and airplane storage. The Auburn University Aviation Department is fully certified by the Federal Aviation Administration as an Air Agency with examining authority for private, commercial, instrument, and multiengine courses.

WHERE IT'S AT

The Auburn University campus consists of more than 1,800 beautiful acres, surrounded by farms and woodlands in the city of Auburn, Alabama (population about 35,000). Auburn is located in the east-central part of the state, 60 miles northeast of Montgomery, 120 miles southeast of Birmingham, and 110 miles southwest of Atlanta, Georgia. Interstate 85 provides easy access to both Montgomery and Atlanta. Auburn is a small residential area and is often referred to as the "loveliest village of the plains." The university and the local community offer that rare blend of mutual support and cooperation evident only in a true university community.

THE DETAILS

Campus setting:	small town
Degrees:	bachelor's, master's, doctoral
Calendar:	semesters
Public/Private:	public state
Number of full-time faculty:	1,177
Student-to-teacher ratio:	16:1
Admissions requirements:	
• **Options:** early admission	
• **Application fee:** $25	
• **Required:** high school transcript, SAT or ACT	
• **Application deadlines:** 8/1 (freshmen), continuous (transfer)	
• **Early decision:** —	
• **Notification:** continuous (freshmen), continuous (transfer)	

Average high school GPA:	3.55
Average freshman SAT verbal/math score:	558 / 568
Average freshman ACT score:	23
Number of applicants:	12,838
Number of applicants accepted:	10,797
Percentage of students from out of state:	32%
Total freshman enrollment:	3,564
Total enrollment:	22,928
Percentage of students who live in campus housing:	15%
Total in-state tuition, fees & expenses:	$12,414
Total out-of-state tuition, fees & expenses:	$21,634
Average financial aid package:	$7,626

AUBURN UNIVERSITY

MAJORS

- Accounting
- Adult and Continuing Education and Teaching
- Aerospace, Aeronautical and Astronautical Engineering
- Agricultural/Biological Engineering and Bioengineering
- Agricultural Economics
- Agricultural Teacher Education
- Agriculture, General
- Agronomy and Crop Science
- Airline/Commercial/Professional Pilot and Flight Crew
- Animal Sciences, General
- Anthropology
- Apparel and Textiles, General
- Applied Mathematics
- Aquaculture
- Architectural Engineering
- Architecture
- Art/Art Studies, General
- Audiology/Audiologist and Speech-Language Pathology/Pathologist
- Aviation/Airway Management and Operations
- Biochemistry
- Biology/Biological Sciences, General
- Biomedical Sciences, General
- Botany/Plant Biology
- Broadcast Journalism
- Business/Managerial Economics
- Business Administration and Management, General
- Business Teacher Education
- Chemical Engineering
- Chemistry, General
- Child Development
- Civil Engineering, General
- Clinical/Medical Laboratory Technician
- Clinical Laboratory Science/Medical Technology/Technologist
- Commercial and Advertising Art
- Communication, Journalism and Related Programs, Other
- Computer and Information Sciences, General
- Computer Engineering, General
- Computer Engineering, Other
- Computer Hardware Engineering
- Computer Software Engineering
- Criminology
- Dairy Science
- Drama and Dramatics/Theatre Arts, General
- Early Childhood Education and Teaching
- Economics, General
- Education/Teaching of Individuals with Vision Impairments, Including Blindness
- Electrical, Electronics and Communications Engineering
- Elementary Education and Teaching
- Engineering, General
- English Language and Literature, General
- Environmental Design/Architecture
- Environmental Science
- Environmental Studies
- Family and Consumer Sciences/Human Sciences, General
- Finance, General
- Fine/Studio Arts, General
- Foods, Nutrition, and Wellness Studies, General
- Food Science
- Foreign Languages and Literatures, General
- Forest Sciences and Biology
- French Language and Literature
- French Language Teacher Education
- Geography
- Geological/Geophysical Engineering
- Geology/Earth Science, General
- German Language and Literature
- German Language Teacher Education
- Health/Health Care Administration/Management
- Health and Medical Laboratory Technologies
- Health Teacher Education
- History, General
- History Teacher Education
- Horticultural Science
- Hospitality Administration/Management, Other
- Hotel/Motel Administration/Management
- Housing and Human Environments, General
- Human Development and Family Studies, General
- Human Resources Management/Personnel Administration, General
- Industrial Design
- Industrial Engineering
- Interior Architecture
- International Business/Trade/Commerce
- Journalism
- Kindergarten/Preschool Education and Teaching
- Landscape Architecture
- Logistics and Materials Management
- Management Information Systems, General
- Marine Biology and Biological Oceanography
- Marketing/Marketing Management, General
- Mass Communication/Media Studies
- Materials Engineering
- Mathematics, General
- Mechanical Engineering
- Medical Microbiology and Bacteriology
- Microbiology, General
- Molecular Biology
- Music Teacher Education
- Nursing/Registered Nurse Training
- Nutrition Sciences
- Operations Management and Supervision
- Ornamental Horticulture
- Parks, Recreation and Leisure Studies
- Philosophy
- Physical Education Teaching and Coaching
- Physics, General
- Physics Teacher Education
- Plant Pathology/Phytopathology
- Plant Sciences, General
- Plant Sciences, Other
- Political Science and Government, General

AUBURN UNIVERSITY

- Poultry Science
- Pre-Dentistry Studies
- Pre-Law Studies
- Pre-Medicine/Pre-Medical Studies
- Pre-Pharmacy Studies
- Pre-Veterinary Studies
- Psychology, General
- Public Administration
- Public Relations/Image Management
- Radio and Television
- Science Teacher Education/General Science Teacher Education
- Secondary Education and Teaching
- Secondary School Administration/Principalship
- Social Work
- Sociology
- Spanish Language and Literature
- Spanish Language Teacher Education
- Special Education and Teaching, General
- Special Education and Teaching, Other
- Speech and Rhetorical Studies
- Speech Therapy
- Teaching English as a Second or Foreign Language/ESL Language Instructor
- Textile Sciences and Engineering
- Trade and Industrial Teacher Education
- Wildlife and Wildlands Science and Management
- Zoology/Animal Biology

BIRMINGHAM-SOUTHERN COLLEGE

900 Arkadelphia Road
Birmingham, AL 35254

(205) 226-4600
http://www.bsc.edu/

BIG IDEA

UNIVERSITY 101
Extended orientation program; special academic advisors assigned to first-year students; upperclassman mentors.

BIG FISH

Birmingham-Southern students spend winter break going to concerts, traveling, or logging hours on the job.

The difference is that BSC students do it for credit. The university's January Interim Term is a monthlong academic free-for-all offering students a chance to creatively explore aspects of their majors. All BSC students complete an Interim project or course on campus, abroad, or through other domestic schools. Projects have included learning about dolphin behavior in Honduras, manning a ship for three weeks in the Caribbean, and creating computer-animated films.

BIRMINGHAM-SOUTHERN COLLEGE

WHAT IT IS

Birmingham-Southern College was created through a merger of Southern University, established in 1856, and Birmingham College, established in 1898. Since 1959, when *Harper's* magazine called it "one of the leading small colleges in the South," BSC continues to be recognized as one of the nation's outstanding liberal arts institutions. The college is recognized by the John Templeton Foundation's Honor Roll as one of 100 schools nationwide that emphasize character building as an integral part of the college experience.

Birmingham-Southern is one of only six baccalaureate colleges—liberal arts, as classified by the Carnegie Foundation for the Advancement of Teaching, to hold both AACSB International (the Association to Advance Collegiate Schools of Business) accreditation and Phi Beta Kappa designation. Each year, Birmingham-Southern ranks number one in Alabama and among the nation's best in percentage of all graduates accepted to medical, dental, or health-career programs. It also ranks high nationally in graduates accepted to law school. The college has more than 80 clubs and organizations and intramural sports.

WHERE IT'S AT

Located on a 197-acre campus in the rolling hills of western Birmingham, the college is just three miles via I-59 from the downtown business district. A combination of the wonderful climate and tree-blanketed, hilly terrain; the hospitality of the people; and educational, professional, and recreational opportunities make Birmingham an ideal place to live. Birmingham, Alabama's largest city, has been honored by the U.S. Conference of Mayors as the "Most Livable City in America" and offers fine restaurants, museums, city and state parks, and theater. BSC's offerings are supplemented by the activities of four other Birmingham colleges. Birmingham's 17,000-seat Civic Center Coliseum is the setting for many outstanding cultural and athletic events.

THE DETAILS

Campus setting:	urban
Degrees:	bachelor's, master's
Calendar:	4-1-4
Public/Private:	private religious
Number of full-time faculty:	96
Student-to-teacher ratio:	12:1

Admissions requirements:
- **Options:** common application, deferred entrance, early admission, early action, electronic application
- **Application fee:** $25
- **Required:** essay or personal statement, high school transcript, letter of recommendation, SAT or ACT
- **Application deadlines:** continuous (freshmen), continuous (transfer)
- **Early action:** 12/1
- **Notification:** continuous (freshmen), continuous (transfer), 12/15 (early action)

Average high school GPA:	3.38
Average freshman SAT verbal/math score:	610 / 589
Average freshman ACT score:	25
Number of applicants:	1,157
Number of applicants accepted:	956
Percentage of students from out of state:	25%
Total freshman enrollment:	367
Total enrollment:	1,453
Percentage of students who live in campus housing:	79%
Total tuition:	$20,425
Total cost with fees & expenses:	$29,135
Average financial aid package:	$16,015

BIRMINGHAM-SOUTHERN COLLEGE

MAJORS

- Accounting
- Art/Art Studies, General
- Art History, Criticism and Conservation
- Art Teacher Education
- Asian Studies/Civilization
- Biology/Biological Sciences, General
- Business Administration and Management, General
- Chemistry, General
- Computer Science
- Dance, General
- Drama and Dramatics/Theatre Arts, General
- Drawing
- Economics, General
- Education, General
- Elementary Education and Teaching
- English Language and Literature, General
- Fine/Studio Arts, General
- French Language and Literature
- German Language and Literature
- History, General
- Human Resources Management/Personnel Administration, General
- Interdisciplinary Studies
- International Business/Trade/Commerce
- Kindergarten/Preschool Education and Teaching
- Mathematics, General
- Music, General
- Music History, Literature, and Theory
- Music Teacher Education
- Painting
- Philosophy
- Physics, General
- Piano and Organ
- Political Science and Government, General
- Pre-Dentistry Studies
- Pre-Law Studies
- Pre-Medicine/Pre-Medical Studies
- Printmaking
- Psychology, General
- Religion/Religious Studies
- Sculpture
- Secondary Education and Teaching
- Sociology
- Spanish Language and Literature
- Voice and Opera

HUNTINGDON COLLEGE

1500 East Fairview Avenue
Montgomery, AL 36106

(334) 833-4222
http://www.huntingdon.edu/

BIG IDEA

UNIVERSITY 101
Required first-year transitional seminar; optional alumni mentors for first-year students; extended orientation program; optional first-year extracurricular and social events.

BIG FISH

Huntingdon College knows how to treat its students right.

All first-years receive a free laptop with wireless Internet connection to use during their collegiate years and take with them upon graduation. Small classes—80 percent of which have fewer than 20 students—are taught by an outstanding faculty, and professors encourage their students to complete independent research and creative projects, take their studies abroad, intern off campus, and participate in service-oriented activities. As if free hardware and individual attention weren't enough, Huntingdon's tuition plan guarantees that once students are enrolled, they'll never see a tuition increase during their four years. What's with all the nurturing and support? It's the pay-it-forward philosophy: Huntingdon's aim is to foster leaders who will give back to society.

HUNTINGDON COLLEGE

WHAT IT IS

Students are welcomed to Huntingdon College, where a deep cultural history, rich traditions, a dynamic student life program, an innovative plan for their future, and outstanding educational programs converge for a college experience that is like no other. Founded in 1854, Huntingdon, a residential liberal arts college affiliated with the United Methodist Church, is a community of faith, wisdom, and service committed to developing skilled leaders to serve a complex world. The Huntingdon experience combines liberal arts education with communication and information technology, hands-on learning, and travel/study. Huntingdon students are provided laptop computers upon enrollment—theirs to keep at graduation—and each student is offered the opportunity to participate in a travel/study experience during their junior or senior year.

Huntingdon's students represent 25 states and 13 countries. In recent years, 96 percent of those graduates who have sought admission to law schools have been accepted, as have 88 percent of those who have sought admission to medical schools. In most other fields, the graduate or professional school acceptance rate is nearly 100 percent. Huntingdon's student life program offers more than 50 clubs and organizations, including national fraternities and sororities, honoraries, special interest groups, fine and performing arts groups, the Campus Ministry Association, service clubs, student publications, and intramural sports.

WHERE IT'S AT

Huntingdon's 58-acre home campus and 13-acre Cloverdale campus are located in one of Montgomery's oldest and most beautiful residential neighborhoods, Old Cloverdale. Montgomery enjoys warm summers and mild winters and is only 80 miles from Birmingham; 170 miles from Atlanta, Georgia; 300 miles from New Orleans, Louisiana; and 160 miles from the spectacular white sand beaches of the Gulf Coast. Alabama's capital city, Montgomery, is home to a breadth of cultural and historic landmarks and performing arts programs, including the world-famous Alabama Shakespeare Festival, the Montgomery Museum of Fine Arts, Blount Cultural Park, the Civil Rights Memorial, the Rosa Parks Museum, Dexter Avenue King Memorial Baptist Church, the first White House of the Confederacy, the Montgomery Symphony, the Alabama Dance Theater, and a host of civic, cultural, and performing organizations.

THE DETAILS

Campus setting:	suburban
Degrees:	bachelor's
Calendar:	semesters
Public/Private:	private religious
Number of full-time faculty:	32
Student-to-teacher ratio:	15:1

Admissions requirements:
- **Options:** common application, deferred entrance, early admission, electronic application
- **Application fee:** $25
- **Required:** high school transcript, letter of recommendation, SAT or ACT
- **Application deadlines:** continuous (freshmen), continuous (transfer)
- **Early decision:** —
- **Notification:** —

Average high school GPA:	3.23
Average freshman SAT verbal/math score:	533 / 527
Average freshman ACT score:	22
Number of applicants:	876
Number of applicants accepted:	555
Percentage of students from out of state:	20%
Total freshman enrollment:	192
Total enrollment:	731
Percentage of students who live in campus housing:	72%
Total tuition:	$15,250
Total cost with fees & expenses:	$22,750
Average financial aid package:	$10,686

MAJORS

- Accounting
- American/United States Studies/Civilization
- Applied Art
- Art/Art Studies, General
- Art Teacher Education
- Athletic Training/Trainer
- Biology/Biological Sciences, General
- Business/Managerial Economics
- Business Administration and Management, General
- Cell/Cellular Biology and Anatomical Sciences, Other
- Chemistry, General
- Chemistry Teacher Education
- Computer and Information Sciences, General
- Computer Graphics
- Computer Science
- Counseling Psychology
- Creative Writing
- Drama and Dramatics/Theatre Arts, General
- Education, General
- English/Language Arts Teacher Education
- English Language and Literature, General
- European Studies/Civilization
- Experimental Psychology
- History, General
- History Teacher Education
- Interdisciplinary Studies
- International Business/Trade/Commerce
- International Relations and Affairs
- Kinesiology and Exercise Science
- Liberal Arts and Sciences/Liberal Studies
- Marketing/Marketing Management, General
- Mathematics, General
- Mathematics Teacher Education
- Multi-/Interdisciplinary Studies, Other
- Music, General
- Music Teacher Education
- Parks, Recreation and Leisure Studies
- Physical Education Teaching and Coaching
- Physical Therapy/Therapist
- Piano and Organ
- Political Science and Government, General
- Public Administration
- Religion/Religious Studies
- Religious Education
- Secondary Education and Teaching
- Spanish Language and Literature
- Speech and Rhetorical Studies
- Sport and Fitness Administration/Management
- Visual and Performing Arts, Other
- Voice and Opera

JACKSONVILLE STATE UNIVERSITY

700 Pelham Road North
Jacksonville, AL 36265

(256) 782-5781
http://www.jsu.edu/

BIG DEAL

UNIVERSITY 101
Extended orientation program; special academic advisors assigned to first-year students; optional first-year transitional seminar; upperclassman mentors; optional first-year residential learning communities.

BIG FISH

You've heard of the International House of Pancakes.

But have you heard of Jacksonville State's International House? While Jacksonville's International House does not offer half-dollar-size pancakes with whipped cream at any time of the day, it does offer some serious opportunities to gain a new perspective on the world. Each year, 40 students—half international students, half American—find out what happens when cultures collide. Every International House member is assigned a roommate from another country for the entire school year and takes part in extracurricular programs that focus on fostering cultural awareness and harmony. Past International House events have included Halloween parties, rafting trips, formal dances, and cultural presentations. Students who participate in IH get to learn about new cultures without ever leaving the dorm.

JACKSONVILLE STATE UNIVERSITY

WHAT IT IS

Jacksonville State University was founded as a normal school in 1883 and later became a state teachers' college before being named a university in 1966. Producing future educators continues to be a major part of the school's mission—more teachers graduate from JSU each year than from any other Alabama university. But students interested in other areas of study will also find plenty of options. The university offers more than 40 concentrations; some of the most popular majors are criminal justice, biology, and computer science. Students with a love of the outdoors can take part in a unique environmental education program in the Little River Canyon National Preserve, and the nationally recognized Environmental Policy and Information Center is also based at the university. Sports are another source of school pride—Jacksonville State is the only NCAA school to have won national championships in football, basketball, and baseball.

WHERE IT'S AT

Known as the "Gem of the Hills," Jacksonville, Alabama, is a quaint town of about 8,400 people nestled in the Appalachian foothills and characterized by Civil War monuments and stately antebellum homes. Though located in a small community, the university, which occupies 58 buildings on a 459-acre campus, has the feel of a much larger school (notable university buildings include a planetarium and state-of-the-art athletic facilities) and is less than two hours east of Birmingham and two hours west of Atlanta, Georgia.

THE DETAILS

Campus setting:	small town
Degrees:	bachelor's, master's
Calendar:	semesters
Public/Private:	public state
Number of full-time faculty:	300
Student-to-teacher ratio:	21:1

Admissions requirements:
- **Options:** deferred entrance, early admission
- **Application fee:** $20
- **Required:** high school transcript, SAT or ACT
- **Application deadlines:** continuous (freshmen), continuous (transfer)
- **Early decision:** —
- **Notification:** continuous (freshmen), continuous (transfer)

Average high school GPA:	3.03
Average freshman SAT verbal/math score:	477 / 475
Average freshman ACT score:	20
Number of applicants:	2,419
Number of applicants accepted:	2,130
Percentage of students from out of state:	12%
Total freshman enrollment:	1,017
Total enrollment:	8,930
Percentage of students who live in campus housing:	20%
Total in-state tuition, fees & expenses:	$8,360
Total out-of-state tuition, fees & expenses:	$12,400
Average financial aid package:	$5,756

JACKSONVILLE STATE UNIVERSITY

MAJORS

- Accounting
- Animal Genetics
- Anthropology
- Army JROTC/ROTC
- Art/Art Studies, General
- Biology/Biological Sciences, General
- Business Administration and Management, General
- Chemistry, General
- Clothing and Textiles
- Communication Studies/Speech Communication and Rhetoric
- Computer and Information Sciences, General
- Corrections
- Criminal Justice/Law Enforcement Administration
- Criminal Justice/Police Science
- Dietetics/Dietitians
- Drama and Dramatics/Theatre Arts, General
- Ecology
- Economics, General
- Education, General
- Educational/Instructional Media Design
- Educational Psychology
- Electrical, Electronic and Communications Engineering Technology/Technician
- Elementary Education and Teaching
- English Language and Literature, General
- Environmental Biology
- Family and Consumer Sciences/Home Economics Teacher Education
- Family and Consumer Sciences/Human Sciences, General
- Finance, General
- Foods, Nutrition, and Wellness Studies, General
- Forensic Science and Technology
- French Language and Literature
- Geography
- Geology/Earth Science, General
- German Language and Literature
- Health and Physical Education, General
- Health Teacher Education
- History, General
- Industrial Technology/Technician
- Junior High/Intermediate/Middle School Education and Teaching
- Kindergarten/Preschool Education and Teaching
- Kinesiology and Exercise Science
- Marine Biology and Biological Oceanography
- Marketing/Marketing Management, General
- Mathematics, General
- Music, General
- Music Teacher Education
- Nursing/Registered Nurse Training
- Occupational Safety and Health Technology/Technician
- Parks, Recreation and Leisure Studies
- Physical Education Teaching and Coaching
- Physics, General
- Political Science and Government, General
- Psychology, General
- Secondary Education and Teaching
- Social Work
- Sociology
- Spanish Language and Literature
- Special Education and Teaching, General

208

JUDSON COLLEGE

302 Bibb Street, PO Box 120
Marion, AL 36756

(334) 683-5100
http://www.judson.edu/

BIG IDEA

UNIVERSITY 101
Required first-year chapel and campus community hours; required first-year transitional seminar; extended orientation program.

BIG FISH

Feeling horsey?

Judson College is the only school in Alabama that is a member of the Intercollegiate Horse Show Association, and students on its equestrian team compete in regional and national competitions. With a small enrollment and a low student-teacher ratio, the academic atmosphere at Judson is designed to encourage women's confidence, strength, and independence. As a result, Judson grads have gone on to great things: One alumna became an Alabama Supreme Court Justice; another co-founded the state's first battered women's shelter. It's not like Judson students don't see any guys during their four years on campus—they often socialize with male cadets at the nearby Marion Military Institute—but there's a lot more to do there than hang out with the boys.

JUDSON COLLEGE

WHAT IT IS

Founded in 1838, Judson College is the nation's fifth-oldest women's college. Named after Ann Hasseltine Judson, the country's first female foreign missionary, Judson provides the students of this liberal arts school with a unique learning environment. The college is affiliated with the Alabama Baptist Convention, and faith is an important aspect of life for its students, with Christian tradition serving as a basis for school etiquette, dress code, and residence hall policies. Classes at Judson are small, and students can choose to major in fields as diverse as criminal justice, music, and equine science. Judson also offers the opportunity for international study through the American Institution of Foreign Study, Capstone International Studies Program, University of Oslo and University of London, Museum of London, Cooperative Services International Education Consortium, and Scandinavian Seminar. In addition to the standard four-year program of study, most majors also offer an accelerated "2-10" option, which allows students to graduate in two years and 10 months. Athletics include intercollegial competition in basketball, volleyball, softball, and tennis.

WHERE IT'S AT

Judson College is located in Marion, a town of approximately 87,000 in west-central Alabama. Nearby, Perry Lakes Park and the Barton's Beach Cahaba River Preserve offer natural trails and white sand beaches. Montgomery and Birmingham are within 100 miles, and Atlanta, Georgia, and Nashville, Tennessee, are just a few hours away. The Judson campus is spread out over 80 acres, and facilities include a state-of-the-art fine arts center; stables and an equestrian area; and recreational areas for tennis, swimming, weight training, and basketball. Howard Bean Hall, a former Carnegie Library, is now the home of the Alabama Women's Hall of Fame.

THE DETAILS

Campus setting:	rural
Degrees:	bachelor's
Calendar:	semesters, plus 2-month term
Public/Private:	private religious
Number of full-time faculty:	35
Student-to-teacher ratio:	9:1

Admissions requirements:
- **Options:** common application, deferred entrance, early admission, electronic application
- **Application fee:** $25
- **Required:** high school transcript, 2 letters of recommendation, SAT or ACT
- **Application deadlines:** continuous (freshmen), continuous (transfer)
- **Early decision:** —
- **Notification:** continuous (freshmen), continuous (transfer)

Average high school GPA:	3.13
Average freshman SAT verbal/math score:	565 / 522
Average freshman ACT score:	21
Number of applicants:	253
Number of applicants accepted:	183
Percentage of students from out of state:	21%
Total freshman enrollment:	69
Total enrollment:	360
Percentage of students who live in campus housing:	60%
Total tuition:	$9,350
Total cost with fees & expenses:	$16,850
Average financial aid package:	$10,001

MAJORS

- Art/Art Studies, General
- Biology/Biological Sciences, General
- Business/Commerce, General
- Chemistry, General
- Criminal Justice/Law Enforcement Administration
- Education, General
- Elementary Education and Teaching
- English/Language Arts Teacher Education
- English Language and Literature, General
- History, General
- Interdisciplinary Studies
- Junior High/Intermediate/Middle School Education and Teaching
- Mathematics, General
- Mathematics Teacher Education
- Modern Languages
- Multi-/Interdisciplinary Studies, Other
- Music, General
- Music Teacher Education
- Psychology, General
- Religion/Religious Studies
- Romance Languages, Literatures, and Linguistics, General
- Science Teacher Education/General Science Teacher Education
- Secondary Education and Teaching
- Social Science Teacher Education

MILES COLLEGE

PO Box 3800
Birmingham, AL 35208

(205) 929-1000
http://www.miles.edu/

BIG FISH

UNIVERSITY 101
Extended orientation program; required first-year transitional seminar; special counseling and tutoring services available to low-income and first-generation-college first-years.

Miles College describes itself as that "really good little school across the way."

This deliberately small, historically black Christian college emphasizes self-motivation. The school's honors curriculum program provides special learning opportunities for participating students. Honors students may attend special on- and off-campus cultural events, leadership workshops, and intensive courses in addition to working on collaborative projects. They must also participate in community service projects, mentor fellow honors students, and tutor other Miles students, contributing to the academic achievement of the campus as a whole.

WHAT IT IS

Founded in 1905, Miles College is a historically black institution with roots in the Christian Methodist Episcopal Church. The school's focus is on providing its students with a rigorous liberal arts education that will prepare them to be responsible members of a global society. Miles has grown considerably in the past decade, with an increased enrollment of approximately 2,000 students and several major building projects designed to improve the campus, including plans for a new dorm and classroom building. Professors promote creativity, instructing the small, mostly commuter student body in majors like social work, communications, environmental science, and education. The college also has programs designed to ease the transition to college, such as the Freshman Interdisciplinary Seminar. Miles College athletics include basketball, track and field, cross-country, men's football and baseball, and women's softball and volleyball. In addition to marching band, gospel/concert choir, and sororities and fraternities, student organizations range from math and drama clubs to an interdenominational ministerial group.

WHERE IT'S AT

The Miles College campus comprises 16 buildings located on 35 acres in the town of Fairfield, a community of approximately 12,000 in north-central Alabama. The campus is close to Birmingham, the state's major metropolitan center, where attractions include a zoo, botanical gardens, the historic Alabama Theater, and the Birmingham Civil Rights Institute. Local events such as the annual Sidewalk Moving Picture Festival (one of the largest film festivals in the country) and the yearly Southern Heritage Festival provide students with culturally enriching diversions. Fairfield is also within driving distance of Montgomery; Nashville, Tennessee; and Atlanta, Georgia.

THE DETAILS

Campus setting:	small town
Degrees:	bachelor's
Calendar:	semesters
Public/Private:	private religious
Number of full-time faculty:	93
Student-to-teacher ratio:	20:1

Admissions requirements:
- **Options:** —
- **Application fee:** $25
- **Required:** ACT, ACT ASSET (recommended)
- **Application deadlines:** 8/23 (freshmen), continuous (transfer)
- **Early decision:** —
- **Notification:** continuous (freshmen), continuous (transfer)

Average high school GPA:	2.5
Average freshman SAT verbal/math score:	—/—
Average freshman ACT score:	14
Number of applicants:	806
Number of applicants accepted:	437
Percentage of students from out of state:	14%
Total freshman enrollment:	430
Total enrollment:	1,716
Percentage of students who live in campus housing:	36%
Total tuition:	$5,242
Total cost with fees & expenses:	$10,734
Average financial aid package:	$6,702

MILES COLLEGE

MAJORS

- Accounting and Business/Management
- African Studies
- Behavioral Sciences
- Biology/Biological Sciences, General
- Business Administration and Management, General
- Chemistry, General
- Communication and Media Studies, Other
- Computer and Information Sciences, General
- Criminal Justice/Law Enforcement Administration
- Early Childhood Education and Teaching
- Education, General
- Elementary Education and Teaching
- English/Language Arts Teacher Education
- English Language and Literature, General
- Environmental Science
- History, General
- Mass Communication/Media Studies
- Mathematics, General
- Mathematics Teacher Education
- Physics, General
- Political Science and Government, General
- Religion/Religious Studies
- Secondary Education and Teaching
- Social Sciences, General
- Social Work

SAMFORD UNIVERSITY

800 Lakeshore Drive
Birmingham, AL 35229

(205) 726-2011
http://www.samford.edu/

BIG FISH

UNIVERSITY 101
Extended orientation program; optional first-year transitional seminar; special academic advisors assigned to first-year students; Office of Freshman Life to help answer questions and solve problems.

Samford will change your perspective on everything from common sense to communism.

As the state's largest private university, Samford offers 80 majors and several undergraduate research opportunities. All first-years must take the two-semester course Cultural Perspectives, which covers major texts from Western civilization. Through Samford's study abroad programs, students can visit countries like China, Germany, Morocco, Brazil, and South Africa, to name a few. Add to that the Samford in Mission programs, which send students and faculty to local areas and destinations around the world, and the opportunities for travel are practically endless.

SAMFORD UNIVERSITY

WHAT IT IS
Founded by Alabama Baptists, Samford maintains a proud commitment to Christian values. The university's academic reputation is due to well-prepared, accessible faculty members who take the time to know and interact with students. Samford offers a lively Greek social system, an honors program, men's and women's intramural and varsity athletics, music and drama groups, an award-winning debate program, and other interest groups that bond the students and the faculty members in a community of friends and scholars. Students enjoy modern recreational facilities, including a concert hall, a theater, an indoor pool, racquetball and tennis courts, and an indoor track. Special student services include an active and successful Career Development Center, which offers guidance in career exploration, as well as ample opportunities for placement interviews. Co-op programs add work experience and business contacts to the rewards of achievement and income for the participants. The co-op program is an excellent source of financial assistance that complements the significant scholarship and federal aid programs available to Samford students.

WHERE IT'S AT
Samford's wooded 180-acre campus is located in the picturesque, mountainous area of Shades Valley, six miles from the heart of Birmingham, Alabama's largest city and the state's industrial, business, and cultural center. The city attracts national entertainment acts to its Civic Center, historic Alabama Theater, and Oak Mountain Outdoor Amphitheater. Gulf Coast beaches to the south and ski slopes to the north can be reached in less than five hours by car. The world's largest space and rocket museum, located in Huntsville, is also only a short drive away. Alabama's abundant freshwater lakes and rivers are sites for enjoyable outings. One of the South's largest shopping centers, the Riverchase Galleria, is only seven miles from the Samford campus. The Samford student enjoys the best of two worlds: a suburban setting for study, contemplation, and social enjoyment, and easy access to the varied offerings of a metropolitan area.

THE DETAILS

Campus setting:	suburban
Degrees:	bachelor's, master's, doctoral
Calendar:	4-1-4
Public/Private:	private religious
Number of full-time faculty:	267
Student-to-teacher ratio:	12:1

Admissions requirements:
- **Options:** deferred entrance, early admission
- **Application fee:** $25
- **Required:** essay or personal statement, high school transcript, letter of recommendation, SAT or ACT
- **Application deadlines:** 12/15 (freshmen), 8/15 (transfer)
- **Early decision:** —
- **Notification:** continuous (freshman), — (transfer)

Average high school GPA:	3.62
Average freshman SAT verbal/math score:	577 / 575
Average freshman ACT score:	24
Number of applicants:	1,952
Number of applicants accepted:	1,717
Percentage of students from out of state:	55%
Total freshman enrollment:	667
Total enrollment:	4,416
Percentage of students who live in campus housing:	65%
Total tuition:	$13,944
Total cost with fees & expenses:	$20,386
Average financial aid package:	$10,608

SAMFORD UNIVERSITY

MAJORS

- Accounting
- Art/Art Studies, General
- Asian Studies/Civilization
- Athletic Training/Trainer
- Biochemistry
- Biology/Biological Sciences, General
- Biology Teacher Education
- Business Administration and Management, General
- Cartography
- Chemistry, General
- Classical, Ancient Mediterranean and Near Eastern Studies and Archaeology
- Classics and Languages, Literatures and Linguistics, General
- Commercial and Advertising Art
- Community Organization and Advocacy
- Computer Science
- Counseling Psychology
- Criminal Justice/Law Enforcement Administration
- Drama and Dramatics/Theatre Arts, General
- Engineering, Other
- Engineering Physics
- English/Language Arts Teacher Education
- English Language and Literature, General
- Environmental Science
- Environmental Studies
- Foreign Languages and Literatures, General
- French Language and Literature
- General Studies
- Geography
- German Language and Literature
- Health and Physical Education, General
- History, General
- History Teacher Education
- Human Development and Family Studies, General
- Human Nutrition
- Human Resources Management/Personnel Administration, General
- Interior Design
- International Business/Trade/Commerce
- International Relations and Affairs
- Journalism
- Kinesiology and Exercise Science
- Latin American Studies
- Latin Language and Literature
- Marine Biology and Biological Oceanography
- Mathematics, General
- Music Performance, General
- Music Teacher Education
- Music Theory and Composition
- Nursing/Registered Nurse Training
- Philosophy
- Philosophy and Religious Studies, Other
- Physical Education Teaching and Coaching
- Physics, General
- Piano and Organ
- Political Science and Government, General
- Pre-Medicine/Pre-Medical Studies
- Psychology, General
- Public Administration
- Religion/Religious Studies
- Religious/Sacred Music
- Science, Technology and Society
- Science Teacher Education/General Science Teacher Education
- Social Sciences, General
- Social Science Teacher Education
- Sociology
- Spanish Language and Literature
- Speech and Rhetorical Studies
- Speech Teacher Education
- Visual and Performing Arts, Other
- Voice and Opera

SPRING HILL COLLEGE

4000 Dauphin Street
Mobile, AL 36608

(251) 380-4000
http://www.shc.edu/

BIG FISH

UNIVERSITY 101
Extended orientation program; optional first-year transitional seminar; special academic advisors assigned to first-year students.

Known as "the Jesuit College of the South," Spring Hill is the Southeast's oldest Catholic college.

Eighty-eight percent of the faculty members have terminal degrees and, perhaps more important, are available to students. The low student-teacher ratio and the small average Spring Hill class size means that students don't have to vie for attention. Another thing Spring Hill students don't have to compete for is a place to live. Three out of four attendees take the school up on its guaranteed on-campus housing for all four years. Paying for Spring Hill is just as easy as finding your place there: More than 90 percent of all students qualify for financial aid.

SPRING HILL COLLEGE

WHAT IT IS

Founded in 1830, Spring Hill College was the first Catholic college established in the southeastern United States. Spring Hill was also one of the first southern colleges to integrate voluntarily, which it did in 1954; Dr. Martin Luther King Jr. commended the school for this action in his famous *Letter from a Birmingham Jail*. The 1,100 undergrads at Spring Hill enjoy a low student-faculty ratio, and professors are accomplished in their fields of study—88 percent have doctorates or the highest degrees in their fields. The liberal arts college has a focused core curriculum, which gives students a solid foundation, and undergrads can choose from one of many majors in the school's eight divisions. Student volunteerism is also an important part of the Spring Hill educational experience—the college contributes more than 10,000 hours of community service each year in the surrounding community.

WHERE IT'S AT

Spring Hill College is located near the picturesque Gulf Coast in the suburbs of Mobile, Alabama's second-largest city. For fun, students can take part in the city's annual Mardi Gras celebration in February, relax on one of the area's many beaches, or eat fresh seafood in one of the port city's numerous restaurants. The college itself occupies 450 acres, and campus landmarks include the striking Avenue of Oaks, a state-of-the-art library that opened in 2004, and an 18-hole golf course. Several of the 23 buildings on the campus are listed on the National Register of Historic Places.

THE DETAILS

Campus setting:	suburban
Degrees:	bachelor's, master's
Calendar:	semesters
Public/Private:	private religious
Number of full-time faculty:	69
Student-to-teacher ratio:	13:1

Admissions requirements:
- **Options:** common application, deferred entrance, early admission, electronic application
- **Application fee:** $25
- **Required:** essay or personal statement, high school transcript, letter of recommendation, SAT or ACT
- **Application deadlines:** 7/1 (freshmen), 8/10 (transfer)
- **Early decision:** —
- **Notification:** continuous (freshmen), continuous (transfer)

Average high school GPA:	3.48
Average freshman SAT verbal/math score:	572 / 553
Average freshman ACT score:	23
Number of applicants:	1,218
Number of applicants accepted:	971
Percentage of students from out of state:	52%
Total freshman enrollment:	309
Total enrollment:	1,427
Percentage of students who live in campus housing:	78%
Total tuition:	$18,722
Total cost with fees & expenses:	$28,252
Average financial aid package:	$16,829

SPRING HILL COLLEGE

MAJORS

- Accounting
- Arts Management
- Art Therapy/Therapist
- Biochemistry
- Biology/Biological Sciences, General
- Business Administration and Management, General
- Chemistry, General
- Communication, Journalism and Related Programs, Other
- Computer and Information Sciences, General
- Drama and Dramatics/Theatre Arts, General
- Early Childhood Education and Teaching
- Elementary Education and Teaching
- Engineering, Other
- English Language and Literature, General
- English Language and Literature/Letters, Other
- Environmental Science
- Finance, General
- Fine/Studio Arts, General
- General Studies
- Graphic Design
- History, General
- Humanities/Humanistic Studies
- International Business/Trade/Commerce
- International Relations and Affairs
- Journalism
- Marine Biology and Biological Oceanography
- Marketing/Marketing Management, General
- Mathematics, General
- Multi-/Interdisciplinary Studies, Other
- Nursing/Registered Nurse Training
- Philosophy
- Political Science and Government, General
- Pre-Dentistry Studies
- Pre-Medicine/Pre-Medical Studies
- Pre-Veterinary Studies
- Psychology, General
- Radio and Television
- Secondary Education and Teaching
- Spanish Language and Literature
- Theology/Theological Studies

TALLADEGA COLLEGE

627 West Battle Street
Talladega, AL 35160

(256) 362-0206
http://www.talladega.edu/

BIG IDEA

UNIVERSITY 101
Extended orientation program; required first-year transitional seminar; required first-year communications, math, natural science, social science, and physical education courses; special academic advisors assigned to first-year students.

Talladega provides innovative programs not offered anywhere else in the state.

Alabama's oldest private, historically black liberal arts college, Talladega requires all first-year students to hone their communication and leadership skills in the interdisciplinary core curriculum. Because of the significant number of required first-year courses, incoming students have the entire year to get to know their peers and professors. Once the two-year general-education requirements have been fulfilled, Talladega students move into any of the school's 19 degree programs, five preprofessional programs, or three combined-degree options. Those who want an MD hanging next to their bachelor's degree can take advantage of Talladega's Minority Biomedical Research Program.

TALLADEGA COLLEGE

WHAT IT IS

Talladega College was founded in 1865 by two former slaves; classes were originally held in a single-room schoolhouse built with salvaged lumber. Students who enroll at this school tend to be highly motivated and eager to take advantage of the low student-teacher ratio and the individualized attention that is a hallmark of the Talladega learning experience. The school strives to improve programs and prepare students for the diverse needs of a changing society, as evidenced by the new course options recently added in media and cultural studies and electronic and visual media studies. The quality of a Talladega education can be seen in the success of its graduates, 80 percent of whom pursue advanced degrees.

WHERE IT'S AT

Talladega College is located in the historic district of Talladega, Alabama, a city about 50 miles east of Birmingham, 25 miles south of Anniston, 85 miles north of Montgomery, and 115 miles west of Atlanta, Georgia. Talladega is home to the International Motorsports Hall of Fame Museum, the Talladega Superspeedway, the International Race of Champions, and ARCA's Mountain Dew 500K. A major campus attraction is the Amistad Murals. These paintings by noted artist Hale Woodruff depict the revolt of Africans aboard a slave ship and their eventual return to Africa. Students can choose to live in one of the college's six residence halls; other campus landmarks include DeForest Chapel, built in 1903, and Fanning Refectory, built in 1928.

THE DETAILS

Campus setting:	small town
Degrees:	bachelor's
Calendar:	semesters
Public/Private:	private nonprofit
Number of full-time faculty:	38
Student-to-teacher ratio:	8:1

Admissions requirements:
- **Options:** common application, deferred entrance, early admission, electronic application
- **Application fee:** $25
- **Required:** essay or personal statement, high school transcript, letter of recommendation, SAT or ACT, SAT and SAT Subject Tests, or ACT
- **Application deadlines:** continuous (freshmen), continuous (transfer)
- **Early decision:** —
- **Notification:** — (freshmen), continuous (transfer)

Average high school GPA:	2.60
Average freshman SAT verbal/math score:	—/—
Average freshman ACT score:	—
Number of applicants:	1,467
Number of applicants accepted:	344
Percentage of students from out of state:	29%
Total freshman enrollment:	88
Total enrollment:	362
Percentage of students who live in campus housing:	76%
Total tuition:	$6,720
Total cost with fees & expenses:	$11,548
Average financial aid package:	$5,000

MAJORS

- Accounting
- African-American/Black Studies
- Biology/Biological Sciences, General
- Biology Teacher Education
- Business Administration and Management, General
- Chemistry, General
- Chemistry Teacher Education
- Computer Science
- Economics, General
- Education, General
- English/Language Arts Teacher Education
- English Language and Literature, General
- Finance, General
- French Language and Literature
- French Language Teacher Education
- History, General
- History Teacher Education
- Marketing Research
- Mathematics, General
- Mathematics Teacher Education
- Music, General
- Music Teacher Education
- Physics, General
- Pre-Dentistry Studies
- Pre-Law Studies
- Pre-Medicine/Pre-Medical Studies
- Psychology, General
- Public Administration
- Science Teacher Education/General Science Teacher Education
- Social Work
- Sociology
- Spanish Language and Literature
- Voice and Opera

TROY UNIVERSITY

University Avenue
Troy, AL 36082

(334) 670-3000
http://www.troy.edu/

BIG DEAL

UNIVERSITY 101
Upperclassman mentors; optional first-year transitional seminar.

BIG FISH

Troy is the college of choice for thousands of motivated undergrads seeking high-quality education with a reasonable price tag.

Troy's design, technology, and innovation major combines graphic design with one other area of study. Students take traditional art and digital design classes but also do a concentration in business, advertising, or mass communications. They learn both the art and technology of the graphic design industry, as well as how both aspects apply to the current job market. For those craving a cooler climate, a special arrangement with Halmstad University in Sweden lets students take classes in their major while studying abroad.

TROY UNIVERSITY

WHAT IT IS

Troy University was founded in 1887 as Troy State Normal School, a teacher-training institution. The university now offers arts and sciences, business and commerce, education, fine arts, health and human services, journalism and communications, applied science, and preprofessional programs. The university system operates four campuses in Alabama and more than 50 sites on military bases in 12 states and eight countries.

There are 5,000 undergraduates enrolled at the main campus in Troy. Approximately half live on campus in men's, women's, or co-educational residence halls or in sorority or fraternity housing. Students participate in the Sound of the South Marching Band, Collegiate Singers, weekly newspaper, yearbook, radio and television stations, University Dancers, debate and forensics, musical theater productions, pageants, foreign language clubs, religious organizations, intramural sports, service clubs, honor societies, ethnic and political organizations, Trojan Ambassadors, social fraternities and sororities, and special interest clubs. A championship golf course is located on campus, and the natatorium building houses an Olympic-size swimming pool, sauna, weight room, and gymnasium. Lighted tennis and handball courts, a 30,000-seat football stadium, a 3,000-seat gymnasium, a baseball complex, a modern field house, intramural fields, an outdoor pool, sand volleyball courts, a state-of-the-art track, and a press box with VIP seating are also among the athletic facilities.

WHERE IT'S AT

The university's beautifully landscaped 577-acre campus is situated in a residential area of Troy in Pike County, Alabama. The city offers numerous cultural resources. The State Theater, home of the Alabama Shakespeare Festival, is less than an hour's drive from the campus. Rivers, lakes, streams, and farmland surround Troy. Birmingham, Mobile, and Atlanta, Georgia, are a few hours away, and the Gulf of Mexico is only two hours away. The Troy University arboretum and nature preserve is located next to the campus and includes more than 300 species of trees, as well as a nature trail with a swamp, stream, and Mullis Pond. Other Alabama-based campuses are located in Dothan, Montgomery, and Phenix City.

THE DETAILS

Campus setting:	small town
Degrees:	bachelor's, master's
Calendar:	semesters
Public/Private:	public state
Number of full-time faculty:	242
Student-to-teacher ratio:	22:1

Admissions requirements:
- **Options:** deferred entrance, electronic application
- **Application fee:** $20
- **Required:** high school transcript, SAT or ACT
- **Application deadlines:** continuous (freshmen), continuous (transfer)
- **Early decision:** —
- **Notification:** —

Average high school GPA:	3.2
Average freshman SAT verbal/math score:	—/—
Average freshman ACT score:	20
Number of applicants:	3,568
Number of applicants accepted:	2,338
Percentage of students from out of state:	15%
Total freshman enrollment:	968
Total enrollment:	8,847
Percentage of students who live in campus housing:	29%
Total in-state tuition, fees & expenses:	$9,834
Total out-of-state tuition, fees & expenses:	$13,684
Average financial aid package:	$3,320

TROY UNIVERSITY

MAJORS

- Accounting
- Art/Art Studies, General
- Art History, Criticism and Conservation
- Art Teacher Education
- Athletic Training/Trainer
- Biology/Biological Sciences, General
- Broadcast Journalism
- Business/Commerce, General
- Business Administration and Management, General
- Business Teacher Education
- Chemistry, General
- Computer and Information Sciences, General
- Corrections
- Drama and Dramatics/Theatre Arts, General
- Education, General
- Elementary Education and Teaching
- English Language and Literature, General
- Environmental Science
- Finance, General
- Fine/Studio Arts, General
- Health Teacher Education
- History, General
- Journalism
- Kindergarten/Preschool Education and Teaching
- Management Information Systems, General
- Marine Biology and Biological Oceanography
- Marketing, Other
- Mathematics, General
- Music Teacher Education
- Nursing/Registered Nurse Training
- Parks, Recreation and Leisure Studies
- Physical Education Teaching and Coaching
- Physical Sciences
- Political Science and Government, General
- Pre-Dentistry Studies
- Pre-Medicine/Pre-Medical Studies
- Pre-Veterinary Studies
- Psychology, General
- Science Teacher Education/General Science Teacher Education
- Secondary Education and Teaching
- Social Sciences, General
- Social Work
- Sociology
- Special Education and Teaching, General
- Speech and Rhetorical Studies

TUSKEGEE UNIVERSITY

102 Old Admin Building
Tuskegee, AL 36088

(334) 727-8011
http://www.tuskegee.edu/

BIG REP

UNIVERSITY 101
Extended orientation program; upperclassman mentors.

Two Washingtons slept (and taught) here.

Since the days when Dr. Booker T. Washington and Dr. George Washington Carver taught at Tuskegee, it's been a premier destination for scholars. With $500 million worth of administrative and academic facilities, including nine university-run research centers and institutes, the school provides an excellent learning environment. Tuskegee is currently the only historically black institution with its own aerospace engineering program, one of four engineering programs accredited by the Accreditation Board of Engineering and Technology. Grammy winners, state supreme court judges, NFL players, four-star generals, and internationally heralded writers are just part of the school's network of grads.

TUSKEGEE UNIVERSITY

WHAT IT IS

Founded in 1880 by an act of the Alabama State Legislature, Tuskegee University is now one of the nation's best-known historically black colleges. Booker T. Washington was the institution's first president, and the university has largely followed Washington's vision of maintaining outstanding educational opportunities for black students in such areas as career preparation in the sciences and professional studies. All majors also include a strong liberal arts component, which complements more technical studies. The university—which offers 35 majors in five colleges—is particularly strong in the disciplines of engineering and veterinary medicine; the institution produces more black graduates in chemical, electrical, mechanical, and aerospace engineering than any other school in the country. In addition, about 75 percent of the nation's African American veterinarians are Tuskegee grads. While not at work in the lab or the library, students can choose to participate in one of the more than 100 groups that are active on campus.

WHERE IT'S AT

In the heart of the South, Tuskegee makes its home in the Alabama city of the same name. The campus sprawls over approximately 5,000 acres, which include the main campus, a forest, farmland, and 100 major buildings. The school is the only historically black college in the country to have been designated as a National Historic Site. The area surrounding the town and the university has a rich history, and students can visit nearby historical landmarks such as the Tuskegee Airmen National Historical Site Museum and Tuskegee Human and Civil Rights Multicultural Center. Montgomery, the capital of Alabama, is 40 miles east of Tuskegee, and students in need of a quick weekend getaway will find that Tuskegee is an easy drive from Birmingham and Atlanta, Georgia.

THE DETAILS

Campus setting:	small town
Degrees:	bachelor's, master's, doctoral
Calendar:	semesters
Public/Private:	private nonprofit
Number of full-time faculty:	218
Student-to-teacher ratio:	12:1

Admissions requirements:
- **Options:** early admission, electronic application
- **Application fee:** $25
- **Required:** high school transcript, SAT or ACT
- **Application deadlines:** 4/15 (freshmen), 4/15 (transfer)
- **Early decision:** —
- **Notification:** —

Average high school GPA:	3.20
Average freshman SAT verbal/math score:	455 / 469
Average freshman ACT score:	19
Number of applicants:	1,326
Number of applicants accepted:	1,068
Percentage of students from out of state:	57%
Total freshman enrollment:	697
Total enrollment:	2,870
Percentage of students who live in campus housing:	63%
Total tuition:	$11,290
Total cost with fees & expenses:	$18,403
Average financial aid package:	$13,824

TUSKEGEE UNIVERSITY

MAJORS

- Accounting
- Aerospace, Aeronautical and Astronautical Engineering
- Agricultural Business and Management, General
- Agriculture, General
- Agronomy and Crop Science
- Animal Sciences, General
- Architecture
- Biology/Biological Sciences, General
- Building/Home/Construction Inspection/Inspector
- Business Administration and Management, General
- Chemical Engineering
- Chemistry, General
- Clinical Laboratory Science/Medical Technology/Technologist
- Computer Science
- Construction Engineering Technology/Technician
- Dietetics/Dietitians
- Economics, General
- Electrical, Electronics and Communications Engineering
- Elementary Education and Teaching
- Engineering Technology, General
- English Language and Literature, General
- Environmental Studies
- Finance, General
- Foods, Nutrition, and Wellness Studies, General
- Food Science
- History, General
- Hospitality Administration/Management, General
- Hospitality and Recreation Marketing Operations
- Management Science, General
- Marketing/Marketing Management, General
- Mathematics, General
- Mechanical Engineering
- Natural Resources Management and Policy
- Nursing/Registered Nurse Training
- Occupational Therapy/Therapist
- Physics, General
- Plant Sciences, General
- Political Science and Government, General
- Poultry Science
- Psychology, General
- Sales, Distribution and Marketing Operations, General
- Social Work
- Sociology

UNIVERSITY OF ALABAMA

Box 870132
Tuscaloosa, AL 35487

(205) 348-6010
http://www.ua.edu/

BIG DEAL

UNIVERSITY 101
Extended orientation program; optional first-year residential learning communities; optional first-year transitional seminar; optional first-year humanities seminars; optional first-year pre-orientation program.

BIG REP

What a deal!

The University of Alabama provides the opportunities of both a heavily populated public university and a tiny private college—for a reasonable price. What a deal! Students who relish the idea of attending a large, research-intensive school will find ample chances for independent and collaborative research, as well as work-placement programs through the school's 27 centers and institutes. Those who prefer to learn in a smaller community have their choice between two liberal arts programs, each designed to feel like a private college. UA also offers residential learning communities and January interim courses to provide learning opportunities for every type of student.

UNIVERSITY OF ALABAMA

WHAT IT IS

The University of Alabama became the state's first university when it was founded in 1831. Although most of the campus was destroyed during the Civil War and George Wallace's infamous protest against integration in 1963 took place here, the school has grown into a large, comprehensive institution of higher education, attracting many students from Alabama and beyond. Academic offerings are diverse, and business is a popular major. UA is constantly adapting educational programs and transforming facilities to meet the needs of a changing society. It is one of two public universities to own and operate a commercial television station. Working at the station provides invaluable experience to students hoping to pursue careers in communications and media.

WHERE IT'S AT

Tuscaloosa is a pleasant southern community on the Black Warrior River, with a historic theater, galleries, museums, and dramatic examples of antebellum architecture. The University of Alabama is a prominent part of this west-central Alabama community of about 80,000. The campus occupies 1,000 acres, and notable features include the Alabama Museum of Natural History, the University Medical Center, and Moundville Archaeological Park. In the main campus quad are the Denny Chimes, a 25-bell, campanile carillon housed in a 115-foot tower. Birmingham is 57 miles away, and Atlanta, Georgia is less than 200 miles away from the university.

THE DETAILS

Campus setting:	suburban
Degrees:	bachelor's, master's, doctoral
Calendar:	semesters
Public/Private:	public state
Number of full-time faculty:	840
Student-to-teacher ratio:	20:1

Admissions requirements:
- **Options:** common application, deferred entrance, early admission, electronic application
- **Application fee:** $25
- **Required:** high school transcript, SAT or ACT
- **Application deadlines:** 8/1 (freshmen), — (transfer)
- **Early decision:** —
- **Notification:** 9/1 (freshmen), continuous (transfer)

Average high school GPA:	3.36
Average freshman SAT verbal/math score:	563 / 564
Average freshman ACT score:	23
Number of applicants:	9,106
Number of applicants accepted:	7,021
Percentage of students from out of state:	20%
Total freshman enrollment:	3,345
Total enrollment:	20,929
Percentage of students who live in campus housing:	22%
Total in-state tuition, fees & expenses:	$10,164
Total out-of-state tuition, fees & expenses:	$18,198
Average financial aid package:	$7,902

UNIVERSITY OF ALABAMA

MAJORS

- Accounting
- Advertising
- Aerospace, Aeronautical and Astronautical Engineering
- American/United States Studies/Civilization
- Anthropology
- Apparel and Textiles, General
- Art History, Criticism and Conservation
- Athletic Training/Trainer
- Audiology/Audiologist and Speech-Language Pathology/Pathologist
- Biological and Physical Sciences
- Biology/Biological Sciences, General
- Business/Managerial Economics
- Business Administration and Management, General
- Chemical Engineering
- Chemistry, General
- Civil Engineering, General
- Classics and Languages, Literatures and Linguistics, General
- Computer and Information Sciences, General
- Consumer Economics
- Criminal Justice/Safety Studies
- Dance, General
- Drama and Dramatics/Theatre Arts, General
- Electrical, Electronics and Communications Engineering
- Elementary Education and Teaching
- English Language and Literature, General
- Family and Consumer Sciences/Human Sciences, General
- Family and Consumer Sciences/Human Sciences, Other
- Finance, General
- Fine/Studio Arts, General
- Foods, Nutrition, and Wellness Studies, General
- French Language and Literature
- Geography
- Geology/Earth Science, General
- German Language and Literature
- Health Professions and Related Clinical Sciences, Other
- History, General
- Hospital and Health Care Facilities Administration/Management
- Hotel/Motel Administration/Management
- Human Development and Family Studies, General
- Industrial Engineering
- Interdisciplinary Studies
- Interior Design
- International Relations and Affairs
- Journalism
- Kindergarten/Preschool Education and Teaching
- Latin American Studies
- Management Information Systems, General
- Management Science, General
- Marine Biology and Biological Oceanography
- Marketing/Marketing Management, General
- Mathematics, General
- Mechanical Engineering
- Medical Microbiology and Bacteriology
- Metallurgical Engineering
- Music, General
- Music Teacher Education
- Nursing/Registered Nurse Training
- Philosophy
- Physical Education Teaching and Coaching
- Physics, General
- Political Science and Government, General
- Psychology, General
- Public Relations/Image Management
- Radio and Television
- Religion/Religious Studies
- Russian Language and Literature
- Secondary Education and Teaching
- Social Work
- Sociology
- Spanish Language and Literature
- Special Education and Teaching, General
- Speech and Rhetorical Studies

UNIVERSITY OF ALABAMA AT BIRMINGHAM

1530 3rd Avenue South
Birmingham, AL 35294

(205) 934-4011
http://main.uab.edu/

BIG DEAL

UNIVERSITY 101
Extended orientation program.

BIG FISH

The second sexual revolution is underway, thanks to the University of Alabama at Birmingham.

Topping the list of major discoveries at the university is the protein that led to the creation of the popular drug Viagra. UAB faculty are also currently testing a potential vaccine to prevent cervical cancer and developing new ways to combat bioterrorist attacks. Undergraduate students wanting to get in on the action can apply for paid researcher positions in the UAB labs. Undergrads in science-related majors also receive campus housing and get paid to work on collaborative projects alongside faculty mentors. In the end, students walk away with money in their pockets and experience on their résumés.

UNIVERSITY OF ALABAMA AT BIRMINGHAM

WHAT IT IS

The University of Alabama at Birmingham is a research university and academic health center. UAB has established outstanding programs through six liberal arts and professional schools, six health professional schools, and graduate programs serving all major units. UAB is committed to education, research, and service programs of excellent quality and far-reaching scope. In terms of research and development funding, UAB ranks 28th nationally and first in the state of Alabama, receiving more funding than all Alabama universities combined. As an autonomous campus of the University of Alabama System, the University of Alabama at Birmingham resides in the largest metropolitan area in the state and offers unique educational opportunities with day and evening classes.

Part of the UAB experience is student life, which consists of a rich mix of academic organizations, honor clubs, social fraternities and sororities, volunteer groups, and activities ranging from sports to performing arts. With more than 200 campus organizations to keep students involved, UAB offers the chance to make lifelong friendships while helping develop skills essential to leadership and teamwork. Student housing is limited and available on a priority basis; early application is encouraged.

WHERE IT'S AT

Birmingham earned the name "the Magic City" during its first boom days. The expression still rings true as the metropolitan area continues to mirror UAB's phenomenal growth and reflects the many cultural opportunities available within the city. With a population of more than 1 million people, Birmingham is Alabama's largest city, with exciting attractions, colorful events, and friendly neighborhood hangouts. With a budget of more than $1.5 billion, UAB is the city's largest employer and the second-largest in the state. Birmingham is easily reached by automobile from major national routes (Interstates 20, 59, and 65), and UAB is only minutes away from the Birmingham International Airport.

THE DETAILS

Campus setting:	urban
Degrees:	bachelor's, master's, doctoral
Calendar:	semesters
Public/Private:	public state
Number of full-time faculty:	785
Student-to-teacher ratio:	18:1

Admissions requirements:
- **Options:** deferred entrance, early admission
- **Application fee:** $30
- **Required:** high school transcript, SAT or ACT
- **Application deadlines:** 7/1 (freshmen), 7/15 (transfer)
- **Early decision:** —
- **Notification:** continuous (freshmen), continuous (transfer)

Average high school GPA:	3.30
Average freshman SAT verbal/math score:	—/—
Average freshman ACT score:	22
Number of applicants:	4,318
Number of applicants accepted:	3,710
Percentage of students from out of state:	6%
Total freshman enrollment:	1,543
Total enrollment:	16,694
Percentage of students who live in campus housing:	11%
Total in-state tuition, fees & expenses:	$5,562
Total out-of-state tuition, fees & expenses:	$11,322
Average financial aid package:	$13,600

UNIVERSITY OF ALABAMA AT BIRMINGHAM

MAJORS

- Accounting
- African-American/Black Studies
- Anthropology
- Biological and Physical Sciences
- Biology/Biological Sciences, General
- Biomedical/Medical Engineering
- Business/Managerial Economics
- Business Administration and Management, General
- Chemistry, General
- Civil Engineering, General
- Clinical Laboratory Science/Medical Technology/Technologist
- Communication Studies/Speech Communication and Rhetoric
- Computer and Information Sciences, General
- Corrections and Criminal Justice, Other
- Cytotechnology/Cytotechnologist
- Electrical, Electronics and Communications Engineering
- Elementary Education and Teaching
- English Language and Literature, General
- Finance, General
- Fine/Studio Arts, General
- French Language and Literature
- Health Information/Medical Records Administration/Administrator
- Health Teacher Education
- History, General
- Kindergarten/Preschool Education and Teaching
- Management Information Systems, General
- Marketing/Marketing Management, General
- Materials Engineering
- Mathematics, General
- Mechanical Engineering
- Medical Radiologic Technology, Science/Radiation Therapist
- Music, General
- Nuclear Medical Technology/Technologist
- Nursing/Registered Nurse Training
- Philosophy
- Physical Education Teaching and Coaching
- Physician Assistant
- Physics, General
- Political Science and Government, General
- Psychology, General
- Respiratory Care Therapy/Therapist
- Secondary Education and Teaching
- Social Sciences, Other
- Social Work
- Sociology
- Spanish Language and Literature
- Special Education and Teaching, General
- Visual and Performing Arts, General

UNIVERSITY OF ALABAMA IN HUNTSVILLE

301 Sparkman Drive
Huntsville, AL 35899

(256) 824-1000
http://www.uah.edu/

BIG DEAL

UNIVERSITY 101
Extended orientation program; required first-year transitional seminar; upperclassman mentors; special academic advisors assigned to first-years.

BIG FISH

A desk by the window or a cart in the mailroom?

At the University of Alabama in Huntsville, students learn that a résumé with plenty of work experience can make the difference. UAH's Cooperative Education program allows students to gain work experience while remaining active on campus. Students take on-campus courses for one semester and work at an area company for the second. The co-op program has students remain with the same employer for a minimum of three terms so they thoroughly learn the ins and outs of their profession.

UNIVERSITY OF ALABAMA IN HUNTSVILLE

WHAT IT IS

The University of Alabama in Huntsville, a member of the University of Alabama System, was founded in 1950 as an extension center of the University of Alabama and became an autonomous campus in 1969. UAH has earned national recognition in engineering and the sciences, and its programs in the humanities, fine arts, social sciences, business, and nursing are outstanding. Students interact with some of the most productive researchers in their respective disciplines. UAH is a partner with more than 100 high-tech industries as well as major federal laboratories such as NASA's Marshall Space Flight Center, the National Space Science and Technology Center, and the U.S. Army. Its unique location provides many co-op opportunities for students to defray much of their college costs and maximize their employment potential. Students have many opportunities to work with some of the top scientists in the country.

UAH has more than 115 active student groups and organizations, including national fraternities and sororities, honor societies, special interest groups, religious organizations, the Student Government Association, the student-run newspaper and literary magazine, minority student organizations, international student organizations, the choir, the chorus, a film and lecture series, service organizations, professional interest groups, and intramural athletics. The Central Campus Residence Hall, a seven-story residence hall that offers private bedrooms, is located in the center of campus and connected to the University Center by an enclosed walkway.

WHERE IT'S AT

The University of Alabama in Huntsville is located in the Tennessee River Valley of north-central Alabama, 100 miles north of Birmingham and 100 miles south of Nashville, Tennessee. Huntsville is home to more than 50 Fortune 500 companies that specialize in high technology, including aerospace engineering, rocket propulsion, computer technology, weapons systems, telecommunications, software engineering, information systems design, and engineering services. Most of these companies are located in Cummings Research Park, one of the top 10 research parks in the world and the second-largest research park in the United States. Cummings is adjacent to the UAH campus.

THE DETAILS

Campus setting:	suburban
Degrees:	bachelor's, master's, doctoral
Calendar:	semesters
Public/Private:	public state
Number of full-time faculty:	271
Student-to-teacher ratio:	16:1

Admissions requirements:
- **Options:** common application, deferred entrance, early admission, electronic application
- **Application fee:** $30
- **Required:** high school transcript, SAT or ACT
- **Application deadlines:** 8/15 (freshmen), — (transfer)
- **Early decision:** N/A
- **Notification:** continuous (freshmen), continuous (transfer)

Average high school GPA:	3.36
Average freshman SAT verbal/math score:	582 / 589
Average freshman ACT score:	24
Number of applicants:	1,743
Number of applicants accepted:	1,559
Percentage of students from out of state:	13%
Total freshman enrollment:	653
Total enrollment:	7,036
Percentage of students who live in campus housing:	16%
Total in-state tuition, fees & expenses:	$10,436
Total out-of-state tuition, fees & expenses:	$15,438
Average financial aid package:	$5,848

UNIVERSITY OF ALABAMA IN HUNTSVILLE

MAJORS

- Accounting
- Art/Art Studies, General
- Biology/Biological Sciences, General
- Business Administration and Management, General
- Chemical Engineering
- Chemistry, General
- Civil Engineering, General
- Computer and Information Sciences, General
- Computer Engineering, General
- Electrical, Electronics and Communications Engineering
- Elementary Education and Teaching
- Engineering, Other
- English Language and Literature, General
- Finance, General
- Foreign Languages and Literatures, General
- History, General
- Industrial Engineering
- Management Information Systems, General
- Marketing/Marketing Management, General
- Mathematics, General
- Mechanical Engineering
- Music, General
- Nursing/Registered Nurse Training
- Philosophy
- Physics, General
- Political Science and Government, General
- Psychology, General
- Sociology
- Speech and Rhetorical Studies

UNIVERSITY OF MONTEVALLO

Station 6001
Montevallo, AL 35115

(205) 665-6000
http://www.montevallo.edu/

BIG DEAL

UNIVERSITY 101
Extended orientation program; optional first year–only rafting trip; upperclassman mentors available through some departments.

BIG IDEA

Undergraduate research opportunities set the University of Montevallo apart from the rest.

Whereas most schools simply prepare students for the research opportunities of graduate school, the University of Montevallo lets undergrads jump right in. Students of all majors are invited to direct their own research or creative projects for credit under the watchful eyes of faculty mentors. Students with outstanding projects are invited to strut their stuff on campus during Undergraduate Research Day and off campus at the National Conference on Undergraduate Research. UM also provides stipends of up to $200 per student to help defray the costs of supplies and travel.

UNIVERSITY OF MONTEVALLO

WHAT IT IS

The university was founded in 1896 and served as the state college for women. Known as Alabama College, the school first admitted men in 1956. In 1969, the name was changed to the University of Montevallo. Montevallo's "small college" experience features classes of reasonable size and an individual advising system. In addition, the university's emphasis on liberal arts is supported by a core curriculum with a comprehensive writing component. The University of Montevallo is one of the 21 public liberal arts colleges and universities that are members of the Council of Public Liberal Arts Colleges. As a member, UM is dedicated to the education of undergraduates in the liberal arts tradition, the creation of teaching and learning communities, and the experience of access to undergraduate liberal arts education.

The Olmsted brothers, landscape architects famous for designing New York's Central Park, Atlanta's Ponce de Leon Avenue Park, and the Biltmore Estate near Asheville, North Carolina, also developed the first plan for the Montevallo campus. Campus activities such as Greek-sponsored events, movies, theater productions, concerts, and athletic and other events are regularly scheduled. Students may also participate in more than 70 campus organizations, including national fraternities and sororities, intramural athletics, clubs, and service and religious organizations. In September 2004, the university opened the Student Activity Center, a state-of-the art, 90,000-square-foot facility that features racquetball courts, an indoor collegiate-size pool, a student fitness center, and a 2,500-seat arena for athletic events and convocations.

WHERE IT'S AT

Located on a 160-acre campus, the University of Montevallo has redbrick walkways and tree-shaded lawns, with central portions of the campus designated as a National Historic District. Approximately 25 miles south of the metropolitan Birmingham area, Montevallo offers students the advantage of living within walking distance of shops, restaurants, and banks. The location provides students with easy access to Birmingham, the state's largest metropolitan area, which offers many cultural, educational, recreational, retail, and employment opportunities. Situated in the geographic center of the state of Alabama, the campus is located approximately nine miles from the Shelby County Airport.

THE DETAILS

Campus setting:	small town
Degrees:	bachelor's, master's
Calendar:	semesters
Public/Private:	public state
Number of full-time faculty:	136
Student-to-teacher ratio:	17:1

Admissions requirements:
- **Options:** common application, deferred entrance, early admission, electronic application
- **Application fee:** $25
- **Required:** high school transcript, SAT or ACT, ACT (recommended)
- **Application deadlines:** 8/1 (freshmen), continuous (transfer)
- **Early decision:** —
- **Notification:** —

Average high school GPA:	3.29
Average freshman SAT verbal/math score:	—/—
Average freshman ACT score:	22
Number of applicants:	1,245
Number of applicants accepted:	999
Percentage of students from out of state:	4%
Total freshman enrollment:	488
Total enrollment:	3,061
Percentage of students who live in campus housing:	35%
Total in-state tuition, fees & expenses:	$9,924
Total out-of-state tuition, fees & expenses:	$15,114
Average financial aid package:	$7,150

UNIVERSITY OF MONTEVALLO

MAJORS

- Accounting
- Art/Art Studies, General
- Art Teacher Education
- Audiology/Audiologist and Speech-Language Pathology/Pathologist
- Biology/Biological Sciences, General
- Broadcast Journalism
- Business Administration and Management, General
- Ceramic Arts and Ceramics
- Chemistry, General
- Commercial and Advertising Art
- Consumer Merchandising/Retailing Management
- Dietetics/Dietitians
- Drama and Dramatics/Theatre Arts, General
- Drawing
- Elementary Education and Teaching
- English Language and Literature, General
- Family and Consumer Economics and Related Services, Other
- Family and Consumer Sciences/Home Economics Teacher Education
- Family and Consumer Sciences/Human Sciences, General
- Fashion Merchandising
- Fine/Studio Arts, General
- French Language and Literature
- Health and Physical Education, General
- History, General
- Interior Design
- Kindergarten/Preschool Education and Teaching
- Management Information Systems, General
- Marketing/Marketing Management, General
- Mass Communication/Media Studies
- Mathematics, General
- Music, General
- Music Teacher Education
- Photography
- Piano and Organ
- Political Science and Government, General
- Pre-Dentistry Studies
- Pre-Law Studies
- Pre-Medicine/Pre-Medical Studies
- Pre-Veterinary Studies
- Printmaking
- Psychology, General
- Radio and Television
- Sculpture
- Social Sciences, General
- Social Work
- Sociology
- Spanish Language and Literature
- Speech and Rhetorical Studies
- Voice and Opera

UNIVERSITY OF NORTH ALABAMA

One Harrison Plaza
Florence, AL 35632

(256) 765-4100
http://www.una.edu/

BIG DEAL

UNIVERSITY 101
Extended orientation program.

BIG FISH

The University of North Alabama knows the meaning of the word *value*.

The school offers four colleges—Arts & Sciences, Business, Education, and Nursing—with more than 75 majors, as well as a friendly student community and enough activities to keep you busy for four years. The university's College of Business is where the Donald Trumps of the South go to get their start. Smart students get the most for their money by taking advantage of high-tech computer labs, off-campus internships, and special scholarships available for business students only. Those who make the grade will receive extra leadership training and get to hear area business leaders discuss the secrets of success during the Honors Lecture Series.

UNIVERSITY OF NORTH ALABAMA

WHAT IT IS

A public university with a personal touch, the University of North Alabama began as LaGrange College in 1830. Since then, the school has changed locations and names a few times, finally settling into its present identity as one of Alabama's public universities (as of 1974). At UNA, professors (not teaching assistants) teach small classes, and undergrads can count on receiving individual attention from faculty. One of the unique academic programs available at the school is a filmmaking major offered in cooperation with the University of California, Los Angeles. Cineastes can also take in new films at the George Lindsey/UNA Film Festival, an annual event that features movie screenings and workshops. The university also operates the Kilby Laboratory School, the only university-run elementary laboratory school in Alabama, providing an excellent opportunity for education majors to observe best practices in teaching. Campus traditions include *Step Sing* and *Step Show*, yearly student revues whose proceeds go to charities such as the United Way, and visiting the two real live lions that make their home on campus, Leo II and Una.

WHERE IT'S AT

The University of North Alabama is located in Florence, a city of about 36,000 on the banks of the Tennessee River. Florence landmarks include Rosenbaum, the only Frank Lloyd Wright house in the Southeast; the Kennedy-Douglas Center for the Arts; and the Indian Mound Museum. W. C. Handy, the "father of the blues," was also born here, and his former home is now a museum. The 130-acre UNA campus includes student housing, multiple auditoriums and performance spaces, and several gallery spaces. A number of university buildings are also listed on the National Register of Historic Places.

THE DETAILS

Campus setting:	urban
Degrees:	bachelor's, master's
Calendar:	semesters
Public/Private:	public state
Number of full-time faculty:	204
Student-to-teacher ratio:	20:1

Admissions requirements:
- **Options:** deferred entrance, early admission, electronic application
- **Application fee:** $25
- **Required:** high school transcript, SAT or ACT
- **Application deadlines:** continuous (freshmen), continuous (transfer)
- **Early decision:** —
- **Notification:** —

Average high school GPA:	2.94
Average freshman SAT verbal/math score:	—/—
Average freshman ACT score:	21
Number of applicants:	1,856
Number of applicants accepted:	1,492
Percentage of students from out of state:	20%
Total freshman enrollment:	763
Total enrollment:	5,961
Percentage of students who live in campus housing:	19%
Total in-state tuition, fees & expenses:	$9,066
Total out-of-state tuition, fees & expenses:	$12,593
Average financial aid package:	$3,508

UNIVERSITY OF NORTH ALABAMA

MAJORS

- Accounting
- Biological and Biomedical Sciences, Other
- Biology/Biological Sciences, General
- Business/Managerial Economics
- Business Administration and Management, General
- Chemistry, General
- Computer and Information Sciences, General
- Counseling Psychology
- Criminal Justice/Law Enforcement Administration
- Elementary Education and Teaching
- English Language and Literature, General
- Family and Consumer Sciences/Human Sciences, General
- Finance, General
- Fine/Studio Arts, General
- Fine Arts and Art Studies, Other
- Foreign Languages and Literatures, General
- General Studies
- Geography
- Geology/Earth Science, General
- History, General
- Kindergarten/Preschool Education and Teaching
- Management Information Systems, General
- Marine Biology and Biological Oceanography
- Marketing/Marketing Management, General
- Mathematics, General
- Music, General
- Nursing/Registered Nurse Training
- Parks, Recreation, Leisure and Fitness Studies, Other
- Physical Sciences
- Physics, General
- Political Science and Government, General
- Psychology, General
- Secondary Education and Teaching
- Social Work
- Sociology
- Special Education and Teaching, General
- Speech and Rhetorical Studies
- Teacher Education, Multiple Levels

UNIVERSITY OF SOUTH ALABAMA

307 University Boulevard
Mobile, AL 36688

(251) 460-6101
http://www.usouthal.edu/

BIG DEAL

BIG FISH

UNIVERSITY 101
Optional first-year transitional seminar; first year–only extracurricular activities and social events; first-year tutoring; optional first-year residential learning communities; extended orientation program; special academic advisors assigned to first-years; upperclassman mentors.

The Essence program is South Alabama's way of saying "welcome" to first-years.

First-years who sign up for the Essence Freshman Experience Program live in one of three first-year dorms and take a transitional seminar that covers first-years' academic and social issues. To help acclimate students to collegiate life, the university assigns these students to residential upperclassman peer advisors. Should students hit a snag in one of their classes, Essence offers free tutoring (Monday through Thursday nights) in English, algebra, calculus, and chemistry.

UNIVERSITY OF SOUTH ALABAMA

WHAT IT IS

The University of South Alabama is one of the state's fastest-growing universities. Since its founding in 1963, the school has awarded more than 55,000 degrees in such areas as computer science, the arts, education, and engineering. This diverse and lively public university is home to several special programs, most notably the USA Cancer Research Institute. The university has also established a new technology and research park to strengthen the institution's relationship with area businesses and support high-tech industry. Students can take advantage of the vibrant campus environment, working with faculty members involved in innovative research and taking advantage of internship and job opportunities at local companies.

The university and its students also take pride in its many traditions, including the homecoming celebration, Greek Week, the Miss USA Scholarship Pageant, and the International Spring Festival. Student clubs are diverse, ranging from the Alliance for Sexual Diversity to the Baptist Campus Ministries. Overall, there are 182 organizations on campus, including eight sororities and 10 fraternities. Students can even get involved in the university-run television station, Jag-TV, which is broadcast in dorms and other buildings on campus.

WHERE IT'S AT

The University of South Alabama's campus is located near the Gulf Coast, in Mobile, Alabama. Students who live in one of the school's four residence halls are within a short walk of most classroom buildings, athletic facilities, the student recreation center, and the library. Mobile itself is a charming southern city of 500,000, known for its beaches, excellent seafood, and annual Mardi Gras celebration. With an average annual temperature in the high 60s and nearby recreational opportunities, including beaches and boating, there's always something to do.

THE DETAILS

Campus setting:	suburban
Degrees:	bachelor's, master's, doctoral
Calendar:	semesters
Public/Private:	public state
Number of full-time faculty:	712
Student-to-teacher ratio:	18:1

Admissions requirements:
- **Options:** early admission
- **Application fee:** $25
- **Required:** high school transcript, SAT or ACT
- **Application deadlines:** 7/15 (freshmen), 8/10 (transfer)
- **Early decision:** —
- **Notification:** 8/10 (freshmen), 8/10 (transfer)

Average high school GPA:	3.21
Average freshman SAT verbal/math score:	—/—
Average freshman ACT score:	22
Number of applicants:	2,883
Number of applicants accepted:	2,695
Percentage of students from out of state:	17%
Total freshman enrollment:	1,278
Total enrollment:	13,340
Percentage of students who live in campus housing:	19%
Total in-state tuition, fees & expenses:	$9,512
Total out-of-state tuition, fees & expenses:	$13,322
Average financial aid package:	$5,702

UNIVERSITY OF SOUTH ALABAMA

MAJORS

- Accounting
- Anthropology
- Art/Art Studies, General
- Atmospheric Sciences and Meteorology, General
- Audiology/Audiologist and Speech-Language Pathology/Pathologist
- Biology/Biological Sciences, General
- Biomedical Sciences, General
- Business/Commerce, General
- Business Administration and Management, General
- Chemical Engineering
- Chemistry, General
- Civil Engineering, General
- Clinical Laboratory Science/Medical Technology/Technologist
- Communication Studies/Speech Communication and Rhetoric
- Computer and Information Sciences, General
- Computer Engineering, General
- Criminal Justice/Law Enforcement Administration
- Drama and Dramatics/Theatre Arts, General
- Early Childhood Education and Teaching
- E-Commerce/Electronic Commerce
- Electrical, Electronics and Communications Engineering
- Elementary Education and Teaching
- English Language and Literature, General
- Finance, General
- Foreign Languages and Literatures, General
- Geography
- Geology/Earth Science, General
- Health/Medical Preparatory Programs, Other
- History, General
- Liberal Arts and Sciences, General Studies and Humanities, Other
- Marketing/Marketing Management, General
- Mathematics and Statistics, Other
- Mechanical Engineering
- Multi-/Interdisciplinary Studies, Other
- Music, General
- Nursing/Registered Nurse Training
- Parks, Recreation and Leisure Studies
- Philosophy
- Physical Education Teaching and Coaching
- Physics, General
- Political Science and Government, General
- Psychology, General
- Radiologic Technology/Science-Radiographer
- Respiratory Care Therapy/Therapist
- Secondary Education and Teaching
- Sociology
- Special Education and Teaching, General

UNIVERSITY OF WEST ALABAMA

Station 4
Livingston, AL 35470

(205) 652-3400
http://www.uwa.edu/

BIG DEAL

UNIVERSITY 101
Extended orientation program; upperclassman mentors; optional first-year transitional seminar; special academic advisors assigned to first-years.

BIG FISH

Want a private college education at a state school price?

The honors program at the University of West Alabama gives students more intensive versions of the basic courses required of all students. Factor in required cultural events, extracurricular activities, interdisciplinary courses for upperclassmen, and a mandatory senior thesis project, and you've got yourself four years of a tough but top-notch education. Social events, field trips, and activities organized by the staff of the designated honors dorm (living there is optional) provide much-needed relief from the pressure of school.

UNIVERSITY OF WEST ALABAMA

WHAT IT IS

The University of West Alabama was founded in 1835 as a women's school. With an enrollment of just a few thousand and a low average class size and student-teacher ratio, this state university is comparable in size and feel to many small private colleges. Each student is directly advised by a professor in his or her major department, and the university offers concentrations in such areas as marine biology, business administration, and pre-law. The school has made major improvements over the past decade, increasing the number of computers on campus, renovating college facilities, and introducing new majors in agribusiness, psychology, and forestry. Popular events and activities at UWA include watching student-cowboys wrangle horses in the UWA Rodeo Complex and the Sucarnochee Folklife Festival, which celebrates the local folk culture of Sumter County and the surrounding area.

WHERE IT'S AT

Home of the University of West Alabama, Livingston is a town of about 3,000 people in the west-central part of the state. The university is about 116 miles southwest of Birmingham and 130 miles west of Montgomery. Major campus landmarks include Lake LU, where students can fish and boat; the Covered Bridge, a popular location for romantic walks; and the Moon House, built in 1834 and one of the oldest homes in the area. The campus environment at UWA is pleasant and relaxing; students can spend an afternoon lounging in the rocking chairs on Webb Hall's long, Southern-style front porch or take a dip in the Olympic-size pool outside of the Student Union.

THE DETAILS

Campus setting:	small town
Degrees:	bachelor's, master's
Calendar:	semesters
Public/Private:	public state
Number of full-time faculty:	88
Student-to-teacher ratio:	23:1

Admissions requirements:
- **Options:** common application, deferred entrance, early admission, electronic application
- **Application fee:** $20
- **Required:** high school transcript, SAT or ACT
- **Application deadlines:** continuous (freshmen), continuous (transfer)
- **Early decision:** —
- **Notification:** continuous (freshmen), continuous (transfer)

Average high school GPA:	—
Average freshman SAT verbal/math score:	—/—
Average freshman ACT score:	19
Number of applicants:	691
Number of applicants accepted:	510
Percentage of students from out of state:	20%
Total freshman enrollment:	260
Total enrollment:	2,667
Percentage of students who live in campus housing:	35%
Total in-state tuition, fees & expenses:	$8,215
Total out-of-state tuition, fees & expenses:	$11,941
Average financial aid package:	$8,870

UNIVERSITY OF WEST ALABAMA

MAJORS

- Accounting
- Athletic Training/Trainer
- Biology/Biological Sciences, General
- Business Administration and Management, General
- Chemistry, General
- Early Childhood Education and Teaching
- Elementary Education and Teaching
- Engineering Technology, General
- English Language and Literature, General
- History, General
- Industrial Technology/Technician
- Management Information Systems, General
- Marine Biology and Biological Oceanography
- Mathematics, General
- Physical Education Teaching and Coaching
- Psychology, General
- Sociology
- Special Education and Teaching, General

SCHOOLS BY CATEGORY

SCHOOLS BY CATEGORY

BIG REP

Auburn University p. 196
Embry-Riddle Aeronautical University p. 13
Emory University p. 118
Florida State University p. 37
Georgia College and State University p. 124
Georgia Institute of Technology p. 127
Tuskegee University p. 227
University of Alabama p. 230
University of Florida p. 74
University of Georgia p. 175
University of Miami p. 77

BIG DEAL

Alabama A&M University p. 190
Alabama State University p. 193
Albany State University p. 97
Auburn University p. 196
Columbus State University p. 112
Flagler College p. 16
Florida A&M University p. 19
Florida Atlantic University p. 22
Florida Gulf Coast University p. 25
Florida International University p. 31
Florida State University p. 37
Fort Valley State University p. 121
Georgia College and State University p. 124
Georgia Institute of Technology p. 127
Georgia Southwestern State University p. 130
Georgia Southern University p. 133
Georgia State University p. 136
Jacksonville State University p. 206
New College of Florida p. 47
North Georgia College and State University p. 148
Savannah State University p. 163
Southern Polytechnic State University p. 166
Troy University p. 224
University of Alabama p. 230
University of Alabama at Birmingham p. 233
University of Alabama in Huntsville p. 236
University of Central Florida p. 71
University of Florida p. 74
University of Georgia p. 175
University of Montevallo p. 239
University of North Alabama p. 242
University of North Florida p. 80
University of South Alabama p. 245
University of South Florida p. 83
University of West Alabama p. 248
University of West Florida p. 89
University of West Georgia p. 178
Valdosta State University p. 181

BIG IDEA

Agnes Scott College p. 94
Alabama A&M University p. 190
Beacon College p. 5
Birmingham-Southern College p. 200
Brenau University p. 106
Eckerd College p. 10
Flagler College p. 16
Florida A&M University p. 19
Florida International University p. 31
Huntingdon College p. 203
Judson College p. 209
LaGrange College p. 139
Lynn University p. 44
New College of Florida p. 47
North Georgia College and State University p. 148
Rollins College p. 56
Savannah College of Art and Design p. 160
Southern Polytechnic State University p. 166
Talladega College p. 221
University of Montevallo p. 239
University of West Florida p. 89
Wesleyan College p. 184

BIG FISH

Agnes Scott College p. 94
Alabama State University p. 193
Albany State University p. 97
Atlanta College of Art p. 100
Barry University p. 2
Beacon College p. 5
Berry College p. 103
Bethune-Cookman College p. 7
Birmingham-Southern College p. 200
Brenau University p. 106
Clark Atlanta University p. 109
Columbus State University p. 112
Covenant College p. 115
Eckerd College p. 10
Florida Atlantic University p. 22
Florida Gulf Coast University p. 25
Florida Institute of Technology p. 28
Florida Southern College p. 34
Fort Valley State University p. 121
Georgia Southwestern State University p. 130
Georgia Southern University p. 133
Georgia State University p. 136
Huntingdon College p. 203
Jacksonville University p. 41
Jacksonville State University p. 206
Judson College p. 209
Lynn University p. 44
Mercer University p. 142
Miles College p. 212
Morehouse College p. 145
Nova Southeastern University p. 50
Oglethorpe University p. 151
Palm Beach Atlantic University p. 53
Piedmont College p. 154
Reinhardt College p. 157
Rollins College p. 56
Saint Leo University p. 59
Samford University p. 215

BIG FISH *continued*

Savannah College of Art and Design p. 160
Savannah State University p. 163
Southeastern University p. 62
Spelman College p. 169
Spring Hill College p. 218
Stetson University p. 65
St. Thomas University p. 68
Thomas University p. 172
Troy University p. 224
University of Alabama at Birmingham p. 233
University of Alabama in Huntsville p. 236
University of Central Florida p. p. 71
University of North Alabama p. 242
University of North Florida p. 80
University of South Alabama p. 245
University of Tampa p. 86
University of West Alabama p. 248
University of West Georgia p. 178
Valdosta State University p. 181

Notes